Every Kind of People

Every Kind of People

A Journey into the Heart of Care Work

KATHRYN FAULKE

FIG TREE
an imprint of
PENGUIN BOOKS

FIG TREE

UK | USA | Canada | Ireland | Australia
India | New Zealand | South Africa

Fig Tree is part of the Penguin Random House group of companies
whose addresses can be found at global.penguinrandomhouse.com.

First published 2024
001

Set in 12/14.75pt Dante MT Std
Typeset by Jouve (UK), Milton Keynes
Printed and bound in Great Britain by Clays Ltd, Elcograf S.p.A.

The authorized representative in the EEA is Penguin Random House Ireland,
Morrison Chambers, 32 Nassau Street, Dublin D02 YH68

A CIP catalogue record for this book is available from the British Library

ISBN: 978–0–241–67248–8

www.greenpenguin.co.uk

MIX
Paper | Supporting
responsible forestry
FSC® C018179

Penguin Random House is committed to a
sustainable future for our business, our readers
and our planet. This book is made from Forest
Stewardship Council® certified paper.

This book is dedicated to care workers everywhere.
And all those we care for.

Contents

Foreword

Mrs Singh is frail and elderly and lives in an imposing Victorian property with an overgrown garden and an unfeasibly large front door. I have never met Mrs Singh before, but I have been given a key to that door and instructions to help her to bed. Inside, it is quiet. The last of the day's light filters through brittle net curtains strung against huge sash windows. The house is so big that it takes me some time to locate Mrs Singh in the basement. The house is also grand, even at this lower level.

Mrs Singh's room has a worn but once expensive rug that almost entirely covers the acres of dark wooden floorboards. She sits in an enormous armchair, the walls around her going up at least twelve feet, the bed far, far away on the opposite side of the room. Mrs Singh speaks little English. When I put my head to one side, eyes closed on my praying hands, she giggles. I raise my eyebrows. Mrs Singh giggles. I mime drinking a cup of tea and she giggles and giggles. I empty her catheter bag and fetch her nightdress. She giggles. 'You come again,' she implores, giggling helplessly. 'You come back, yes?' And we continue getting on like a giggling house on fire until I try to help Mrs Singh to her giggling feet and discover that she cannot walk.

Flummoxed, I cannot immediately think what to do. I only know what I cannot do. I cannot do nothing because I am Mrs Singh's care worker for the evening and the last person she will see today. I look at that far, far-away bed and sigh. I look at Mrs Singh. Mrs Singh giggles. I consider how little she will be giggling if she's left to sit in her chair all night, and have a silent but firm word with myself. Then, I take a deep breath and straighten up. Of course I can get her safely into that bed. Whatever it is that getting her into it turns out to entail.

I once thought that I'd become a care worker by chance, but now I wonder if it was simply inevitable. I come from a rather humble, country background with parents who were kind and practical. My father, an expert mechanic, was always mending other people's cars and appliances as well as our own, and my mother found clever solutions to problems of mending and sewing and making do. They looked after me and my sister and our pets and other people and plants and baby birds that fell from nests and hungry hedgehogs and vegetable plots. They took care of everything.

I grew into a rebellious teenager. Hitch-hiking into the nearest town and staying out all hours, going barefoot in winter and booted in summer, taking my skirts up short and ironing my hair down long and playing jagged, distorted music with savage lyrics far too loudly from behind my tightly closed bedroom door. I didn't appreciate the beauty of the countryside or the values of my parents. I am ashamed to say that I was just bored. I couldn't wait to leave. In those days, school was only compulsory until the age of sixteen. My school, convinced that I was no academic, wasn't about to try to persuade me to stay on but I didn't mind at all. I think my mother was heartbroken when I caught the train to London. I'd thought I was only carrying a suitcase. It wasn't until much later that I discovered I was carrying my parents' kindness, compassion and practicality inside me too. I had absorbed the tenets of care. I just didn't know it back then.

London was a playground in those days. Albeit a danger-ous one. I spent the first few nights sleeping on the floor of the house of a man I thought had befriended me until he finally accepted I wouldn't be going into his bed any time soon. He kicked me out, suitcase and all, in the middle of a winter night and I slept outside a Tube station, warm air coming up from the underground through the gaps in the closed metal grilles. I slept there several more nights, learning a bit about fear and loneliness, until I talked myself into a live-in pub job.

From then on, work provided money for fun and for travel – not so much to other countries but to places in them that I had seen in pictures or on the telly. I went to the Pyramids I'd seen on an archaeology programme I'd watched with my dad. I went to the Eiffel Tower I'd seen in a presentation in my school French lesson. I went to the Dead Sea that I'd seen my grandad floating on in a photo he'd sent home to my grandma from his army service. What I did for work didn't seem important until long after I'd met my husband and we'd had children. Surrounded by other young parents who were largely professionals, I suddenly needed to *be* something. Struck by the desire to get properly educated, earn a proper wage and become a proper person, I decided to attempt university. I wasn't sure I could do it. I wasn't sure we could afford it. But once I began, I loved it. Now I understood biochemistry and anatomy, knew the periodic table inside out, learned how a heart beats. I could even, miraculously, do mathematical equations. The day I learned how muscles move I explained it in molecular detail to anyone who would listen. Then, at last, I got my proper job. In a hospital as a clinical dietitian. And I did it so well that no one, not my husband, not my friends, not even my colleagues, knew how difficult I found it. Well, almost no one. No one except for Greg.

Greg busked outside the local greengrocer's. He was always there. Every year, week after week. He'd seen my children grow up as we passed him on the street playing his guitar. He was shabby, dirty even. His fingernails were black with grime, face lined, thin chin speckled with stubble, but he had a skinny swagger and I liked the way he dressed. Always in shades, coloured scarf, leather jacket. Despite the jacket you could see the sharpness of his shoulders, and despite the swagger he had no attitude. He was all smiles and friendliness, helping grannies with their bags, chatting to the little kids, strumming and singing in the high street, whatever the weather. I would often stop to talk to him. I was overwhelmed with the responsibility I felt for my patients, the fear of appraisals, the officialdom, the form filling, the outcome measuring. I couldn't tell my family or my friends about this. But I could tell Greg. Greg was the only person I knew who was worse than me at having a proper job. He couldn't do appraisals or officialdom either. He was an absolute expert at avoiding form filling and he'd ensured that the only outcome measurement he was about to do was to count the coins people threw into his guitar case at the end of the day. Greg understood me perfectly.

In the end, I quit the job.

It didn't make things better. It made them worse. Now, I felt guilty as well as anxious. My lack of employment became the elephant in the room and my husband's patience – understandably – was running out. Children still at home but grown up, not needing me, I became depressed, no longer caring about much at all until, one day, I learned that Greg was ill. He was frightened and I remembered how that felt. Indeed, I knew how that felt now. So I began to pour all my energy, all my attention, into keeping him safe and getting him well. Although this was futile, I got something else out of it too. I got a place to escape to, physically and psychologically. I hid myself in caring for Greg and I discovered

4

I was pretty good at caring so I decided the best plan of action would be to get a job as a care worker. And that's how I've ended up here, with Mrs Singh.

I point to Mrs Singh's legs, then to the bed and say, 'How?' She giggles. I ask again and she giggles again but is quite able to tell me how. Just, of course, not in English. I shake my head. She giggles. I pretend to frown at her. She giggles again and points up. I look up at the enormous ceiling rose. Mrs Singh giggles. Then I notice it. A track runs over the ceiling from our side of the room to the bed a million miles away where a bar dangles from it. There really is, I realize with a sinking heart, such a thing as a ceiling hoist. I frown for real. Mrs Singh giggles. I feel cross. She giggles. I look at her sternly. Mrs Singh stops giggling.

I call the office. Berate them. Insist that, no, I have never been to Mrs Singh before, and no, I have never been taught how to use a ceiling hoist. Listen to their instructions. Tut when they tell me Mrs Singh knows how it all works. Feel quietly terrified at having to figure it out on my own but think we should be able to safely crack it if we take things slowly. So long as we refrain from all the giggling.

Mrs Singh is silent as I press the remote control several times to watch the bar of the hoist swing back and forth across the chasm between her chair and the bed. She looks at me, sombre, as I examine the sling. She peers, grave, as I slide it between her back and the chair and gazes, solemn, as I pull two ends out underneath her armpits. Sits stony faced as I take the other two ends and pull them up between her legs. Remains unsmiling as I press the control pad and make the bar go up and down a couple of times before lowering it to the level of her sling. Nods seriously as I attach four loops on the sling to the four hooks on the bar.

I press the button that raises the sling with one hand and

guide it with the other. My precious cargo rises, hushed, into the air, knees at the height of my chin. I hold my breath. The track overhead looks about as robust as the ones fitted to my shower curtains. I push the button that advances the sling toward the bed and am so focused on keeping it well clear of the wall as it glides up and along that I don't notice the sound until we are halfway over.

'Honestly, Mrs Singh,' I say, 'you really are the giggliest person I've met in my entire life.'

Mrs Singh safely tucked in, I go on to my next calls. Calls to other new customers and to my regulars. Calls that are unlikely to contain as much giggling but might be just as fun. Calls that are easy and calls that are difficult in a myriad of different ways. Calls that run smoothly or contain as much emotion as a Hollywood blockbuster. Because care is like that. I have learned that care work is fascinating. Also boring. And exhausting. That it contains both despair and euphoria. And large quantities of meaning. The one thing it doesn't contain is, of course, money. But it is chock full of everything else and replete with characters. Care work is so full of stories that I could not help but begin to write them down until they became this book.

Come with me on my journey into the world of care work. Meet my customers. Let me introduce you to my gentle friend Veronica Rose, to the outrageous Mr Radbert, to sociable Patrick, to sweet and funny Ina, to wise and tender William and to the feisty fiend that is Beryl. Meet Greg, his friends and his philosophy. Come with me and see the extraordinary drama to be found in ordinary lives. Come with me and feel how it is to be in this place that is valued so little but is so vital. I believe that caring is the most important thing one can do and that everyone should know about it.

And, of course, one day so many of us will need it.

I.

The only option

Maggs had been surprised to see me. 'You're not our typical applicant, you know? I mean, you've got a degree.'

'I'm sure I can do it though,' I said, looking at the carpet tiles. They were charcoal grey.

'Oh, I don't doubt that,' said Maggs, 'but, really, why would you want to?'

We were sitting opposite one another, a pale grey formica tabletop between us. The legs of the table were steel grey, the walls were pewter grey and by the window an iron-grey heater threw little warmth into the chilly side room. Everything was grey except for Maggs. Her green cardigan was unbuttoned over a yellow dress, and she wore raspberry-pink lip gloss to match her shoes.

Having left my job as a hospital dietitian, I was looking for work. The last time I'd looked for casual employment had been so long ago that the employer had tested my typing skills on an actual typewriter. Later, I'd got jobs through word of mouth. But now that I was middle-aged, word of mouth no longer existed and job hunting largely took place online. I'd found two different types of employment websites. One was for hotshots and listed positions under categories such as Arts and Heritage, Legal, or Finance and Accounting. The roles on offer included Lecturers, Managers and Department Heads, and the pay was given as yearly salaries in thousands. The other type of website was for non-hotshots and, apart from a smattering of oddball opportunities, listed jobs in hospitality and care. The roles on offer included catering staff, support workers and security guards, and the pay was given as hourly rates in pounds.

The complexity of applying even for the non-hotshot jobs had shocked me. I remembered being able to just walk into those. I'd once got hired on day one, been fondled in the lift on day two and found a new job by close of play on day three. It was all so simple back then. Apart from the getting-fondled-in-the-lift side of things, of course. But now there was no more pub work unless you were bar trained and no more waitressing unless you were server trained. In fact, there was pretty much no more anything without studying a candidate pack, completing a questionnaire with essays and giving a fascinating reason for wanting the job. Earning money just to get by was no longer acceptable. Everything had become a career.

Then I'd seen the advertisement that Maggs had placed.

It said that in exchange for honesty, patience, compassion and reliability, she would forgo experience and really long application forms, give training, and pay nine pounds fifty an hour. Nine pounds fifty didn't sound much but, since I'd have to commit to covering at least two evenings and every other weekend on top of working most weekdays, I doubted I'd have the time or the energy to spend any money.

The company was based in a shared office building on an industrial estate in South London close to where I lived, and the brief introductory form I submitted had barely been with them five minutes before I was summoned up the narrow stairs, past a tiny kitchenette, through a corridor lined with boxes of blue latex gloves and into the main office where three desk-bound workers tapped at computers and fielded phone calls. A mannequin with fuzzy brown hair wearing a lilac tunic and black trousers stared blankly from one corner and there was a medical bed and a standing hoist in another.

'So why do you want to be a carer?' Maggs asked again. 'Come on, Kate, it's not a rhetorical question. It's part of the interview.'

I'd have been better able to answer that question before Maggs had reminded me I was in a job interview. Being so anxious that I was no longer capable of job interviews, I definitely couldn't answer it any more. Maggs tried again. 'Perhaps it's because you like working with people? Or that you'd like to help them remain safe and independent in their own homes? Kate?'

'Yes,' I said. 'Put that.'

'Which?' Maggs asked.

'Either,' I said.

Of course, you can't possibly tell Maggs the real reason you want to be a carer.

For months now you've been making days out of cleaning an already spotless house, doing the laundry, cooking up gastronomic delights night after night and putting the bins out on time. But all that is superfluous to helping pay the bills. You've run out of excuses not to get a new job and you hate the idea of it. But not as much as you hate yourself for having failed at your previous job. Your own version of a hotshot job.

You tell yourself you failed at that job because it required more attention than you, being responsible for homework, for parents' evenings and sports days and bake sales, for taxi services to judo and tennis lessons and parties, for revision and cramming and timetabling of exams, for nightlong nursing of broken bones or broken hearts, could possibly give it. It was difficult doing all that as well. But to say that is why you failed is not true. The truth is

*you failed because you were scared. Scared you would make a cata-
strophic mistake. Scared someone would come along and ask why
on earth you'd been given a job meant for a cleverer, worthier
person. Scared you weren't good enough, and tired of worrying
about it.*

*So eventually you'd quit, but you're still scared now. Scared
that, after all these months out of work, you will no longer be able
to get any other job at all. Except, perhaps, for the one that Maggs
is offering. The one you've been fumbling your way toward as you
try and help Greg, who has been growing sicker and who lives,
precariously, alone. You suspect that being a carer is so awful a
prospect that anyone who passes the security check will get hired.
But even that is not the real reason you're applying for it. The real
reason is because somewhere deep down in your sorry-for-itself,
middle-aged brain you think it will be punishment for failing to
make a success of that last job, the job that you were once given
precious resources and time – utterly unrecoverable, lost time – to
study for.*

In a world where staff were in such short supply, the success
of my application for care work was inevitable. 'Morning
all,' said Rita a fortnight after my interview. 'I hope you slept
well because we're going to be covering a lot of ground this
week, yaaah?' Like Maggs, she was dressed in vibrant colours,
her hair a rigid blonde helmet around her fully made-up
face. She had heels on, and pulled biros and biscuits from
her faux-leather aqua-blue handbag. It seemed that, in the
world of caring, if there was an opportunity to dress colour-
fully one took it, yaaah? I wondered if this was because the
job was so drab that when you weren't doing it you were
compelled to compensate for the gloom you'd had to withstand when you were.

The trainee carers were all women, of various ethnicities,

aged from just nineteen to fifty-three. There were supposed to be eight of us, but four hadn't shown up. I was silently alarmed by this attrition rate, but everyone else cheerfully ignored the empty chairs and shuffled up together to watch Rita's lengthy presentation and fill out our workbooks. If we didn't know the answer to one of the questions in the workbook, Rita happily supplied it, and if we were taking too long she would rapidly dictate half a dozen answers to save us spending too much time on thinking. When one of the absent trainees arrived two hours late, Rita, unperturbed, spent half an hour bringing her up to date with dictation while the rest of us ate the biscuits in the kitchenette.

'Any questions?' Rita said, toward the end of our third and final day.

'How do we get into people's houses?'

'Customers, we call them customers. Mostly your customer will let you in.'

'What if I've got a customer who can't walk?'

'They'll have keys outside. In a key safe. With a code. Now I need to teach you how to hoist, yaaah?' Rita said and we returned to the main office. The three admin staff were shouting back and forth about how to cover Radbert because Fatima's daughter was ill and who could go and do a review on William now he was out of hospital and was it possible for Itzie to switch to Beryl if Sheila could go to Franklyn because Danny was off and there was no way the number sixty-three would get Sheila to Mrs Gibson on time otherwise? Only the mannequin paid us any attention as we loaded one another into a sling and used the freestanding hoist to transfer ourselves lumpily from floor to bed and back again. The mannequin did not look impressed.

'Any other questions?'

'We need to have a phone?'

'Oh yaaah. We have an app for phones that gives you your rota and the customer details. You'll write your notes onto it. For each visit.'

'Do you give us a phone, then?'

'No,' said Rita, 'but we give you a contribution toward your phone, yaaah?'

'How much?'

'Three pounds a month. And for travel we pay twenty-five pence a mile.'

Before I or any of the other applicants could express our dismay, Rita had moved on. 'Now, uniforms, they cost twelve pounds each and I suggest you buy a spare. So you can wash them regularly, yaaah? You should probably buy a fleece as well. For when it's cold. Those are fifteen pounds. And you'll need to pay for the security check.' We swapped outraged eye contact at realizing we might be working several hours before we were even in profit, but none of us walked out. I guess that showed me I wasn't alone in seeing this as my only option.

And that was it. I was working. One doesn't really learn how to do care work from a lengthy presentation, nor from any of the other desk-bound training sessions that will occasionally crop up. One learns about care work by shadowing and assisting other care workers out in the real world, and I learned it from some of the calm and patient best. I learned from Itzie that a carer should always keep their customer at the centre of everything they do. I learned from Julie that a carer should advocate so that the voices of those who are most vulnerable are heard. I learned from Chrissy that a carer should provide companionship where it is needed even if time constraints make this challenging. I learned absolutely everything from these carers who do their job so well.

Of course, there are bad carers. I've met only a few. But

why wouldn't there be when the price paid at the coalface of care work is so low? Caring is considered low-skilled work, but my co-workers were largely hard-working, dedicated experts, out in all weathers, at times when the majority of the population were still asleep, eating lunch or watching the evening's television. Many would spend their own time sitting with those who were lonely, accompanying people on hospital visits, or solving unscheduled problems from blocked sinks to overgrown lawns. They moved people with many different disabilities and frailties using specialized equipment, could spot weight loss, pressure sores and dehydration before they'd barely become established and, most crucially, understood the importance of dignity, autonomy, a cup of tea and a bloody good natter.

Caring is the toughest thing I've ever done but also by far the most rewarding. Early on, when I asked one of my colleagues why she did the job, she said simply, 'It's a passion,' and she was right. But a magical thing happened too. There were times when my customers helped me through exhaustion, grief and heartbreak. They provided me with comfort and advice. They gave me love.

There were times, many times, that the caring went both ways.

2.

Three weeks

Up by six, you put on clothes you laid out the night before. A pair of cheap black trousers you bought just a couple of days ago, an old work shirt, trainers. Your uniform tunic is pale lilac with white piping. The fabric, not yet washed, is stiff. Maggs said to buy a size fourteen to give you extra room for a jumper underneath, but this size fourteen is enormous. It drowns you and now you're wondering whether Maggs had just ordered too few smaller sizes and saw you coming.

You shove a couple of aprons, torn from the enormous roll of white plastic you were given, into a grubby, khaki backpack, along with two pairs of plastic shoe covers and a box of medium-sized plastic gloves. Then you force down a piece of toast, suddenly nauseous at what you have done. You've called your own bluff in a game of dare gone horribly wrong. Thrown several babies out with the bathwater. Burned down an entire street of houses. Taken a pneumatic fucking drill to a perfectly ordinary nut and thoroughly wrecked your curriculum vitae. You'll never get another decent job again after this.

The teenager floats in, bleary-eyed. 'Hey, that's my backpack.'

'My God, you're up early. All right if I borrow it?'

'Dough shift.' He clicks on the kettle. 'Got to be at the bakery by seven. Keep the bag, it's on its last legs.' Then he frowns, 'Are you OK?'

'Not really,' you say. 'I mean, look at me,' and you stand up, hold out your arms and spin sarcastically around in the too-big

polyester tunic as though you're modelling Moschino. 'I never,' you say, 'ever, thought life was going to turn out this way.'

'Oh, Mum,' he says, 'it's not so bad. You love people. You might enjoy this. If only you'll let yourself.'

And so it was that one morning in the middle of winter, I found myself waiting outside Franklyn's house. I was going to wash him. I'd never washed a stranger before and I was nervous. I was going to wash Franklyn with Itzie. Apart from my fellow trainees, I'd never really met another carer before either, but I'd seen stories about them in the news. They always seemed to be hitting people or stealing things, so I was quite nervous about meeting Itzie too. But I was mostly nervous about the washing.

I'd been up half the night trying to comfort my friend Greg. When he first became sick, I'd made him go for chemotherapy. He'd tolerated just one session. Not because of the side effects but because, having spent so much of his life happily on his feet playing music outside, he could not bear to spend so long in miserable silence on his back inside. Greg has now chosen to pay as little regard as possible to his wretched predicament. He dislikes the attention of strangers, including those from the medical professions. Instead, I go to him. Almost every day now. To dish out the few medications he is willing to take, to clean, to cook tiny portions of tempting meals for him to pick at, to keep him company and to provide a whipping post for his fears and frustrations. Last night, we had stayed up too late and talked too much, using infantile codewords, about the tasks I might soon have to undertake that would fill him with shame and me with disgust. We had wept. Then he'd had yet another cigarette and we'd both had several large glasses of Scotch before I'd gone home to bed just four hours ago.

Now, as I stood stamping my frozen feet against the cold, I heard singing. Then I saw her. Itzie didn't so much walk as sashay down the street, well wrapped up in a long coat, scarf and bobble hat. Despite her garb and large girth, Itzie was graceful. She had a voice like honey and her teeth were sugar-white in a generous smile. Regardless of that smile, I was nervous about the number of questions I'd be able to ask before Itzie's patience ran out.

'You're Kate,' she said, ringing the doorbell.

'I am,' I said. 'I don't really know what to do.'

'You'll be fine,' Itzie said, but I didn't know how she could possibly tell that, since I didn't yet know myself whether I'd be fine.

A middle-aged woman opened the door. 'Good morning, Lucille,' said Itzie, taking off her bobble hat. Under the hat her hair was knotted neatly on top of her head like a crown. 'How's Dad today?'

'Morning, lady, much the same,' said the woman.

She turned and followed the sound of breakfast television down the warm hall, while Itzie and I put on plastic aprons, shoe covers and gloves. Itzie looked like an empress being made to do the cleaning. 'You go fill this with soapy water,' she said, handing me a plastic bowl.

It's surprisingly difficult to find the bathroom in a stranger's house, especially if you don't want to use up one of your annoying questions by asking where it is. I tiptoed through two doors before I was able to fill the bowl, squirt in soap, throw in a couple of blue flannels and return to Itzie. She was in a room containing a man asleep in a medical bed, an armchair on wheels, a metal hoist and a chest of drawers from which she was pulling clothes, towels, bed-linen, tissues and an adult incontinence pad. I'd seen an adult incontinence pad once before. It had been lying on the floor of a swimming-pool changing room years ago. I'd complained and asked one of the lifeguards to clear it up. I don't remember that it was even dirty, but I'd been disgusted anyway.

'Oh, not two blue ones,' Itzie said, looking in the bowl. 'One blue and one brown, please.' I swapped one of the blue flannels for a brown one.

Itzie motioned me round to the other side of the bed and swept down the bed rail on her side. I pressed the catch on my side, jiggled the rail, caught my apron in the mechanism, swore and blushed. 'How?' I said, as the rail slammed down so hard it sounded like a car crash. The sleeping man's arms flew up into the air, but he didn't open his eyes. 'God. Sorry,' I said, 'the training didn't cover how to lower bed rails.'

'Mr Franklyn, sleepyhead,' sang Itzie, grinning. She pushed the button on the bed control that raised the mattress to the level of our hips. 'We going to wash you, Mr Franklyn,' she continued, as she lifted the blanket and pillows away.

Franklyn was wearing a pink T-shirt with a green palm tree on it. I tried to take his right arm out of it, but his right arm didn't move. 'Sorry,' I said, 'how?'

Itzie took Franklyn's mobile left arm out first, so that the T-shirt slipped easily over his head and down his frozen side leaving him naked except for the wretched pad. I had never seen a man so thin. His skin, burnished brown, was stretched over prominent cheekbones and all the way down his long limbs, hip bones jutting up like sails. You could have slotted toast between his ribs, and the lumps where they attached themselves to the sternum looked like two rows of tiny brown pebbles. He reminded me of a television programme I'd once seen about prehistoric burials.

'And the sheet?' I said. Itzie replied by tugging it out from under the mattress and pushing as much of it under Franklyn as she could. Then she rolled him toward her and I pulled the sheet out from under him. The bed was stripped.

I smelled frying. Lucille was in the kitchen.

Itzie used the blue flannel to wash Franklyn's face. 'Mr Franklyn,' she sang, 'is morning, wake up.' She washed his face a second time and he opened his eyes. 'Well, hello!' sang Itzie. 'Is me, Mr Franklyn.' Franklyn smiled at her.

'Hello, Franklyn,' I said, 'I'm Kate.' Franklyn did not turn his head.

Itzie washed Franklyn's left arm and passed me the flannel while she used the towel. The triangular hollows beneath Franklyn's collarbones were deep enough to hold water and as I washed his right arm I could feel the exact shape of the humerus and the bones of his radius and ulna. I washed the pit of it, deep as a cup. Then I turned his hand to its paler side. The lines over it were like a child's crossings-out in dark brown felt-tip pen. I washed everything twice, like Itzie did, swapping the flannel and the towel back and forth. In this way, she and I cleaned Franklyn from top to toe except the middle bit. Water and soapsuds had trickled onto the blue plastic mattress, so that Franklyn seemed like a swimmer floating motionless on his back in an ocean, eyes fixed on the sky. We dried the bed and moisturized him, and the fragrance of the cream mingled with the smell of Lucille making coffee and eggs.

Itzie did not put the blue flannel back into the bowl. There was just the brown flannel now. It was waiting for the Velcro fasteners to be undone. When Itzie pulled the front of the pad away, Franklyn's nakedness shocked me. I watched her lift and wash and inspect, and wipe down the pelvis where the spindly legs joined on. Then she rinsed the flannel, squeezed it out and gave it to me.

'I'm a bit nervous.'

'You'll be fine. Have you been to Beryl yet?'

'No. This is my very first visit.'

'Give it time. Soon you'll find it's nothing. Nothing at all.'

I wondered how *much* time I would have to give for this to become nothing. I remembered reading that it took twenty-one days for people to change their self-image, to form new habits, to adapt. As I used the flannel, I imagined washing my husband and my father. I imagined washing Greg. I silently gave myself just three weeks, and not a day more, to get used to this before quitting. Then, after I had washed and dried the front of him from my side, Itzie bent Franklyn's right leg up and rolled him toward me and I held him there with one hand on his bony spine and the other behind his knee and I saw the pad open underneath.

Lucille walked back through to the lounge to eat. I glimpsed her plate carried past the door, but I could no longer smell fried eggs and coffee. Or moisturizing cream. Three weeks, I thought again. If I can't handle it in three weeks, I'll give up.

Serene, beautiful Itzie folded the pad back onto itself to contain the mess and began to wipe. She wiped, discarded, wiped, discarded, wiped, discarded, and the tissue came away slightly cleaner every time but never clean enough and all I could think of was, three weeks.

Franklyn yelped. 'Sorry, Mr Franklyn,' said Itzie. But he could not see her.

'Sorry, Franklyn,' I said and he looked at me.

Eventually, the tissue came away white and then Itzie took up the brown flannel again and washed and put on barrier cream. She put the dirty pad into a plastic bag and laid out a fresh one, rolled Franklyn back onto it and eased him toward her. I reached under him for the other side of the pad and we rolled him onto his back again, pulled the clean, dry softness of it up between his thin legs and fastened the Velcro on either side.

Franklyn needed dressing. We put on a fresh T-shirt, a red and navy striped one with a collar, and pulled jogging bottoms up to his knees. I bent his leg, pulled him toward me and hugged him there and said, 'Nearly done, Franklyn,' and Franklyn smiled at me as Itzie pulled the joggers up over the pad on her side. Then I rolled him back toward her and pulled them up on my side. We took up one sock each.

'Stop!' said Itzie.

There was a tiny red patch on Franklyn's left heel. Itzie massaged and moisturized it. 'You need a pillow against the footboard,' she said. 'You're a lo-o-o-o-ong man, Mr Franklyn.'

The grey sling was difficult to fasten onto the hoist with Franklyn's immobile body inside. I was alarmed at his dangling frame, but Itzie calmly raised him clear of the bed and told me to make sure he didn't swing his brittle legs against the hoist's hard, metal ones as we hefted it over to the big black armchair and poured him into it. 'Morning, sir,' she said, stroking his face.

I wheeled Franklyn through to the lounge and Lucille made porridge while Itzie showed me how to clean and remake the bed and write up notes. Then I fed this man I'd never met before, loading the spoon and touching it to his lip to remind him to open his mouth and waiting the slow minute for his swallow to finish and offering water and reloading. He looked at me, unblinking but smiling, indents the size of the cereal bowl in the sides of his dark temples and his eyes set far back in their sockets, but bright.

And at the end of an hour you leave, having earned a little under ten pounds to help clean and feed a complete stranger. It feels extraordinary. And satisfying. You've helped make someone's day more comfortable. Two people, actually, if you count Lucille. For a second you wonder if this job really is the penance you'd thought it would be. But only for a second.

Less than a fortnight later, Chrissy and I arrive at Beryl's house to find the place covered in grapes, cigarette butts and glass. Having become frustrated during the night, Beryl has thrown her ashtray at the wall. I clean up the mess and encourage Beryl to take her medications.

'Faaack off,' she says when I offer her the medicine cup.

'Beryl, please,' says Chrissy.

Beryl smiles, tips the tablets into her mouth, closes her lips and then spits them out all over me.

I take a step backwards, but not because of the tablets. 'Beryl,' says Chrissy.

'What?'

'We need to change your pad.'

Beryl slams her hands down onto the sheet, tips her head back and screams at the ceiling. Visits to Beryl are always like this. Entertaining, but exhausting and slightly hazardous.

'Beryl,' I say, 'it won't take long.'

'Faaack off.'

'You born in London, Beryl?' I try.

She raises one thin eyebrow. 'I'm a Canning Taaan girl,' she says cautiously.

'You evacuated during the war?'

'To Norwich.'

'Wow,' I say, 'I was born near Norwich.'

Beryl raises her other eyebrow. 'I,' she whispers poisonously, 'got nits in Norwich.' Her face is all peevish grin. 'They cut all my faaackin' hair off in faaackin' Norwich,' she shrieks, hysterical with triumph.

I sweep the bed rail down and lift Beryl's nightdress while

Chrissy fetches hot, soapy water. I undo the Velcro fasteners, pull the pad away and fold it over to contain the soiling. Chrissy coaxes Beryl onto her side, Beryl continues cackling, and I wipe, discard, wipe, discard, wipe, discard, and then I take the brown flannel and begin to wash.

And in the end, it hasn't even taken three weeks. Until it's nothing. Nothing at all.

3.

Being very specific about tea

You're mean, scrambling noisily out of bed to let everyone know just how early you're having to get up on a sleepy Sunday morning to do this job. You dress angrily, throw your bag together, don't even bother to sit down to eat the toast, fling open the front door and are stunned. The world is white silence, the street a sculpture. Snow-capped telegraph poles throw slender shadows onto unblemished powder.

You briefly wonder if you should take a bus, remind yourself buses cost money and you don't know anything much about their routes, and step back inside for wellies. Your booted feet are clumsy on the pedals and every now and again the bike slips on the camber of the road, but it's the perfect morning to be the earliest person out, the very first to make their mark on the day. You breathe in cold and you breathe out clouds and your wheels weave satisfying black lines behind you, bad mood forgotten, heart soaring at the smooth, clean beauty of it all.

'I'm not sure about a shower today, missus. It's awful chilly,' says Ina as Sheila and I stand, roasting, in the hall, snow melting from our boots and all four gas hobs of the cooker burning in the nearby kitchen. It's dark apart from their blue-yellow flames because the light bulb in the hallway has blown, there are few windows and a large picture of a forest in a gilt frame has been placed over the one in the kitchen. Ina is short and stocky and wobbly, and wearing an ankle-length black polyester skirt and a navy sleeveless blouse. The blouse wasn't originally sleeveless and whoever cut its sleeves off didn't know anything about hemming. Under this amputated blouse is a pink sweater, sleeves still intact. Sheila pulls the rucksack from her shoulders and delves for tissues to mop not snow but sweat from her face, overly wrapped in a thick brown scarf. 'Me head hot but me feet cold.'

'Awful chilly,' repeats Ina. 'Wouldn't you say so, missus?' She leans in to my face and squints.

'Someone stolen your glasses again, Ina?' Sheila says, turning off the burning hobs.

'I'm not sure I'd say stolen, missus. Borrowed maybe.'

'Oh, when will you learn to stop letting those people in?'

'They're friends, missus.'

Sheila snorts. 'They're not friends. They're thieves.'

'You just can't keep 'em out, missus – friends,' continues Ina blithely. 'They're like rodents when you buy bacon.' She turns to me again. 'Top tip, never eat bacon.'

'Bacon?'

'They love the smell. Rodents. Don't keep it in the house. You'll be run over with 'em.'

'Overrun? With rats?'

'Yes, missus.'

Sheila kisses her teeth. 'She's run over, you're overrun. Well, I'm run out. All out. Of patience. Hurry up and get in that shower.' She corrals Ina into the bathroom like a shepherd driving a wayward sheep into a pen.

Ina slips off her blouse, reaches back over her shoulders for the sweater, and for a moment her voice is strangled, until her curly hair pops out again. 'They're not always the enemy though, missus. Rodents.'

'They're not?' I crouch down to remove Ina's shoes. Each

is laced only through alternate eyelets and she wears a sock on just one foot.

'Not if you're having a war with somebody. It's the land-mines, see?'

'What've landmines got to do with rodents?'

'You send 'em in, missus. Rodents.'

'Oh! I get it!' I love quizzes and Ina is a bit like one of those quizzes that are difficult enough to be interesting but not so impossible that you become bored. 'I've read about that,' I say. 'The rats detect landmines. Well, not exactly detect them but the landmines explode if a rat hits one and that makes it safe for the soldiers to go in.'

'Correct,' says Ina seriously, like Magnus Magnusson compering *Mastermind*.

'But there aren't any landmines round here.'

'Well, *I* feel,' says our Magnus, looking sideways at Sheila, 'that there might be.'

The bathroom is cramped with three of us in it. Ina plonks herself down on the plastic shower stool and I help-fully switch on the shower. We all get thoroughly soaked as Ina leaps, shrieking, out of its way before Sheila snatches up the flailing shower head and points it at the floor to allow the freezing water to heat up. She sighs. 'How about you go and get Ina a change of clothes?'

Ina's wardrobe is a jumble sale that's got out of hand. I rehang the tumbled clothes at the bottom and find unopened toiletries, chocolate, an important-looking A4 envelope, pens and a pouch of tobacco underneath. When I've assem-bled a fresh outfit, I remember Sheila talking about Ina's light-fingered friends and put a couple of jumpers back over the things at the bottom again.

Back in the bathroom, Ina's been thoroughly moisturized so the clothes do not go on easily. Furthermore, I have brought the wrong blouse. One with its sleeves still on. Eventually, we get down to the feet again.

'One sock or two?'

'Just this one.'

'Doesn't the other foot get cold?'

'Helps with the balance, missus,' says Ina. 'I'm a bit heavy on that side so I can't put a sock on that foot. Otherwise, I'd be a goner, I really would.'

The sock is one of those sports socks that always shrink in the wash and lose every bit of the tiny amount of elasticity they ever possessed. It goes over the toes just fine, but I have to grab the heel and ease it up over the rest of Ina's sole. She's ticklish. I lose a nail even under my gloves before I get the shoes on. Laced into their alternate holes. 'For balancing?' I say.

'No, missus. Saves on laces. They last twice as long like that.'

We all waddle through to the sitting room and Ina begins rolling a cigarette.

'Breakfast?' I say.

'Cereal and tea.'

'Milk and sugar?'

'Milk, three teabags, two sugars.'

The kitchen drawer holds a disparate selection of cutlery and crockery. I separate out three teaspoons, some old forks and two table knives. Straighten up an incongruous palette knife. Tuck the remaining half of a cheese grater and a solitary eggcup to the left. In the cupboard, cereal and sugar have been decanted into jam jars. I line them into neat rows, a little army of sugar and a huge army of cornflakes.

'Ah, no, missus,' Ina says when I present breakfast.

'You should've left the teabags in,' says Sheila, 'and Ina likes hot milk and hot cornflakes and hot sugar. The whole lot hot. Cooked, in fact. Sorry, you weren't to know.' She begins typing notes into the phone app and I offer medications to Ina while the cereal's in the microwave.

'Ah, no, missus,' Ina says, the minute she sees the tablets.

'But you have to take your medications.'

Ina raises her eyebrows. The quizmaster's back again. 'No, missus, I don't.'

Sheila sighs, puts away her phone and squats down at eye level with Ina. 'Why don't you want your tablets, Ina?' The question seems obvious. I wish I'd asked it.

'They make me ill, missus.'

'Let me explain what they're for,' Sheila says. 'Look, this one's for your heart. I take it every single day. And this is for your blood pressure . . .' She goes through each tablet until she gets to the last. 'And this is to keep you feeling, umm, well, straight.'

'Straight?'

'Balanced,' Sheila says firmly. 'You'd be a goner without it, you really would.'

My next call is some distance away. I wait outside the door for ages before calling the office who tell me to go inside and begin doing what I can until the lead carer arrives. I ring the bell with reluctance.

Mrs Andino answers. 'I'm waiting for another carer,' I tell her as I step inside. She frowns. I point to myself and indicate the space next to me where the other carer might stand were they actually, by some miracle, to appear. Mrs Andino looks confused. 'One more,' I say. She turns to stand alongside me, two sentries in a beige hallway. Someone shouts from beyond a door. I don't understand the language, but I understand the sentiment. Mrs Andino breaks rank to pull my sleeve. I frown. She pulls. I follow. Mr Andino is in bed under a shiny blue blanket in the sitting room in front of the television.

Having managed to soothe Mr Andino's anger, change his pad and give him his medications, I'm feeling pleased with myself as I wash my hands. 'Tea?' I say to Mrs Andino. She nods. I open the fridge for milk. Put the kettle on. Mrs Andino shakes her head and gets a little saucepan. Pours a mugful of milk into it. I put it on the hob, pick up the teabag and raise my eyebrows. She nods. I drop the teabag in, light the hob and boil the milk.

When I exit the building, a woman wearing a blue rain-coat over a lilac tunic is standing outside in the snow. 'What the hell's going on?'

'It's all right, I've done it,' I grin.

'For fuck's sake,' she screams. 'I been here ages. You're not supposed to go in without me.'

'But the office said—'

'You called the office? What the fuck did you do that for?' And she walks off, leaving me hoping she won't remember what my face looks like if we ever meet again.

Next, I wait at the bottom of Mrs Gibson's tower block for Anna. I wait and wait. Eventually, a woman wearing a black coat over a lilac tunic exits the building.

'Anna?'

'Kate? You're a bit late.'

'But I thought I had to wait outside for you.'

'Well, next time, go straight in,' she says. 'But not to worry, everything's done.'

I just manage to get to my last call of the morning on time. Despite Anna telling me not to wait outside, I don't want to go in alone, but the buses must be taking far longer than my bike in the snow. Not daring to grass up Itzie's late-ness, I ring the bell. The door of the building clicks open. I wait in the entrance hall for a minute, willing Itzie to appear. She doesn't. Up on the second floor, Lorna's flat is decorated in pale green and cream with elegant furniture, fitted book-shelves and stylish curtains. Her bedlinen matches the decor and she has rumpled but well-cut blonde hair, brown eyes and a bright smile.

'Hello, where's Itzie?'

'The snow. I think the buses . . .'

'Must be awful. How did you . . . ?'

'Cycled.'

'In this weather? You're brave!'

'Can I do anything while we're waiting?'

'Cup of tea would be nice.'

'How d'you like your tea?'

'Just milk, thanks.'

'But with water, yes?'

'Obviously!'

'One bag or more?'

'More? No, just the one.' She giggles.

'Shall I leave the teabag in?'

'Why would you do that?'

I sit at Lorna's bedside, and we chat while we wait for Itzie. Eventually, the intercom rings. As Itzie's coming up in the lift, Lorna takes my hand and says, 'I think you're going to be good at this.'

'You do?' I'm thrilled at this vote of confidence from such a charming woman.

'Oh, you'll be good,' she says, 'because you're nice to talk to. And,' she winks, 'really very specific about tea.'

In the late afternoon, I make my way up to check on Greg. I've known Greg a long time, but I'd never been to his home before he became ill. He was simply a local busker back then. The person with whom I shared my moans and grumbles and jokes, occasionally confiding in him how anxious I was, how invisible I seemed to be now that my children no longer needed me, how I sometimes felt lonely in my marriage. I seemed to do all the confiding. Until, one day, Greg had confided in me. And his confession made mine look like peanuts. He was terribly ill.

As he became sicker, Greg was trying and failing to navigate the medical system and, living alone, had to collect prescriptions, fetch the shopping and feed himself, even on days he felt particularly unwell. Unable to busk, he was also suddenly without money and relying on the donations of those few friends of his who were not living on the extremities of society. Most of those friends had partners so they could not spare a great deal of time for Greg's predicament, much as they loved him. I also had a partner. The difference was that I'd already upset mine by stubbornly jacking in a well-paid job with normal hours for a poorly paid one with ridiculous hours. It seemed to me that spending a bit more time caring for Greg couldn't really make me much less popular with the husband but would make a world of difference to Greg.

Of course, Greg didn't ask for help. But he began to need so much of it. I started to visit the flat often and, despite the increasing amounts of time and energy needed to look after him, Greg's home has become something of a refuge. Another world. A world where I don't feel odd or invisible because Greg and most of his friends from the street are far from normal and rarely visible to outsiders. A world where no one asks questions about why I've quit a good job for a lower-paid one because all those who live in it have lower-paid jobs if they have any jobs at all. My husband is concerned that caring for Greg will take too much of me, too much of us. He asks how long I think it will be likely to take. I don't answer. I don't want to think about that.

The flat is in a low-rise block that sits in its own small car park, dwarfed by the Grade II listed town houses that surround it. Rich and poor, side by side, now that those grander dwellings have been reclaimed from long-ago squatters and gentrified. The richer side is easily seen, the poorer side less obvious. I'd been along this road many times before I knew Greg lived here, but I'd never noticed his block back then. Nor had I seen the homeless hostel a bit further down that he has pointed out to me, or the cheap parade of run-down shops I use now when I'm here.

Outside, the letterboxes are stuffed with unclaimed post, some of it littered over the tarmac and more lying in the stairwell beyond the broken main door that opens if you kick it hard enough. Sometimes there are sleepers lying inside on a mattress under the green lighting that comes from the fire-exit sign. Mossy brown stairs edged with steel and bathed in the green glow go up four floors. All the occupants, aside from Greg, have been rehoused into hostels. The housing association want to renovate this building and pass it on, but have recently accepted that Greg cannot live in a hostel with his terminal illness. He has been given a stay of execution in his home until his illness does the executing for them.

Today, Greg has a friend with him – Marble, a man I'd met before outside on the street. One of many characters who used to drift in and out of Greg's orbit while he busked for money. Marble has forged a thirty-year career out of manipulating the benefits system and washing windows really badly for cash in hand. In skin the colour of jaundice, a half-zipped tracksuit and branded trainers, he yabbers and smokes. Greg once told me that Marble had called him at two in the morning, wanting to know how to spell 'plonker' so he could write it in a letter to the council. Marble. Because he's about as sharp as one.

'How's the job, Kate?' Greg says.

'More complicated than it looks,' I tell him. 'Everyone likes things done differently. I love the snow, though.'

'It's like the Snowman,' Marble says. 'Abominable. You know. The Yeti.'

'Or the Sasquatch,' I say, 'if you're in America.'

'But in the snow,' says Greg, 'he's the abominable one. Snow's all right until it refreezes and gets all slippy. Someone gave me some crampons last year to put on my boots. I played in those and fingerless gloves. Hurt like hell but, you know, the show must go on and all that.'

'Is there only one?' Marble says.

'One what?'

'Abominable Snowman.'

'Yes, Marble,' sighs Greg. 'The hairy one.'

'How did he get to the snow though?' Marble muses.

'The Yeti? He must've walked,' I say.

'That's a stretch, man,' Marble says. 'I don't think he could've walked. It's too far from America to the snow.'

'There's snow in America.'

'America hasn't got snow,' Marble insists. 'America's the desert.'

'It's got nothing to do with snow, Marble,' says Greg, winking at me. 'He can walk it because he's suitably dressed. He's simply got the barnet for it.'

'Oh yeah,' Marble nods seriously, 'that makes sense.'

'You want a cup of tea?' I ask them. 'Frankly, I'm fully up to date on several different ways to make tea.'

Marble salutes me with a can of super-strength lager. 'Nah, we're all right for brews, thanks.'

4.

Ghosts

You'd thought it would give you satisfaction, telling your friends. That they'd see what you'd been driven to, martyr that you are. Instead, it feels embarrassing. Like having to make a confession or report a sentence you've been handed down. 'I'm doing care work.'

One or two of them look briefly aghast before straightening their faces into an interested expression. A few ask why, and you launch into your bogus explanation of it being the only thing you can do, having been denied enough support to do that other, proper job. One simply says, 'Oh . . . Kate . . . no,' in a sad and disappointed voice that makes you feel ashamed of trying to engender sympathy.

Almost all of them are curious about how you can do it. They mean how you can do the bottoms. Bottoms are what most people think it's all about. To be fair, bottoms are turning out to be a significant part of it. You tell them that bottoms are doable. When they belong to strangers, that is. You imagine it would be different with relatives.

Telling them that makes you think of your father. You'd never known your father cry until he'd had to look after your grandfather in the last few weeks of your grandfather's life. You didn't actually see your father crying. You just heard him because you were far away on the other end of a phone. You should have been there, you think now. You, busy partying your pants off and working non-hotshot jobs to pay rent on a run-down flat in a thrillingly dodgy area of London all those years ago, should have helped.

Cleaning your mother, your father, your grandfather must be horribly difficult, you tell your friends, but cleaning the bottoms of people who aren't related to you turns out to be straightforward.

With the door closed behind me, the outside world is silenced. Inside, there is only the hum of electricity and a faint mumbling of disembodied voices. A long corridor ahead is lined with blood-red doors, complemented by a bone-grey floor, with walls and ceiling the colour of yellowing teeth. I walk under plastic lights, some dead, puddles of dark beneath them. Through a set of fire doors, I find a day room, with armchairs and a coffee table. I stop, take off my coat, reach into my bag for my uniform tunic and, when I look up, am startled to see an old woman sprawled in one of the chairs. She lies, head back, mouth open, chest soundlessly rising and falling, beneath a picture hanging on the wall behind her of horses galloping through surf. They look wildly terrified, the whites of their eyes flaring, their grey manes the exact colour of the sleeping woman's hair. I tiptoe out and find Eddie's flat on the next floor up just before I realize I've left the key on the coffee table and sprint back. The sleeping woman has vanished. The key is still there, thank God.

Eddie's flat is much like the rest of the block. Very tatty, very red and seemingly deserted.

Drying washing is pegged from string nailed to the hall ceiling. Trouser legs and shirtsleeves hang like corpses, brushing my face as I walk past a bedroom door. Next a kitchen, red of course, with an ancient stove and a modern fridge. A blue formica table with two matching dining chairs holds a flotsam of crockery and a sticky microwave with a yellow plastic clock propped on top of it. Souvenir tea towels from Wales are pinned up everywhere, decorated with Welsh flowers, Welsh phrases, maps of Wales, recipes for Welsh dishes. I stand in front of this tea-towel art gallery for a few seconds, listening to the yellow clock ticking time away.

At last I find him, a tiny, balding man in a big chair in the living room, wearing a beige shirt with a large collar, a pair of navy tracksuit bottoms and burgundy slippers. He has a spillage of what I hope is tea at his feet. All the windows are firmly shut, the central heating is full on and so is a perilous-looking four-bar heater with imitation flames. Eddie is frowning at the black leather sofa opposite him. There's nothing on it except for a stained tea towel printed with a picture of an old woman in traditional Welsh dress.

I wait. He says and does nothing except stare at the sofa. 'Hello, Eddie. I'm your carer today. My name's Kate,' I say timidly. 'Pleased to meet you.' He looks up only briefly.

'How are you today, Eddie?' I try.

'Bit low.'

'Sorry to hear that. Perhaps you'll feel better after some food. What would you like? Let's start by clearing up this tea, eh?'

I go to the kitchen for a cloth, taking his empty mug and half-eaten breakfast. In the fridge, I find bread, milk, eggs, half a banana and a pack of a dozen chicken legs that would take longer than my allotted half-hour to cook. Elsewhere, sugar, coffee and a collection of Marvel dried milk tins filled with biscuits, teabags and gravy granules.

'Eddie,' I say when I've cleaned up the tea. 'D'you want to keep me company in the kitchen while I make you something?' It takes an age for him to Parkinson's-shuffle through behind his walking frame, but eventually he settles onto one of the dining chairs and perks up a bit while I try to work out which of the sticky black knobs works which of the sticky black hobs.

Eddie eats his omelette while I tidy up and find his medications, and then we walk painfully back to the living room, his inner ankles scraping together as he hobbles along three inches to a step. At one point, he comes to a complete standstill and I have to say, 'One, two, three, go,' to start him off again. I'm so anxious he might fall that I walk behind him holding one of the kitchen chairs. When he reaches the living room, I smuggle it back on the premise of fetching more tea so he won't know I didn't have faith in him.

'Comfortable now, Eddie? I'll be off in a tick.'

He takes a deep breath. 'Can I ask you a question?'

'Course you can.'

There's a long pause before he says, 'Who's that man there?' He points to the sofa.

'I don't see a man there. What does he look like?' I say.

'He's a nasty-looking man,' says Eddie, 'a dirty man. He's no good. Can you not see him?'

I look to my right at the old Welsh woman on the crumpled tea towel. 'No, I can't see him.'

'Why's I seeing him then? He's laughing at me.'

The room is very hot. There's no noise except for the whirr of the motor animating the fake flames of the electric fire.

'Eddie,' I say, 'I think some medications can make you think you're seeing things. But I want you to know you're quite safe.'

'That's right!' Eddie yells at the sofa. And then quietly to me, 'That's what the doctor said.'

I'm just in time for my next call. It's a two-carer, double-up visit at the top of one of my favourite tower blocks with the lovely Jen. 'Busy day?' Jen chirps in the lift on the way up.

I tell her where I've just been. 'Ah,' says Jen, 'that place. None of us like going there. No way you get me going there on my own after dark. I get my son to drive me and wait outside.'

'It does seem lonely,' I say. 'Eddie thought he could see someone sitting on the sofa. I told him it was the medications playing tricks on him.' Jen raises an eyebrow. 'What?' I say brightly. 'What's wrong with that?'

'Oh, for heaven's sake,' she says. '*I* don't think it's medications. Not for a minute, I'm telling you. That place is bloody spooky.'

That night I lie awake, imagining being in Eddie's flat all by myself. I wonder if he's sleeping or shuffling about or sitting in the kitchen beneath the tea-towel art gallery. I try to imagine how it must feel to see a nasty-looking man sitting on your sofa in the shadows created by street lamps coming through gaps in the curtains. It makes me worry about Greg, alone in his building. The next day, I go early to him.

I let myself in with the key that I keep now. I've dissuaded Greg from going out because three weeks ago he phoned me at four in the morning having gone for a night wander. This was not an odd thing for him to have done. Greg is used to spending most of his time outside. Before his illness, he'd rarely been in. He'd be busking to shoppers outside the greengrocer's all day where I'd often stopped to talk to him, then he'd play to people going home from work, and then to partygoers on their way out for the evening. Finally, when he'd packed up his stuff, he'd get a beer and some grub and go sit on a wall to have a chinwag and a fag with any Tom, Dick or Harry who happened to come by. Once, when I'd come out of the pictures at eleven thirty, he was squatted on the cinema steps. I'd sat down with him when all the film-goers had gone and I was still there, chatting, a couple of hours later. That's just how it was with Greg.

But during that last night wander, he'd collapsed, and I'd had to leave my bed to help him home so now I've decided it's too dangerous for him to attempt the stairs, let alone roam the streets. He often wants to try, but I don't want him to fall and break himself any more than he is already broken.

We spend this, my day off, as we do many of my spare days now, together. Weirdly, I love these times, just the two of us. He, estranged from his family, ashamed of his predicament and me, avoiding my anxiety. We're in a stricken spaceship that's lost all power, drifting. There seems nothing we can do to alter our course, and this is oddly blissful because we no longer have to worry about things we should be doing. Should give up smoking. Should eat properly. Should drink something other than coffee or alcohol. Should take his temperature to check for infection. Should let my family know where I am. It's all too late. None of the shoulds would make any difference. Instead, Greg plays records from the sofa and I sit reading in the comfy chair opposite him and we are pulled slowly, relentlessly, on toward a black hole as he tells me about music.

'Listen. Underneath all that, you can hear the triangle. I've known some of the best percussionists in my time. Absolute experts. Jody Linscott was always good on the triangle. Could play it like a demon or an angel. What a lot you can get out of a triangle if you know how. Just a little piece of bent metal and a stick. Brilliant.'

'Oh,' I say, 'yeah, I hear it now. You think you could manage a scrambled egg or two?'

He manages one egg and half a slice of toast smothered in butter. That's two hundred calories, I think, going back to my book.

'Kate, is this all there is left?'

'What? Of the eggs?'

'No. Of life. This. In here. I mean, I love you coming, and you're a great friend and all that, but it's miserable just waiting for you or death to arrive. Sometimes, I'm not sure who's going to show up first.'

'Just tell me more about this track,' I say.

'You hear Mick Ronson clicking the strings with his plectrum as he plays?'

I listen. Proper listen. Music was once just one sound that made me want to dance or sing. I didn't hear its individual components until Greg showed me the strands of them. The way a bass line trucks on through the song, dragging the percussion with it, and the strings swoop in and out over the vocal story. Now, every time I hear a track repeated I notice something new in it. I can hear the plectrum clicking against the guitar between notes as we float, uncaring, through the day, focusing only on sounds and words and eggs. Occasionally, we bicker.

'I have to get out. See people. I hate being inside all the time. The walls and the ceiling are so close. And so straight. It's like being inside a fucking envelope. I can't see anything in here.'

'Oh, please don't, it's too risky. You might fall. People should come here instead.' Those wretched shoulds.

'It's miserable here. My eyes are terrible. Glued shut. It's that gel stuff you keep putting in.'

'Ointment. But it can't be that. You don't let me put enough in to make any difference.'

'What are you talking about? You're always putting it in. Morning, noon and night you're putting that stuff in. It's fucked my eyes.'

'I've only done it twice. When can I do them again?'

'In a second.'

'That means ages.'

'No, it doesn't, it means a second. What're you doing?'

'Getting the ointment.'

'No, not yet. In a minute.'

'God, it's getting longer.'

'Go the whole hog and give it an hour,' he grins. 'I might be ready for it by then.'

I throw a cushion at him and return to my book.

The following week, I'm back on a call to Eddie, relieved to be visiting the eeriness of his block in daylight hours and delighted that he's pleased to see me. Eddie has good news. He's going with social services to look at a nursing home. It's in a modern building and they have a room on the ground floor so he's hoping they'll let him have a cat.

'There's a cat in *Postman Pat*,' he says, 'I think I'll call it Pat.'

'Pat's the postman, though,' I tease. 'The cat's called Jess.'

And then, without warning, Eddie's jollity disappears. His voice is flat and serious. 'I want to leave here.' He stands absolutely still and then he starts to cry. Silently and without moving, like his face is behind a windowpane with rain running down. He sniffs. Recovers himself a little. 'I'll be glad to leave these things behind.'

'Yes, it'll be good to get rid of stuff you don't need.' I'm thinking of the tea towels and the Marvel tins and the fake, electric fire.

'The ghosts!' he shouts suddenly, his voice fierce, defiant even. The word is shocking, out in the open, no hiding from it. 'I can leave them ghosts behind.'

Maybe a cat would chase away Eddie's ghosts. Certainly, caring for one might improve his quality of life more than anything. Everyone likes to be needed but it seems that at the end of your days, the problem is finding someone or something to need you. I doubt any nursing home will let

Eddie have a cat really, though. I squeeze his hand and hope this one will be the exception.

You'd started out thinking you'd do this job efficiently but without becoming too fond of anyone. That you wouldn't get attached. Caring without caring, if you like. Your friend showed you a news article the other day. It was written by an expert in artificial intelligence who said that robotics are becoming so advanced that we'll soon have automatons to care for our elderly relatives. You'd felt like telling her that the robot's already here. That you're the robot. You were so determined to be a robot carer at the beginning. But somehow this doesn't seem to be quite how things are panning out, does it?

I don't have much time before my next call, but I rush up to Greg's flat.

'God, am I glad to see you,' Greg says.

'What happened?'

'Nothing new. It's been a miserable day. I'm hurting. I need to see your cheerful smile.'

'And I need to see your grumpy one,' I say. 'And you need something to do. You'll end up talking to the walls otherwise. Or,' I add, thinking of Eddie, 'seeing ghosts. You need a project. Something to take your mind off things.'

'I've got one.'

'Really?'

'Yeah. Are you listening to this?' Gil Scott-Heron's *I'm New Here* sounds, as all music does, fantastic in Greg's flat where he has rigged up line-ins and line-outs from various half-defunct turntables, radios and CD players to speakers assembled on the coffee table in front of him, on shelves and side tables and over the kitchenette worktop. 'I'm compiling a list of top-ten death albums. The best music made by artists who were about to die.'

'Oh, great. That'll really take your mind off things. Anyway, Gil Scott-Heron wasn't actually dying, was he? When he made that. He didn't die for another six months.'

'Oh,' says Greg, 'believe me. You know when you're dying, mate.'

5.

I don't like it when they do this

'I'm sorry,' Mrs Rose says, 'but I wasn't expecting you. Where's Chrissy?'

'I don't know.'

Mrs Rose, like Eddie, is among the first of the customers I visit alone, having now, after two weeks, been deemed capable of doing so. Experienced carers generally dislike the two-carer calls that were part of my training because, although they get to see a colleague, the colleague is sometimes late. This is not necessarily because the colleague is to blame, but because the gap between visits is often shorter than the length of time it takes on public transport or walking to get from one to the next. Nervous of going to new people on my own, I miss those double-up calls. Having stuttered who I am into the intercom, waited while Mrs Rose decides whether to let me in or not, found my way to the right room and introduced myself with a smile I don't feel, I'm now trying to make myself look as capable as possible of getting her efficiently through her morning routine without ever having gone about it myself.

Mrs Rose sits, demure, in her bed, a large woman in her seventies partially paralysed by illness. She has bobbed hair greying only at her temples, a prim cotton nightgown firmly buttoned up to her chin and one hand on the shiny, hard-shelled handbag in her lap. Her other hand is holding a mobile phone at the ready to call the office and complain.

I hear someone waking and moving in another bedroom along the hall. Her partner, I assume. Mrs Rose glares. 'I don't like it when they do this,' she repeats.

Neither do I. I feel unwelcome and awkward. 'I'm sorry.' I try to imagine how I would feel in her situation. To have a stranger appear in your own home without warning. A stranger who has been given instructions to wash you. Who will see you naked. Remove your incontinence pad. Witness you at your most vulnerable. A person you have never met before. I know I wouldn't like it.

'Why have they sent *you*?'

'Perhaps Chrissy's not well?'

'I'm not happy. Do you know how to work the hoist?' Now I see she is not so much stern as tearful. She is afraid, not in control of this unexpected alteration to her day.

I look at the hoist that takes up a good portion of one corner of the room. I haven't seen this type of hoist before. 'No, I'm afraid not.' This sounds stupid. Now I wonder if I would trust a stranger to lift me using a hoist they'd never encountered before. I think not.

'Then how?'

'Would you like me to leave?'

She tuts. 'I can't stay in bed all day.'

I'm at a loss as to how to reassure her that I'm a safe pair of hands. Am I even a safe pair of hands? I've had three days' training in the office that doesn't really amount to any more than ticking boxes to say I've been told things, and a few weeks out on the job with experienced carers.

If I'm going to do this visit, we need to get started because I know I'll be slow. I know for a fact I can't get it done in the time given while I'm learning how it all goes. I long to walk away but take a deep breath. 'Look, I know I'm new but if you can tell me how to do it, I'll do it properly. It might take longer than usual, but I don't mind. If you can bear me taking it slowly, I won't leave until you're happy.'

Later, she'll refer to this as the moment she knew we were going to get along.

Veronica Rose patiently instructs me through some complex manoeuvring to get her stubborn legs out of bed. Many of our customers' rooms are, like hers, small with little space for the equipment they require. Detailed methods of moving are developed to complete tasks that must seem straightforward on paper but are challenging on the ground within the restrictions of space and time, the entanglement of cables, the distance of plugs, and the precariousness of urine bottles, mugs and piles of books and magazines. Sometimes the instructions given by remote social services and hospitals are laughable and the bemused carers and their customers *do* laugh at them. But they get them done somehow, with routines adjusted as new equipment comes on board or the customer's condition changes, or when they and their carers come up with fresh ideas on how to make things run ever more smoothly. They make it look easy, but outsiders cannot tell how expert carer and customer have become at carrying it all out and struggle to do it if they try it for themselves. On this first visit, of course, *I'm* the outsider who's struggling. When I was at university, I remember being given some sort of test to find out what learning style I preferred. I can't remember all the different learning styles, or even what mine was, to be honest, but it definitely didn't involve being shoved in at the deep end without first being shown how.

On his way downstairs, Mr Rose puts his head of wild black hair into the room to say hello. Although it is his wife who needs care, he appears quite frail himself. When he leaves the room, I hear each individual stair creaking as he treads slowly down, one careful step at a time.

I line things up precisely, moving pieces of furniture around as Veronica and I begin our manoeuvres. It takes me a good few minutes to discover that the wheeled shower chair only fits close enough to the bed when the bed is raised to an exact point where a soft part allows it to be pressed an extra inch into the blue mattress. As Veronica slides onto the chair, it's difficult to grip it against her moving weight with my right hand while I'm reaching over with my left to stop the bedlinen coming with us. The brakes on pieces of equipment, like the instructions for using them, can be flimsy and customers are heavy. It's hard work. My back complains. Then we execute an eight-point turn within just four square feet, Veronica's possessions balanced all around us. It's like having to push a shopping trolley with wonky wheels through a china department. One false move and I'll have the lot of it over.

I lift a wooden stool out of our way to free up the route to the bathroom. Corners and doorways in the narrow corridor must be taken at particular angles in order not to graze the toes that I can't see because I have to pull the chair backwards. Next, I must undress Veronica and extricate the incontinence pad with her still sitting in the wheeled chair. With practice this will become easy, but at first it's a conjuring trick. And it's embarrassing not being very good at it, for Veronica as well as me. There is a skill in doing these tasks. It is not something that one studies for or takes examinations in, but it is a skill nonetheless and it involves not only the practical aspect of the job but also ensuring that everything is carried out efficiently and discreetly so that the dignity and privacy of the customer remain intact.

While Veronica showers, I remake the bed and carry out her instructions to ready the sitting room. Since she cannot walk, she must have everything she needs within reach.

I must be her hands and feet by helping her anticipate and remember what these things are. Some items are standard to everyone and, by now, have become a list in my head. Drinks, snacks, TV remote, spectacles, telephone, door intercom, and falls alarm. In time, as I come to know people, I will become familiar with the extra items unique to each of them. Veronica's turn out to include handcream, the household correspondence file, a notepad and pen, a shawl and her precious Bible. Other things come and go depending on what's happening that day. Her hymnbook when church members are due to visit. Her purse when her great-nieces are expected. Of course, Veronica could ask her husband to bring her what she needs, but when you are chair-bound, having to do this makes you feel like a dependent, useless nuisance no matter how much your elderly partner loves you.

Gathering everything onto Veronica's side table, you catch your lilac tunic reflected in a mirror. For a second you feel guilt that you're here and not in the hospital where you once worked. Then you feel relief. Here, there's no paperwork reducing your contact time with people to an amount too small to be effective, no supervision to prepare for, and no managers asking how you think they can save yet more money but never acting on any of the answers.

Above all, there's no decision to be made over one treatment option against another. Doctors, nurses and allied health professionals accept that, despite their best efforts, some patients will die. You tried for a long time to get used to that. Sometimes one treatment had to be chosen against another. Of course, it almost always turned out to be the right choice but very occasionally it wasn't. When that happened to patients you were helping to care for, you felt grief, failure, horrible anxiety. With this fear of losing people getting ever larger in your mind, you found yourself checking and rechecking your care plans, visiting patients more often than your limited time would allow or ringing the ward in the middle of the night to make sure your instructions had been correctly carried out by the brilliant but overstretched nurses.

Everyone thought you were an excellent and diligent practitioner. Your managers couldn't praise you enough. In reality, you were simply terrified.

'Ready,' Veronica calls. I pull her out of the shower and wheel her just close enough to the sink to be able to clean her teeth before we go into the sitting room where she will spend her day. I inspect her flawless skin and help her dry and cream it. The moisturizer smells of citrus and vanilla.

'What did you use to do?' I say.

'Midwife,' she says. 'It was wonderful. I couldn't have children of my own, but I loved helping other women have them.'

We chat, as we will go on to chat in my many visits that follow, about our previous jobs, about our families, about being women, mothers and wives. I'm in awe of her undertaking a successful career when I have failed at doing the same. She, decades older than me, came to England as a young Ghanaian immigrant, was able to withstand racism and shyness to maintain her dignity and values while qualifying, and then gave her life to our National Health Service. Was able to work nights and look after the house during her tired days, did not ever complain or give up. Unlike me. I trust her from the outset.

I begin to trust Mr Rose too. I will go on to meet him in the kitchen on most of my visits. He's a natural environmentalist. Always fixing things, just like my father does. Recycling plastic packaging into intricate towers of plant-potting containers taped and balanced together on the windowsills.

Holes in the little yoghurt pots strung along the top drip water into the big ice-cream tubs below when Mr Rose tips water saved from the washing-up bowl into them. He pushes seeds from fresh tomatoes harvested in his front garden straight back into the soil to grow into what he calls *tomayto slips*. Ignores sell-by dates as things intended to make us throw away perfectly good food in order that we'll spend money on more. Spending money on more, Mr Rose feels, is foolishness. 'Spending money on things to love! What is that? The earth is what we should love. All this talk about the earth going extinct,' he says. 'What nonsense! It is us that is going extinct. This foolishness that we think we are extincting the earth! The earth was created by God. The earth will simply go on. She has no opinion about us going extinct. She will not miss us. And never mind our foolishness, we will go on with her anyway. Not as human beings. And certainly not in heaven. As compost! We are but God's compost!'

'You're quiet today,' says Veronica, after her shower, a few visits later.

Instead of saying I'm fine, that it's just my age, a lack of sleep, I tell the truth. 'I've got this friend,' I say. And it all spills out. I tell her about Greg. I tell her how our friendship has gone from an exchange of greetings on the street to me spending time looking after him. I tell her how he's stubborn but funny and that I really can't remember when I first knew his name was Greg. Probably on a day when I'd stopped to chat for longer than usual, perhaps a day when I was particularly fed up. I tell her how, with my children grown into young adults and the house often empty, some days I didn't talk to anybody else *but* Greg.

Veronica was staring at me, but I continued.

'All of a sudden, he wasn't there,' I said. 'Eventually, I spotted him in the market. All crouched down. He had a cough he couldn't shake, and his breathing was funny. He'd been to the doctor who thought it was TB. The hospital wanted to talk about scan results, but it was difficult for him to get there on the bus. So I took him in the car and went on to do the shopping. He called me while I was in the check-out queue.'

Veronica didn't interrupt.

'It isn't TB,' I said. 'I wish it was. But it isn't. I felt dreadful that he'd been on his own when he was told that. He hasn't any family near him. He has lots of friends but not many of the sort who can help, and I couldn't bear for him to have to go through everything alone. Not after he sort of kept me company all those years. So now I'm looking after someone I've become fond of who's busy dying in an otherwise aban-doned building. He's refused to move out. He refuses most things, to be honest. But I think he's right. There's nowhere better for him to be than in his home at the end of his days.' I stop speaking, embarrassed at having talked for so long. It was unprofessional, I think. I'm here for her not me. Sharing secrets is not on the task list.

Veronica continues to stare for a few seconds, perhaps she's making sure I've finished talking. When she speaks, I am dumbfounded. 'He sounds like someone who used to come here,' she says. 'Skinny chap. Always wore sunglasses. Two pairs, actually. One on his eyes and the other on top of his hat. My God, he was a grubby bug.'

'He's been here?' It doesn't seem possible that Greg could once have stood where I'm standing now with this calm and graceful woman.

'My husband used to stop and talk to him when he was out getting the shopping,' Veronica says, 'and sometimes Mr Rose would ask him to come and cut the grass or shift some rubbish for us. We used to give him a fiver for doing it, but I think Mr Rose just wanted a chat really. He's a great talker, is Mr Rose. And so was your busker friend, Greg.'

I can well imagine the lively conversations that would have been had between Greg and Mr Rose about God, the earth and human foolishness.

This inclusive attitude is one that I will come across frequently in my customers. I'm not sure many of my friends would welcome Greg into their homes so readily, without any references or recommendations, in such a trusting manner. Certainly, my husband is wary of him. He wishes I didn't have to spend so much time at the flat. Especially when I'm also working such unsociable hours. He misses me at the dinner table. But I seem to have committed myself to all this caring now. The paid caring with its rules and boundaries and safeguards, and the unpaid caring for Greg with none of them.

6.

Beryl

You begin to amuse yourself by categorizing your visits into two T types: Tender or Ticklish.

She thinks the world is spinning and that when she's being washed she's in danger of falling from the ceiling. Her fingernails scrabble up an invisible cliff, slashing the air in front of your face, almost taking out an eye. You tell her she's safe and she screams that she's not and you tell her she is and she screams that she's not until, finally, you admit that, good God, you're having a tricky old time this morning.

She stops screeching and asks why. 'Because you're wearing me out, is why,' you tell her with a wink. And she clasps her hands about your shoulders, kisses your cheek, pats your back and croons, 'There, there, there,' like a mother to a child and you file this visit, as is so normally the case, under Tender.

He's contrite at the door, head bowed, dressing gown belted over his bobbled blue tracksuit, blocking your way inside. 'Before you come in,' he says, 'I want you to know I won't do that thing I did the last time.' You're keen to be out of the cold but he doesn't budge, just looks up through hair that falls uncombed over his eyes, his face lined with both age and anxiety. 'You know,' he says, 'when I took your hand and I sort of licked it.'

You tell him you don't mind him taking your hand but he's right, you didn't appreciate the licking. Again, he looks up through his hair, coyly this time, like an elderly grey-haired Princess Diana. 'I was afraid you wouldn't come again and, well, I've become quite fond of you.' It makes you happy, this affection, and you're just filing his visit, like hers, under Tender when he adds, 'You're quite pretty, you know.' Now you feel chuffed. 'Quite pretty,' he repeats. You swish your hair. Until he adds, with absolute seriousness, 'But definitely no beauty queen.' You're brought right back down to earth. But it tickles you. It's Tenderly Ticklish, in fact. Could almost put him in either category.

Tender or Ticklish, the customers are never Terrifying. Even those that lash out or refuse their medications. Turns out only other carers can be Terrifying. You've only met Terrifying once in the carer who was resentful, late and bad-tempered. Who spoke to you in bites and snarls. Called you foolish when you didn't know what to do. Threw the towels at you and swore at you for not catching them. A carer who simply didn't want to be there, really. During your first week on the job Itzie had told you this could happen. You hadn't really believed her, but had asked what you should do in that situation anyway. Itzie had said, 'Just focus on the customer. They're the priority. Remember they're what really matters.'

You got weepily through that Terrifying visit on the strength of those words and now you know you'll be unlikely to encounter Terrifying ever again. You've begun to care enough about caring to challenge any co-worker you come across who doesn't. So – even though the occasional customer might come a little bit close to it – that's actually the end of Terrifying right there.

Beryl likes Chrissy and she likes Sheila and she likes Jen but she doesn't like me. It isn't because of my age, my colour, my gender or anything I've done. I reckon it might be because she thinks I'm posh. Or perhaps it's just because I'm new. Not yet broken in by her acid tongue.

Beryl's the kind of girl who's been generating rumours all her life, and she's still generating them now. She's entirely bedbound, but was found on the floor first thing yesterday. Chrissy and Jen were the first carers in, but what everyone wants to know is who was the last one out. The rumour is that the last carer out has been suspended and Beryl's family want her skewered on her own mop in front of a jury for not pulling up that bleedin' bed rail properly.

Beryl's lunchtime and bedtime calls are done single-handedly, but in the morning it takes every ounce of the efforts of two to get her washed, dressed and ready for the day's television game-show viewing. Sheila's just taking our key from the key safe when I arrive.

'It was Julie,' she says, as we get in the lift. 'Last carer out.'

'Julie would never leave a bed rail down,' I say when we reach the third floor.

'*None* of us would ever leave a bed rail down,' says Sheila.

The sheltered housing of the type Beryl lives in is uninspiring. The interior decorators of these buildings must be in competition to find the most dismal colour scheme possible. It's the only explanation for the shades of old candlewax, dirty sand and overcast skies used as the colour palette for their decor. Over the years, the walls have been scuffed with black streaks and the woodwork chipped by all the badly driven wheelchairs and mobility scooters that sit behind most of the identical doors of each of the flats. The one opposite Beryl's flat is open and belching cigarette smoke. Someone becomes visible through the smog.

'Morning, Colin,' says Sheila. He grunts and shuffles back into the gloom.

Beryl is asleep in a pair of Minnie Mouse pyjamas with red polka dots on them, scattered with crumbs and cigarette ash. Her long grey hair has been partly pinned up into a pink hairband. It reminds me of the silky-ribboned topknot that my friend used to tie on the head of her elderly

Yorkshire terrier in an effort to make the miserable old dog look cute.

'Morning,' says Sheila, squeezing the sleeping woman's hand.

'Morning, Beryl,' I say.

'Oh, bleedin' hell, Sheila,' says Beryl, without opening her eyes. 'What's she doing 'ere?'

'Don't vex now,' says Sheila. 'Wakey, wakey.'

Beryl's getting on for a hundred, but she pouts like a child and her eyes remain closed. 'I'm knackered. I been up all night.'

'Oh,' I say, 'you weren't comfortable?'

'No. I was dancing a bleedin' foxtrot,' snaps Beryl. 'What do you faaackin' think?'

Sheila squeezes the hand again. 'Fetch a bowl of water, Kate,' and Beryl's toothless howl chases me into the bathroom as I grab a pad, soap, water and a pair of fresh pyjamas with Daisy Duck and pink polka dots on them.

When Sheila washes her face, Beryl opens her eyes. She has the sunken temples typical of those with chronic malnourishment, and cheekbones like blades that a supermodel would kill for. Naked, she's all ribs and clavicles; breasts and tummy like dead balloons. We soap and rinse her scrawny arms, just bones wrapped in onion skins, muscle and fat all stripped away. Veins run like blue worms over hands that end in fingers yellowed by the tar of a lifetime's cigarettes and rings rattle, loose as beads strung on string, between the knots of Beryl's prominent knuckles and enormous arthritic first-finger joints.

This is what the anorexia of old age looks like. Not anorexia nervosa, the eating disorder. Just plain old not eating. There are all sorts of reasons why elderly people don't eat and Beryl has several of them. No teeth, blunted taste buds, too many medications and the immobility that comes of having to spend life in bed that, together with her smoking, means she rarely feels hungry. Her pyjama trousers would be too small for most twelve-year-olds, and when we try to remove them Beryl becomes as rigid as a baby refusing to get in its pushchair, flattening herself to the bed and shuffling down until her feet are against the footboard. I'm trying to gently prise them loose when someone grunts, 'Borrow your lighter, Bee?'

'Colin,' snaps Sheila, in her fierce Jamaican accent, hands on her large hips. 'We busy here. Out with you.' I throw the clean white towel over Beryl's nudity. It looks like a shroud.

If Beryl is a skinny old terrier with a topknot, Colin is an enormous balding walrus. Dressed in brown, extra-plus-size jogging bottoms and a khaki T-shirt that finishes well above his ample belly, he has whiskery patches from a bad shave all over the trembling of his double chins. The exertion of crossing the corridor has left him breathless.

'Col,' shrieks Beryl from under the towel, like a cadaver come to life on Hallowe'en. 'They're killing me. Get in 'ere!' She stamps on the footboard. 'If you go an' leave me with 'em, Col,' she screams, 'I'll never let you in my gaff again. Nevva, you 'ear?'

'Colin,' says Sheila, marching around the bed toward him. 'Out. Now.'

He lumbers off, scraping up the pink plastic lighter from Beryl's bedside table as he goes.

'Coliiiiiiiiin, don't you never come back,' screams Beryl as we take the sliding sheet, a square of slippery green material, and roll Beryl onto it to pull her safely back up the bed again. Beryl kicks out when Sheila takes up one of her feet, but Sheila begins to tickle. Beryl giggles. I take down the pyjama trousers and, while Sheila keeps Beryl cackling, I undo the pad and clean her.

I'd thought it would be more difficult cleaning a man than cleaning a woman, but cleaning a man has become just lift, wash and dry. Cleaning a woman feels somehow more intimate. I'm concentrating on keeping it gentle but efficient, when Beryl stops moving. I sense a ripple of exhilaration run through her body. In the seconds before she yells, the satisfaction on her face tells me she's about to shoot me down but it's not until the noise of cars on the road outside is silenced by a red light that Beryl chooses to open her mouth.

The phrase tears through the air like a bullet. 'Get your bleedin' fingers out of me!' I wince. I've done nothing invasive but still I can't help blushing. I can hear the news on Colin's television and the couple in the room next door having breakfast. I can hear the sounds of conversations on the street outside. 'Get your hands out of my faaackin'—'

'Enough, Beryl!' says Sheila, rubbing Beryl's shoulder. 'All done now. Let's get you dressed.'

Beryl's not one of my regulars but I see her once a week on my own as well as during this morning double-up call. I dread the times I'm here alone. The bit I hate most is when Beryl holds me to ransom over her medications, making me wait before refusing them in imaginative ways. Dropping them in the sheets, spitting them at me, allowing them to fall from her mouth over the edge of the bed while she stares provocatively. Or just screaming, 'Help me! Help me, someone! She's faaackin' killing me!' Our little battle is good news for the carer who works with me on the morning I'm here with them, though. It makes giving the medications so much easier for them.

'Here's your tablets, then, Beryl,' says Sheila.

'Thank you, Sheila,' Beryl says, looking me in the eye for the first time this morning and opening her mouth wide so that Sheila can put the spoon easily into it. She swallows the medications down with gusto and smirks at me where I'm standing in the open-plan kitchen putting cereal into a bowl and buttering some toast. I grip the butter knife hard and slam the milk carton down onto the worktop. Milk splashes out of it and all over the floor.

'Look at that. What a bleedin' nuisance,' says Beryl. 'Causes about as much chaos as a puppy shitting razor blades.'

I say nothing for the rest of the visit. Beryl doesn't care.

'You know what I think?' Sheila says in the lift on the way down.

'Go on.'

'I reckon it was the family that left that bed rail down. Maybe her son came here after Julie had gone that night. To get some peace and quiet.'

'Peace and quiet? With Beryl?' I say. 'Are you kidding?'

'Honestly, the daughter-in-law's worse,' says Sheila.

The following evening, I manage to get Beryl to take her medications by bribing her with a Crunchie bar. We've got fractiously through the pad change and I tuck her in. 'Right then,' I say, 'I'll love you and leave you.'

'Don't lock the door,' Beryl says, in an unusually timid voice.

'Don't lock the door?' I finger our key to her flat in my pocket. 'But anyone could get in.'

'Don't you lock that faaackin' door.' The voice is stronger now.

'I have to.'

'Colin's lost the other key!' she screams. 'Don't you lock the door with your one.'

'Oh,' I say. 'Colin.'

'Yes. Colin,' she glares. 'Miss Goody Two-Shoes is what you are. Locking my friend out so's you don't get told off.'

'But what if someone else comes in? What if something goes wrong?' I say.

'I don't care if something goes wrong, lady. I'm stuck in 'ere day in day out. I just want to 'ave a drink and a fag and a laugh sometimes.' She spits at me. 'But what do you know about that?' She stops. Lets her skinny chin drop onto her skinny chest. Morosely.

I can hear the couple next door clearing away their dinner table. I can hear *Emmerdale* on Colin's telly. I can hear some-one outside on the street talking about how Luiz should never have been sent off last night. Beryl sighs into the hush. Then, without raising her head, she murmurs to herself. 'I bet you never even swear, do you?'

All my pent-up humiliation comes to the front of my brain in a rush of reaction without filtration or reflection. 'Well,' I say through gritted teeth, 'I can't force you to have your fucking door locked, so I won't fucking lock it, but on your fucking head be it if something goes fucking wrong.'

We are both stunned silent. Jesus, I think. That certainly wasn't on the bloody task list. I hope there's not a camera in the room.

Beryl stares at me, mouth wide open. Then she squeals, tips back her head and laughs like a drunk hyena. 'I bleedin' love you, nursey,' she yells and, in that moment, I realize we have become partners in crime, brothers in arms, best friends forfuckingever. 'Have a peaceful night then,' I say. 'Don't let him put the bed rail down this time, though, eh?'

Outside, I call the office and tell them Beryl hasn't allowed me to lock the door because Colin comes into her flat at night, but that he only puts the bed rail down so they can chain-smoke side by side more comfortably. He probably didn't leave it down on purpose. He just forgot to pull it up again.

When I get to Greg, he's watching reruns of *Porridge* on the telly. We've seen all the episodes at least twice.

I pull open the fridge. 'Hey, well done.'

'Huh?'

'You ate the cheesecake. But what about the sandwich?'

'Couldn't be bothered.'

I take a deep breath, thinking of Beryl. 'You know what,' I say, 'you're right. Of course you can't stay here, in this flat, for the rest of your life.' He looks up. 'I'll borrow the car. Get you into town. You can see people. Have a drink and a fag and a laugh.'

'Next Saturday?'

'Can't it be Friday? My day off.'

'There'll be more people about on Saturday.'

'OK, Saturday. But I can't stay with you. I'll just have to take you and bring you back in between people, yeah?'

'Cracking,' he says. 'Thanks, Kate.'

'You'll need a haircut though.'

'What?'

'A haircut. You look a state.'

'Hold on a minute,' he frowns. 'A haircut's a bit more of an operation than you think.'

'Why?'

'Well, we need a lot of equipment for a start. Mirror, newspaper on the floor, towel around the neck.'

'Clippers.'

'Yes,' says Greg, 'clippers. And a cut-throat razor.'

'Both?'

'Oh, the razor,' he says, 'is just for when you do it all wrong.'

7.

Spoiling people

I have my regular customers now. Beryl gets swapped for Margaret, a delightful elderly woman who lives nearer to me, and after I've helped her wash and dress I usually cycle on to Veronica Rose, and then to Mr Radbert.

Mr Radbert is not an easy call. A big man from St Lucia, living alone, who has survived a stroke and is now in the early onset of dementia, it takes two of us to hoist him out of his often-wet bed, onto the toilet and through the showering. His home is on the ground floor of an old Victorian house. Both the house and Mr Radbert are more than a little the worse for wear. Bits of them are always malfunctioning or falling off. I've only been to Mr Radbert a dozen times but I'm already familiar with jammed key safes, lensless spectacles, gluey eyes, defrosting freezers, armless wheelchairs and blocked ears. Anyone else's sanity would be smashed to pulp by it all, but Mr Radbert's relentless fortitude and bawdy sense of humour aren't so much as bruised.

When I first met him, Mr Radbert kept an electric wheelchair under a storage cover in the small patch of yard in front of his house. He used to have minor but increasingly frequent accidents in it, regularly losing all power in distant branches of Argos and the Nationwide Building Society. After one too many rescues, social services have concluded he can no longer be safely in charge of a motorized vehicle and have swapped his electric wheelchair for a manual one.

When we've lowered him comfortably into it, my fellow carer departs, leaving me half an hour to tidy up, give Mr Radbert his medications and make him breakfast.

Back when I didn't know any better, Mr Radbert asked me to cook him eggs. I'd thought he just wanted a change from cereal, but it turns out he believes eggs can cure baldness. Once I'd begun to incorporate them into his diet, he wanted to buy argan oil too so, no longer able to get there under his own steam and despite it not being on my task list, he'd persuaded me to take him out of the house on an impromptu outing to the health food shop.

Now, on the mornings when I see Mr Radbert, I rub argan oil onto his shiny brown scalp while he eats eggs cooked according to his preference on that day. With his one good hand chasing them around the plate, he tells me about being a self-taught motor mechanic in the seventies, how he'll exact revenge on those responsible for removing the electric wheelchair, and when he'll finally get Itzie, his favourite carer, into bed with him. It takes ten extra, unpaid minutes of my time but I don't mind because Mr Radbert makes me laugh, his optimism is inspirational, and he's promised to give me his car. He's forgotten where it is, of course, but it's a sexy black BMW and it's definitely mine when we find it. Just so long as I drive him back to St Lucia first.

Occasionally, after I've seen Mr Radbert, I'm asked to help with seventy-nine-year-old Mrs Gibson. Several years ago, she began to develop a neurological illness and then suffered a massive stroke that left her bedbound in the tower block where she lives with her husband. The block is a bleak 1960s construction, its paintwork peeling and the intercom spattered with something coughed up, but I like coming here. The Gibsons live on the very top floor where the view is incredible.

Mr Gibson is welcoming. He organizes our pads, wipes, towels and flannels neatly into a tower of plastic boxes. Too infirm himself to carry much, and without a car to collect or a computer to order in, Mr Gibson has to go out for groceries on most days. His wife lies in a medical bed where her armchair once was. The window beyond the flat-screen television at the foot of this bed spans the entire wall. Today the sky is unbroken blue, with cold spring sunshine glinting off distant skyscrapers. I've heard this weather called *severe clear*. It makes that incredible view go on for ever.

I don't know the Gibsons well but today I can see they are troubled. Sheila walks in shortly after me, carrying a bunch of flowers. Daffodils. 'Morning, Mrs G,' she says. 'I brought some of the spring in for you. They're from my garden.' But the flowers do nothing to ease the worry on our customers' faces.

'Catheter's playing up,' says Mr Gibson. Mrs Gibson winces. Sheila asks if she should call the district nurses.

'I called them last night,' says Mr Gibson gloomily. 'They said they'll try to come today but couldn't give a time.' He sighs. 'We're almost out of milk.'

'Tell you what, Mr G,' says Sheila, 'my next call isn't till two and I've got my lunch with me. Why don't I eat it here with Mrs G and wait for those nurses while you go to the shop? Let's get these flowers in a vase,' she says to his wife. 'We'll be all right, won't we?' And to him, 'You enjoy the sunshine. It's a lovely day. Take your time.'

I love Sheila's compassion and I wish I saw it in all the carers that I meet, but I don't.

Late in the day, I have a new call. It's another double-up with Ruth. Ruth's hardly said hello before she's barking orders as we make our way up four flights of stairs to a grubby door that was white several decades ago.

'Keep out of her room. Stay in the kitchen. She'll talk for England if you let her. They made her a double-up when she came out of hospital but it's not necessary. They'll cut it to one carer again soon.'

Inside, it takes time for my eyes to adjust to the dimness of the hallway. The red carpet is worn to brown strings through which I can see black flooring, and the walls are lined with cardboard boxes and carrier bags packed with papers and magazines. In between the boxes and bags are old-fashioned household items. There's a floor sweeper with a long handle like the one I remember playing with at my grandma's house when I was a child, several old mops, a couple of broken lamps and two dusty sewing machines.

The narrow hall ends in three doors, one on the right, one on the left and one straight in front of us. Ruth stands me at this doorway junction before going through the door on the right. She comes back out with a tiny plate and a tiny plastic cup from one of those old-fashioned Thermos flasks that people used to take on long car journeys.

'Wash these up and make a fresh cup of tea.'

Behind Ruth a tiny voice says, 'Bit of cake, please,' but Ruth doesn't answer.

The door on my left leads into a tiny kitchen with a tiny cupboard and two tiny tables. One table is completely covered in half-sized tins of food and on the other is a mini fridge. Next to the sink is a tiny saucepan. 'Where's the kettle?' I shout.

Ruth comes stamping into the kitchen. 'Shut up. If she hears you, she'll give you a million things to do. There's no kettle. Use the pan. Milk no sugar.'

The tiny voice yells, 'Cake!'

Ruth leaves the kitchen. I hear her say 'Teeth,' in a firm voice.

The sink is stainless steel turned brown by tea. Limescale runs from the base of the taps like flowstone in a cave. I do the pitiful amount of washing-up and take a fresh cup of tea out to the hall. Ruth sticks a hand out of the other doorway and swaps the tea for a set of dentures. 'Scrub them with the toothbrush. Then fill the box on the bathroom windowsill with water, put the teeth in and leave them there.'

The remaining door leads into a tiny bathroom with a tiny bucket next to a powder-blue pedestal sink, and a bath. There is an old shower set attached to the bath taps. Not the sort of vintage shower with brass fittings that you find hanging over clawfoot baths in expensive bathrooms. The sort made of a shower head connected to two ribbed plastic tubes that are each pulled up over one of the bath taps. I remember a shower like that at my grandma's house too. The bathroom has a single tiny window. On the windowsill is a hinged plastic box next to several tiny flowerpots filled with dry earth and cactuses. The box, pale pink tinged slightly yellow, is the exact same colour as the dentures. I scrub them and put them in it as instructed.

'All done,' says Ruth, coming back into the hall.

The tiny voice is even tinier behind the door as Ruth closes it. 'Cake, please!'

'We're just going to ignore her?'

'Getting cake is not on the task list,' hisses Ruth. 'Undress her, change her, put her to bed, give her a cup of tea. That's it. Cake is at teatime. It's bedtime. We'll run late if we stay.'

'Cake!'

'Oh, for heaven's sake,' says Ruth, looking at my face. 'You'll spoil her.' She shoves the key at me and leaves.

The door on the right leads into a living room with an armchair and a tiny woman in a bed. If she'd been lying down, her feet would barely have reached halfway, but she's sitting up, her grey hair in a long plait pinned up on top of her round, rather beautiful face, her pale skin crinkled around clear blue eyes. I know I'm going to run late. But I also know that I'm going to fetch that cake.

It doesn't take long to plate up a piece but I have to spend a bit more time adjusting the bedcovers and making sure Tiny Annie's alarm clock is well within arm's length and re-arranging three carrier bags of papers and some knitting further up the bed so she can reach them. She tells me she was once the housekeeper of a small hotel so she is used to sewing and mending, and that she has no children, that it's her great-nephew who made the fruit cake for her. She wants to know about me. I tell her where I live and that my mother used to make my clothes when I was a child but I'm no good at sewing myself.

When Tiny Annie's satisfied, my last call is back with Mr Radbert where Kenny's already waiting. When we've hoisted him into bed, Mr Radbert says, 'Kate, I've a bit of a thirst on me.'

'Cup of tea?'

'Please.'

Kenny looks at me, raises his eyebrows and, even though he's grinning, it makes me sad to hear him say it. 'You'll spoil him.'

Spoiling people. How is it even possible to spoil a half-paralysed, elderly man who has to suffer the indignity of having his bottom wiped? You realize it's impossible to fit spoiling people into the time given to you, that it's against the rules to overstay unless it's an emergency, but it seems you can't help doing it anyway, glad that many of your colleagues can't either.

Wondering where this compassion comes from, you recall your mother when you were young. There were plenty of mothers around back then who stayed at home, but most went out to work. Yours was a bit of both. She was always there during the holidays and when you got home from school but during the day in term time she looked after people in their own houses. Your mother did lots of other things too. She cooked every meal from scratch and sewed matching capes for you and your sister and made jumpers with complicated patterns on a knitting machine. But she also worked as a home help. She was slim and trim and funny and she sometimes told you about her customers.

Your mother's customers loved her. She was always doing things that weren't on the task list. The job took patience and kindness. She was good at it. But you didn't talk to your friends about what your mother did. Perhaps you were just allowing them to assume she was one of the stay-at-home mothers. You and your friends played make-believe games. You pretended to be hairdressers, shop-keepers and librarians. You pretended to be teachers and secretaries. You pretended to be nurses. But, you realize now, you never, ever pretended to be home helps.

'Kate!' Mr Radbert yells as I take his tea through. 'I think that electric wheelchair's with my car. Micky Donagh must have stolen them both.'

I've not yet worked out who Micky Donagh is. Someone from Mr Radbert's murky past.

'I bet they're at the police station,' Mr Radbert continues. 'Do you have a car?'

'Well, my husband has one . . .'

'Is it a big one?'

'It's an estate.'

'Good. My boot's too small for a wheelchair. You can drive us to the station, we'll put the wheelchair in the back of your husband's car and I'll drive my Beamer home. Let's go tomorrow.'

'Actually, I'm a bit busy tomorrow, Mr Radbert.'

'When then?'

It's unlikely Mr Radbert will remember wanting to retrieve his non-existent car for more than a few hours, his brain being filled with so many other ambitions. 'Next Thursday? I've got the afternoon off.'

'Good.' He picks up the mug of tea but stops with it half-way to his mouth. 'An estate,' he muses. The mug begins to shake with excitement. 'An estate! We can stop off at Argos and pick up a double bed!'

Kenny and I look at each other and then back at Mr Radbert.

'Itzie,' he says solemnly, 'is a very big woman.'

8.

My memory's getting terrible

You never noticed them before, but you can spot them now. Waiting at bus stops in the darkness of the early mornings among the army of low-paid workers going out to office cleaning jobs, walking the streets, perched on benches checking their phones or eating a sandwich. Often older women, they wear trainers and black trousers, their pastel-coloured uniforms peeking out from beneath dark coats, rucksacks slung across their backs or big, roomy bags over one shoulder. Suddenly care workers are everywhere.

Now that you know there are several customers behind each one, you find yourself imagining what would happen if, one day, all these care workers disappeared. All that care would fall onto the shoulders of friends and relatives. You think, then, of your father and it seems oddly fitting that, having not helped care for your own grandparent, you are now helping care for several belonging to other people. But not all of your customers have friends or relatives. You try to imagine how they would survive without their carers and conclude that this would be miserable. And lonely. Perhaps even impossible. This job, then, is an essential part of the fabric of a decent society.

And that, of course, is the very best reason of all for doing it.

On the day he's due to go on his little outing, Greg opens the door looking sleepy. 'What day is it?'

'Saturday. I'm taking you into town, remember? You've got five minutes to get out of here.'

He dons boots and the greatcoat that now weighs more than he does. 'Fags, keys, lighter . . .'

'Hurry up.'

'There's always four things. Lighter, fags, keys . . . Keys, lighter, fags . . .'

'Oh, please,' I say. I have to get to Patrick. And after that I've got Brenda. Goodness knows who she is.

'Wait. Fuck, my memory's getting terrible.'

'Fags, keys, lighter, *phone*. Idiot.' I grab it from the worktop and help him down the stairs and out of the building. He emerges, blinking, into the brightness of the car park, unshaven, with a dirty face and nails like claws, as though he is some kind of werewolf. In the car, the werewolf turns into a destitute member of royalty, waving regally to everyone he recognizes while I complain about the freezing breeze coming in through the window that he's wound right down. I leave him in the market, dump the car back home and am only just in time for Patrick's call. That doesn't matter though, because Patrick has no idea who I am, much less what time I'm supposed to be here.

I know a lot about Patrick. Where and when he was born, which wife he loved the best, what he did for a living, when each of his parents died, and that he played the local church organ until his seventieth birthday. Despite the many hours we've spent chatting, however, Patrick knows nothing at all about me.

'Morning, Patrick. It's Kate. One of your carers.' I pick up an empty plastic water bottle lying at the bottom of the stairs.

Patrick is dressed in crisp trousers, a shirt and a cardigan of the sort one sees in the more expensive department stores, but his brown hair is greasy. 'Who? Why? What do you want to do?'

'Whatever you need. Shall we make a meal?'

'Don't be silly,' Patrick snaps.

'Any laundry that needs doing?'

'No. Who *are* you? I'd just like a chat, to be honest.'

'Lovely,' I say. 'Shall we get ourselves a drink first?' And we go into the kitchen where I eyeball the medications. Patrick hasn't missed any of his tablets so I tick that task off my list. As he opens the fridge, I peer over his shoulder. His neighbour's done the shopping. Tick.

Patrick feels along a line of bottles in the door compartment. 'I make sure to keep plenty of cold water in here.' There's a gap where a bottle is missing. I hand him the empty one I'm holding, and he puzzles over it, and then goes to the sink. 'I always count to fifteen as I'm filling them,' he says, 'because I can't see when they're full any more.' When he's counted out loud to fifteen and the bottle is, indeed, exactly full he turns off the tap, puts it in the fridge and takes out a cooled one.

'Oh, that's a nice quiche you've got in there.'

'Would you like a slice?' This is the real Patrick, generous and sociable. He cuts two portions of quiche and I say I'd like some tomatoes too. On our way to the living room, we pass the laundry basket. It's full. We sit together on the sofa. Patrick's house is full of elegant furniture, fine vases and books. I begin with my usual opening, 'What lovely books you have.'

'Collected by me and my late wife,' says Patrick. 'We ran into one another in an airport bar. I can't remember where I was going now, but if my taxi hadn't arrived early, we'd never even have met because I was living in Crouch End and she was living in Tooting. Can you imagine?'

'Fascinating,' I say. 'Now you eat and I'll tell you how I met my husband.' Patrick takes two bites before launching into his next memory.

'I've never visited the Middle East myself,' I say, during another chink in the conversation. 'I have been to Asia, though. Let me tell you about it . . .' Patrick manages a little more food before cutting in again. Eventually, when he's finished, I swap the plates and he eats my portion too. As usual, I get up and look out of the window. 'You've a lovely view.'

'Even better upstairs.'

'Oh, may I see?'

Upstairs, used nightclothes litter the bed. While Patrick looks out of the window, sadly assessing how little he can still see, I silently swap them for fresh pyjamas. Patrick says he needs the toilet and asks me to wait outside the en suite. After ten minutes, I hear swearing.

'Are you all right?'

He screams. Not in fear but in anger. I look around the door. He's reaching behind him. Scrabbling. Scratching. I put out of my mind a younger Patrick who would without doubt have been beyond horrified at this version of himself.

'Come,' I say. 'Would you like a shower?'

'Not today.'

'Let's clean your hands then.'

'Is this the right soap?'

'Yes. Wait. Let me do under your nails. Shall we wash your hair?'

'Thank you,' he says, as I wash it. 'Thank you, thank you, thank you,' over and over.

The bad temper of illness comes back with the hair-drying. 'You'll burn me! Silly girl! No! It's taking too long! Stupid! Ugh!'

Despite his outburst, Patrick's disappointed when it's time for me to go. 'It's so lonely. I can hardly see anything at all now. I can't read. I can't watch television. Not that I ever really liked television.'

'Well,' I say, dropping his dirty nightclothes in the laundry basket, 'you've rather a lot of washing. Why don't we put it in the machine and I'll come back later and help you hang it all out?'

'Would you?'

'Of course.'

'Who are you again?'

Having left Patrick, Brenda is my next call but before I head on to her I drop in at the market to check on Greg. He's sitting on a low wall, holding court and looking frail but happy. The kebab man's given him samosas and he's chatting to a wiry Scotsman. 'This is Smitten,' Greg says to me. And to the man, 'This is Kate. She's my angel.'

'*Rogue* angel,' I say to the man. 'I keep doing things that aren't on the bloody task list. For him and everyone else. Why do they call you Smitten?'

'Because he's in love with someone who isn't in love with him,' explains Greg. 'His next-door neighbour. He's painted their initials together in a heart on the bins.'

'So I can torture myself looking at them every time I leave the house,' says Smitten. 'It hurts so exquisitely, the waiting.'

'Masochist,' I tell him. 'You need to get over this woman who doesn't want you.' And to Greg, 'Do you need to get home yet?'

'You crack on, girl. I'm nowhere near wanting to get back to that depressing old gaff.'

If I'd known what was to come, I'd have frogmarched him back while he still had the energy.

I struggle to find Brenda's house. She has appeared, as commonly happens, without warning on my rota so I know little about her, just a few scant details with the instructions on my task list.

Eventually, having wrestled with a rusting key safe, I find

myself standing in her living room. Brenda's in front of me on her sofa, wearing a bathrobe over the top of her skirt and sweater. She stares at me, rubbing her brow in the manner of someone trying to get rid of a persistent headache. I'm standing in front of a magazine rack stuffed with old newspapers, having been instructed to give Brenda breakfast and medications. She has recently taken one too many tablets so the medications will soon be put into a locked box but, until it arrives, they have been temporarily well hidden. I squat slowly down until my eyes are level with Brenda's knees and rummage behind my back in the newspapers. Brenda's slippers twitch on the carpet. 'What *are* you doing?'

'Just tidying up,' I say brightly. 'And now let me get you some tea.'

In the kitchen, I phone Julie. 'For crying out loud. Where is it?'

'Magazine rack.'

'This is ridiculous,' I hiss. 'It's not there. Does this happen every fucking day?'

'Only since Thursday, when I had to call the ambulance. We were definitely putting it in the magazine rack, but maybe someone's moved it. Try that display cabinet with all the funny glass animals in it. Get her to leave the sitting room so you can have a good search.'

'How?'

'Ask her to make you some tea.'

'I'm making *her* tea,' I say.

'Hello?' Brenda shouts. 'What *are* you doing?'

Back in the living room, Brenda stands up, brows knitted, and stares at me. I feel like a kid in a sweetshop being watched by a shopkeeper in a shop coat made of purple towelling. 'Actually, I was just wondering,' I say, 'if I could have a drink of water?'

'Of course!' Transformed by the thrill of being needed, Brenda wafts happily out to the kitchen.

I leaf again through all the newspapers. Nothing. I try behind the television as I hear her taking a glass from the cupboard. Look in the display cupboard with the funny glass animals in it as she turns on the tap, and rummage down the sides of the sofa to the sound of the glass filling. I drop to my knees and look under the armchairs. Go desperately back to the magazine rack and, just as Brenda returns, I find it. Not mixed in with the newspapers but stuffed between the wall and the rack itself. Someone just hid it extra well. I whip out an old magazine and stand up with the medication blister pack hidden between its pages.

'What've you got there?' Brenda is puzzled.

'*TV Times*. Just checking out a few programmes.'

'You know what,' Brenda says, seeing another way to be useful that again transforms her irritability to sweetness. 'You can have that. In fact –' she bends down and, holding the glass of water in one hand, begins to shove magazines at me with the other – 'you can have these as well. I never look at them. I haven't been in that rack down there for years.'

'That's very kind of you, Brenda. But I think you need your tablets.'

'Oh, I've had those already,' she trills.

'You have?' My God, I think. She can't have taken them twice for a second time this week, can she? Not on the same day there's a werewolf loose on the streets? 'Where do you keep your tablets then, Brenda? Just so I know for the future.' Brenda leads me back to the kitchen. She gives me the glass of water, reaches up on top of the fridge and brings down a dusty brown plastic medicine bottle that's clearly been empty for years.

'Ahhh, perfect,' I say.

'What *was* I doing?' Brenda says.

'You were about to take your tablets. Look, you'd just poured the water.' I hand back the glass and pop the tablets from the blister pack.

'Lovely,' says Brenda.

We return, medicated, to the living room. The doorbell rings. 'Morning,' I say to an elderly man with a terrier standing on the doorstep. I shake the dog's jaws from my leg. 'And you are?'

'Come in, Tony,' Brenda yells.

'Breakfast, Brenda?' I say.

'No, I've had that already.'

'Cup of tea?' I ask weakly.

'Milk and two sweeteners, please,' Tony says.

I return with a tray of cereal and hot drinks. Tony's delighted, Brenda starts tucking in and the terrier happily begins attacking me again as I'm folding the blister pack back into the newspapers. 'What *is* she doing?' Brenda whispers as I jump about, swatting at the dog who is snapping and snarling at my sleeve.

I'm still a little shaken up when I arrive at Stevie's flat. Stevie, a burly blonde Irishman, isn't much of an early riser. As is so often the case, it transpires he didn't want to get up during his hour-long morning call. He wants to get up now instead, during his half-hour lunch call.

'You know they come to me too early, Kate. I can't get up at eleven. Not on a Saturday.'

'But I've got to make your lunch.'

'I'll have a bacon sandwich. We'll get me out of bed and dressed while it's cooking. I like my bacon crispy anyway.'

Stevie has forgotten to ask anyone to buy bacon.

By the time I've got Stevie into his chair, been for bacon, cooked it, taken it to him and administered his medications, it's almost time to be at Lorna's. It's then that my phone rings.

'Help.' It's Greg.

'Now?'

'I'm nearly dead on my feet.'

'Well, that's true,' I say, 'but it'll have to be quick.'

It isn't quick. Greg gets into the car easily, but we're in trouble as soon as he gets out. He has to sit on the pavement outside his block for ten minutes before he can even attempt the stairs.

'You have to hurry, I need to be at Lorna's.' I pull him to his feet and push him through the door toward the bottom of the first flight of stairs.

'I can't.'

'Fucksake.' I push. He takes two steps up.

'Please.'

'Stop.' He's bent double, panting.

I begin to panic. 'Only four more steps and you can rest on the landing. Give me the keys, I'll fetch a chair.' I fetch the chair but leave it on the third landing. 'Take your coat off, it's heavy.'

'Too cold.'

I pull it from his bony shoulders. We struggle painfully up to the chair-bait. He sits. There's only one flight left between me and Lorna's call, but it might as well be Everest. I heave him up by the armpits. He shrieks. 'Please,' I yell. 'I'm going to be running so late if you don't move.'

In the end, I drag the chair up the last flight with Greg in it, step by agonising step, the thud of the legs of it against the stairs shuddering through his fragile bones. Then I drive home, dump the car, cycle to Lorna's, cook her dinner, get her into bed and hurtle on, making up lost time on my bike.

By the time I reach Mr Radbert's house, I'm only five

minutes behind schedule but there's a shape already waiting for me on the road outside. It yells into the dark.

'Hey, you!'

'Blimey. How did you get out here? What are you doing?'

'I got them upstairs to bring me out. I was looking for you. I trust you, Kate.' His voice is soft.

'Aw, thanks,' I say, moved almost to tears by this tender declaration after such a difficult afternoon.

The dark shape sits up tall. 'So,' it bellows, 'did you phone the DVLA about me getting a replacement driving licence or what?'

'Jesus.' I turn the wheelchair around and push it back up the garden path. 'Yeah,' I lie.

'Good. I knew you would. And?'

'Actually, I was hoping you'd tell me a bit more about that shop you're going to build first,' I implore. I begin to warm to my theme. 'I mean, I suppose you'll need my help to get planning permission.'

He looks dumbfounded. Then roars with laughter. 'Planning permission? Not in St Lucia, Kate.'

'St Lucia?'

'Of course!' He's crying at the very thought of needing such an insignificant little thing as planning permission in St Lucia. 'Whoo-hoo-hoo,' he shrieks.

'We're in St Lucia?'

'Of course!'

'My God,' I say, 'there was me thinking I was trekking around in the cold on a pushbike in South London and all the time we're in the tropics. Well, that's bloody marvellous.'

Kenny arrives and we get Mr Radbert ready for bed and hoist him into it. 'Planning permission,' he squeaks every now and then until he's safely bedded down in front of *Dad's Army*. 'For a rum shop. Whoo-hoo-hoo!'

Back home, I'm just nodding off when Greg phones. 'Thanks, Kate. I had a good day. Sorry you had to work. Would've been great if you'd been able to stop off and have a drink and a yabber.'

'Oh, don't worry about me,' I say sleepily. 'I probably had a better time than you did. I've been all the way to the West Indies and back today, mate.'

9.

A four-letter word beginning with F

When I was little, I had some toys called Weebles and a tortoise called George. Weebles were egg-shaped plastic people, weighted so they wobbled but always stayed upright. George was different. He propelled himself about the garden, slow on the rough, faster on the concrete path, but often tumbled over onto his back trying to climb up the kitchen doorstep. Once he began to topple there was no stopping him. Without me to pick him up and put him back onto his feet again, George would have died from exposure or thirst, or been eaten by rats or foxes. Young, fit people usually wobble without going over. If they do, they tend to bounce right back up again. But when people are frail or elderly, they are often more like George.

Every Wednesday evening for several weeks now I've shouted 'Hello!' into Walter's house and waited for him to yell 'Come in!' before going inside to fix his dinner. Today, he doesn't immediately respond. I open the door a few more inches. Stick my head in. 'Hey, are you OK?'

'Everything's quite all right,' he calls. 'Give me a moment, please.'

We spend ten minutes shouting back and forth about how quite all right everything is before I go inside. Walter's stranded in the middle of the lounge, arms outstretched like a wire-walker. For added difficulty, his trousers have slipped to his ankles. I heave them back up and wait to see if he can make it to safety. He sways as though a gust of wind has wobbled his tightrope. I grab his hands and steer him to the recliner. He wears a fresh white shirt, has neatly combed hair and is clean-shaven. But all this tidiness is destroyed by the purple violence spread over one half of his face.

'Crikey, how'd you get the black eye?' I say.

'Going out for the paper. It's only two hundred yards, for heaven's sake. I was almost home and dry when I went down. Right outside. You can't believe it. There's just no getting up again. Lying on my back, legs in the air. You know those boys? From the estate?'

'The ones that hang about on the corner?' Vermin, I think, gritting my teeth.

'Well, they were brilliant. They called an ambulance. I was cold and one of them put his coat over me.'

'Good lads,' I say, reprimanding myself.

Eddie's another slow mover, liable to be upended at the slightest obstacle. The two-millimetre step of the aluminium carpet bar was once almost enough to have him over. I was quick enough to stop it happening by coming alongside and allowing him to glide down me into a nearby chair. Because he didn't make it to the floor, it didn't count. If they get that far, we have to call an ambulance. Waiting for one takes for ever – you need pillows, a blanket and a long chat when you're waiting for an ambulance. I once found Mr Radbert on the floor having accidentally undone the lap belt of his wheelchair and slipped from the seat of it whilst trying to push himself around his flat with his feet. Marooned on the footplates of the wheelchair, he told me all about fleeing from St Lucia to London because he'd stolen someone else's girl. It was a great story.

Two weeks later Walter sits in front of the TV while I ready his medications. I watch him out of the corner of my eye. He's waited until I've arrived to practise standing and sitting but doesn't dare take a single step forward. I hold his hands, he stands again and we practise walking, me with one palm on the small of his back. He can go a few steps with my presence to reassure and prompt him but remains afraid, and rightly so. His rigid legs keep forgetting to move without someone else to tell them how. Walter, who has seen far more of the world than I, and entertains me with his tales of travel, can no longer confidently go alone as far as the kitchen.

'I can't even make a cup of tea.' He's embarrassed when he starts to cry.

It happens to Margaret during my weekend off. On my return, I inspect the palette of green, blue and yellow down the back of her thigh. She rises from her bed with difficulty and hobbles to the bathroom, me behind her with my hands on her waist. Getting into the shower is impossible so we wash with her sitting on the toilet. Margaret's leg is too painful to stand up again easily. She tries to pull herself up using the towel rail, but her arm is stiff and sore. 'I can't do it.'

'Take your time.'

'I'm slipping! My feet are going!'

'No,' I say, 'you won't go over with me here,' and I anchor my feet against the front of hers. Eventually, she rises. It takes ages, and almost as long to get to the armchair.

'I'd better come back at lunchtime.'

'You can't do that, you're busy.'

'I'll just pop in. Help you get to the loo. Get your lunch.'

When I'm not on duty, other carers do the same. This comes out of our own time until a lunchtime call is officially instated. We're so worried about Margaret that sometimes two of us turn up at once. We all say the same thing with slightly different words: 'You won't fall if I'm here,' 'You're quite safe,' 'I've got you.' But when I hear Marieme who is from Senegal say it, I like her way the best. Marieme is slim and graceful and gentle and when she walks behind Margaret, she says, 'I keep you, I keep you, don' worry, I keep you,' softly, like a little mantra.

Every morning, Margaret makes the painful journey to the bathroom before hobbling slowly to the television where she is high and dry in her desert-island armchair until the lunchtime carer ferries her to the toilet, and then again until the evening when one of us tows her to bed. A physiotherapist calls, takes Margaret through an exercise session, then leaves her a paper grid with the exercises listed down the left-hand side and tick boxes on the right.

'Why does she want me to fill that in?' Margaret says. 'I can't stand up when no one's here. How can I do exercises?'

I stay as long as I can on my visits. It isn't enough time for the full exercise session, but we practise standing up and sitting down and do extra walking. One day, I find she's attempted the toilet but been stuck on it for over an hour. Another time she hadn't dared sit down at all and had stood over the washing basket instead.

'Good thinking. It doesn't matter. I'll give it a good rinse out.'

'I feel silly. I'm useless. I'm not trying that again. I can't do it any more.'

'Don't be daft. Honestly, one day we'll laugh about you peeing in that.'

Day after day, I float behind Margaret, telling her to lift her feet.

You like to move quickly. You're used to getting lots done. Your family sometimes complain that you don't stay on track long enough, that you get bored and move on to other things too easily, that your conversations jump around all over the place. You don't like being still. When you worked in hospitals you used to clack, clack, clack down those corridors so fast that no one could ever keep up with you. You just didn't feel you were actually working unless you were working at breakneck speed.

Now you still do things quickly, and all at the same time if you can. You ready medications while you cook breakfasts, you write your notes as you're tidying up. But you can't hurry your customers. You are forced to be patient and go at their pace. When people are recovering you have to be even slower. Going slowly is effective. Safe. And in this slowness you notice things.

In the hall, the flowers in the vase which you thought were real are made of silk. 'My sister-in-law bought them for me,' she says. In the picture above the fireplace, that smart-looking man is wielding shears. 'My husband was a gardener,' she tells you. Through the window, the small tree you glimpsed coming up the garden path is actually an enormous yucca plant. 'It used to be on the kitchen table in a little pot,' she explains. 'One of the children bought it donkey's years ago. And when it outgrew the pot we planted it outside. We didn't think it would survive. I never noticed it growing, but look at it now. You never notice yourself getting old, do you? And then one day you just are.'

We work with Margaret's lovely family, buying and trying several different pairs of slippers. She apologizes endlessly: 'I'm so afraid. I went over so quick. There was just no way of getting up again.' She is bemused at the ridiculousness of such a simple thing becoming impossible, and sees a future that she had not realized was even there. One that might be closer than she'd have imagined. 'What happens when people can't walk at all any more, Kate? How do you get to the toilet then?'

'It'll be all right. There's lots of equipment to help you

get around, but I honestly don't think we're there yet. Let's keep trying.'

Walter doesn't eat. I buy fish and chips, bring treats from home. Nothing tempts him. I ask him what his favourite country is, get him to describe his most intrepid expedition, starting a climb at midnight to reach a summit at sunrise, ask him to tell me how long it takes to go over oceans on cargo ships or by bicycle in a hot climate over a land of red sand. Nothing that was previously joyful engages him in the slightest any more. I call the doctor to ask for a review not so much of Walter's physicality but of his mood. One evening I arrive to find the flat in silence. Walter isn't asleep. He's sitting in the recliner in the dark.

'You're fed up?' He doesn't answer. 'I'm worried about you,' I say, switching on the lights and the kettle. 'Come on, sunshine. Be honest now. Let it all out.'

'What's going to happen to me, Kate?' And we have the saddest conversation we've ever had, me trying to be comforting without telling any lies.

Margaret stops putting on lipstick. She tells the hairdresser there's no point in her coming while she can't stand over the sink to have her hair washed. Eventually, weeks after the injury and with no sign of improvement, even I feel like giving up.

Then, I see something. It's so small I cannot even say for certain what it is, but I know it's there. Perhaps she stood a little more steadily twice in a row or maybe she took five minutes rather than six to get from bed to bathroom. I say nothing in case I'm wrong. But soon it's obvious. Although she's slow, she rises on the first go every time she tries. 'See?' I say. 'You *can* do it.'

In Walter's flat, things are not as optimistic. He's sunk twice this week.

Margaret begins to navigate gingerly around the walls of

the lounge like a non-swimmer negotiating the sides of the deep end of the pool. I am reminded of the days when my children were learning to swim. I want to sail beside her like a protective tug boat. Instead, I hover on my side of the room trying not to let her see that I'm watching to make sure she doesn't get into trouble.

That Wednesday, Walter has another black eye. 'Oh God. You had another f—'

'Don't even say the word.'

On the day that Margaret sets out to the middle of the room for a newspaper left on a table, I stand in the doorway clenching my fists, ready to dive in if necessary. She doesn't so much walk as drift, returning with the television section gripped under one hand on the walker. When she attempts a complete crossing to turn on the heater, I can't breathe until she's made it past the halfway mark.

I find Walter on the carpet after an attempt to open the living-room curtains. 'Just help me up.'

'I need to call an ambulance.'

'Oh no. I'm fine. Please, not that.'

'I have to, honey. You might have hurt yourself, or perhaps your meds need adjusting.'

The following week, Margaret's hair has been washed, cut, coloured, blow-dried and set to perfection in enormous blonde curls. Another week in and we're really celebrating. She can get on and off the toilet unaided! I scream in delight and hug her. Three days later, she's hung out the laundry. We're as pleased as if she'd swum the English Channel. She gets back to normal quickly now.

The physiotherapist returns. 'You didn't do the exercises?' She holds up the tick-box grid.

'How could I do the sodding exercises?' says Margaret. 'I couldn't stand.'

'Well, you're up and about now,' says the physiotherapist. 'That's great. I'm discharging you.'

After she's gone, Margaret says, 'How much do you reckon she gets paid for delivering that ruddy exercise book?'

'At least twice what we do,' I say.

Later, Margaret feels able to talk about it. 'Remember when I got stuck on the toilet?' she giggles.

'Don't, you'll make me wet myself.'

'Fetch the washing basket!'

The following Wednesday, Walter's house is empty. I never see him again. Hibernation in the nursing home.

A few nights later, I'm struggling to sleep. I phone Greg after midnight. He is, as usual, wide awake. 'You OK?' I ask him.

'Course I'm OK. Well, as OK as possible under the circumstances. Why?'

'Just checking,' I say, but I take a screwdriver with me the next time I go up to the flat. It's a gorgeous spring morning. Greg spins tunes and music floods out of the balcony door into the sunshine. I'm in the bathroom with the screwdriver. When I lift the door from the screwless hinges, it smashes to the floor.

'What the fuck are you doing in there?'

'Taking the bathroom door off.'

'What? Why? You didn't even ask me.'

'I knew you'd say no,' I say, going through into the sitting room. 'Sorry, I had to. I was losing sleep worrying about what would happen if you fell in there. You'd be trapped, see? I wouldn't be able to open the door if you were out cold against it.'

Missing ingredients

He says he wants to tell you something that he's never told anyone before. Well, no one except the priest. You're a good secret-keeper. You've never seen secrets as currency to be spent on sharp intakes of breath and a gain in popularity. You are curious but, more than that, you feel delighted that he's sharing his secret with you. It makes you feel special. You've pulled the laundry from the machine and are beginning to hang it up. 'Go on then, what's this secret?'

'You won't tell anyone?'

'Of course not.'

You hang the shirts.

'It was in the last place I lived,' he says, 'thirty years ago. In an area that was full of thieves and people like me who had no one. I was bullied mercilessly. You can't imagine what that was like.'

You hang the sweaters.

'It was late afternoon,' he tells you. 'I was lying on my bed but I promise you I was awake.'

You hang the jogging bottoms.

'I had a vision,' he says, as you're hanging the underpants. 'A beautiful woman with long blonde hair and a flowing dress appeared on the other side of the room and floated toward me. Like she was skating. An angel,' he says, 'with outstretched hands. I promise you,' he repeats, 'I was not dreaming.'

You tell him you believe him. And then you say you'll tell him a secret in return.

'No one's ever told me a secret before,' he says.

'Well, I'm telling you one now,' you say. 'My secret is that I was bullied at school as a child. Mercilessly. So I know what that feels like.'

He nods. Takes your hand. Squeezes. And you think to yourself, my goodness, the things you get told doing this job are extraordinary. An angel when you're hanging out the underpants. Who'd have thought it?

It's Pancake Day, but Ina wants pasta instead. She's been to the corner shop. 'I bought some cheesy sauce, missus.'

'Sounds good,' I say before I find not a jar but a sachet of cheesy powder on the kitchen side. Blending cheesy powder with milk to make cheesy sauce sounds straightforward, but in Ina's house it's virtually unviable. For a moment, I consider telling her it simply can't be done. Then I think of my mother.

My mum is good at cooking traditional British meals. Casseroles and comforting crumbles with proper custard on winter days, pan-fried fish in the summer. She can dress a crab or joint a rabbit, and her batter puddings are to die for. Plump, crisp, golden and served the old-fashioned way, two on a plate with plenty of gravy as a starter.

Mum doesn't use recipes for her everyday meals, but she has a cookery book from the 1970s full of razzle-dazzle dishes that were new back then. They looked so exciting that she sometimes expanded her repertoire by trying to cook them, but could rarely find all the ingredients in the village shop. Undaunted, she'd substitute as she saw fit, so that an Asian curry might be made with lemons and honey, or an Italian ragù from minced beef and tinned tomato soup. My mum would not be daunted by the culinary limitations of Ina's kitchen.

Like most customers, Ina mainly eats frozen meals chosen

from a catalogue and delivered in weekly batches. They are nutritious and easily cooked in a microwave. Admittedly, the fish and chips lose all their crispness in the reheating, but most of the others provide a decent hot meal to people who otherwise live on sandwiches, cereal or basic meals that we are tasked to cook.

I've heard people complain about carers if they're unable to cook these simple dishes. They are, after all, so easy to make that my children were able to cook some of them when they were of primary school age. Most people ought to be able to manage them without too much difficulty.

Unless, that is, you are cooking them as a carer.

Working in someone else's kitchen is more complex than working in your own. Things are in the wrong places, you're without your familiar spices and blenders. Like washing machines, grills and microwaves are often unexpectedly incomprehensible. Ovens are slightly different at best and, at worst, require the skill of a fire juggler once you've found a suitably flammable piece of paper to light from the hob, squeeze inside with and waggle around at the back with the gas hissing at you from God knows where. But most difficult of all, like my mum in the 1970s, you're usually missing at least one key ingredient.

William had wanted beans on toast. 'I like the toast with plenty of butter.'

'I have grated cheese on mine.'

'That sounds nice. I think there's cheddar in the fridge.'

The missing ingredient at William's house wasn't baked beans or butter or cheese. There were plenty of those, easily found. It wasn't even bread, really. The missing ingredient was memory. William couldn't remember where he'd put the loaf. He had me looking everywhere. In all the cupboards, the fridge, the shopping trolley. Perhaps, William thought, they didn't unpack all the groceries properly yesterday. I wasn't sure the shopping had been done yesterday. I thought the shopping got done on Fridays and today was Monday but, nevertheless, I went through all the old carrier bags stacked next to the mop, bucket and vacuum cleaner in the cleaning cupboard. In the end I found the bread going mouldy in the humidity of the rarely used oven.

'Don't they make half-sized loaves any more?' I asked the shopkeeper.

'Not much call for them now.'

Back at William's I decanted half the new loaf into an empty hot cross bun packet. 'William,' I said, as I helped him eat, 'I've put some bread in the freezer compartment of the fridge to keep it fresh. Can you remember to tell the other carers?'

He looked doubtful so I wrote a note saying 'MORE BREAD IN FREEZER'. Then I spent ages failing to find Sellotape. Eventually, I stuck the note to the fridge door using a still-gluey label I'd picked off an empty cough syrup bottle.

Lorna and I agreed I'd put the potatoes on as soon as I got in the door, and cook the salmon and broccoli after I'd helped her to the toilet. That way we'd be able to make her dinner inside my allotted half an hour. Lorna's not at all forgetful and her kitchen is well equipped but as we were moving, her shaky hands upended a full cup of juice.

The carpet now an orange swamp, our missing ingredient immediately became time. Most of our late-afternoon calls, when dinner usually gets made, are thirty minutes long. You *can* medicate, toilet and cook for someone safely and hygienically inside half an hour but it takes skill to do so and when things go wrong it also takes enormous amounts of patience.

I soaked up the stickiness and squeezed it into a bucket,

changing my gloves as I went back and forth to the kitchen. The spuds were done long before the carpet, so I switched them off and continued working on that, while Lorna wept and raged at her motor neurone disease and the clock ticked relentlessly on. Eventually, with Lorna toileted and back on the sofa, I stood at the stove willing the broccoli to steam faster, hating the salmon and trying to convince myself that food tastes better when it's cooked with love.

Then there was Stevie, looking livid in his day chair in the sitting room.

'Jesus, what's the matter with you?'

'I wanted an egg for my lunch.'

'Right. And?'

'Look at it.' He gestured toward a plate on the table that contained a piece of cold toast and an eggcup with an egg in it. The top of the egg was smashed, and pieces of shell floated in clear, uncooked albumen.

I picked up the egg and poured it, raw, out of its shell onto the plate. 'Ew,' I said. 'Why's it like that?'

'I asked Niya to make me an egg,' Stevie said. 'That's all. I said she could boil it or poach it, but poaching's quicker. She said, "So sorry, but how long does it take?" I said I thought about three minutes.'

'Right.'

'And she came back with this and was out the door before I realized the bloody thing was raw.'

'Three minutes might be OK for poaching,' I said, 'though just for future reference, I do usually give it four. But three isn't anywhere near long enough to boil one of your eggs because you keep them in the fridge. It's a good thing you didn't eat it. I mean, you can get salmonella from—'

'Christ, Kate!' he yelled. 'I know that and you know that but how come she didn't bloody well know that?'

The missing ingredient at Stevie's home certainly wasn't culinary knowledge. It was more like *cultural* culinary knowledge. Niya is an excellent cook. I once tasted the curry she'd brought for her lunch so I know she can make meals that have your taste buds singing *Aida*. But Niya eats a diet that is strictly plant-based. 'Sorry,' I said to Stevie, 'but Niya's vegan. She'd probably never cooked an egg in her life.'

At Ina's, I contemplate the cheesy sauce packet and rummage under the sink and in the drawer to pull out every last bit of available equipment to confirm that none of the missing utensils I need have materialized since I was last here. The implements I have to hand remain one blackened frying pan with no handle, several old forks, two plastic plates, one cereal bowl, a mug, half a cheese grater, two table knives, a dessertspoon, three teaspoons, the palette knife, an eggcup and a tea strainer. With nothing remotely useful for making cheesy pasta from powder, I briefly consider trying to cook the actual spaghetti in the electric kettle.

In fact, there's nothing for it but to do the whole lot in the frying pan that I sometimes fry Ina's eggs in. The eggs slip together toward the front of it because the cooker's two or three inches higher at the back. I normally hold the pan level until they've solidified, but I figure I won't be able to hold it up when it's full of boiling liquid, so I adjust the cheesy sauce instructions down to half a pint of milk and half a pack of powder to stop it all slopping over at the front. It heats up nicely but, without a whisk, there's just one of the forks to get out all the lumps.

Ina is singing Motown as she rolls cigarettes next door. She's had enough time to get through all of 'My Girl', 'Heatwave' and 'Signed, Sealed, Delivered' by the time the sauce is finally smooth. Then the handle-less frying pan has to be lifted off the hob. Easy with eggs, but nigh on impossible with it full of pasta sauce. Pouring the sauce into Ina's cereal bowl is tricky too. I wash the spillage from the worktop before rinsing the frying pan for the next part of the operation. Despite all the challenges, everything is going so much better than I'd expected that I begin to sing along.

The real problems start when the pasta takes so long to boil in its shallow depth that the cheesy sauce in the cereal bowl cools. I put the bowl of cold sauce into the microwave and drain the spaghetti by holding it against the palette knife as I pour off the water. Unaware of the added complication that is about to rear its head, I puzzle at the unlikeliness of Ina having such an unusual item. I thought palette knives were what pâtissiers used to spread frosted icing onto cakes. As my fingers get scalded on the rapidly soaking tea towel with which I'm holding the handle-less frying pan, I can't help imagining Ina – who is stocky with short curly hair and a big nose – as a pâtissier in chef's whites. She'd look like Joe, the chef who cooks spaghetti for Lady and the Tramp in the Disney film. Joe certainly wouldn't spill pasta into the sink in the way that I'm doing, but there's plenty left to put onto one of the pink melamine plates.

When I take the sauce from the microwave the shriek that comes out of my mouth harmonizes perfectly with Ina, Marvin Gaye and Tammi Terrell singing about mountains not being high enough in the sitting room. Ina breaks off to call out: 'Everything all right in there, missus?'

The sauce has set like rock.

'Don't worry,' I yell, teeth gritted, 'all under control,' and slam the frying pan back on the stove with more milk and the last of the cheesy powder. With an eye on the kitchen clock ticking my time down, I chisel the sauce from the bowl with one hand, blend the second attempt with the other and press the button on the microwave with my elbow to reheat the plate of pasta.

I slam the plate down on the coffee table in front of Ina just a bit too forcefully, but she doesn't notice. She tucks in with gusto. 'Very convenient, isn't it, missus?' she says as I stomp back to the kitchen.

'I'm not so sure about that,' I shout, crumpling the empty cheesy powder packet in a clenched fist and hurling it into the bin.

'Well, it's much easier to carry than those jars,' she calls. 'Cheaper too, missus. Good thing I bought a dozen packets of the stuff, eh?'

For Greg, the missing ingredient was usually money. Busking, he and Spud tell me later, isn't as lucrative as you'd think. Like Marble, I'd seen Spud before out on the street. When I'd first met him, he'd been sitting on the pavement in the rain, masquerading as a sad young boy who needed looking after. His disguise had been so convincing that I'd given him a fiver. In the flat, he is a small man who might be anywhere between twenty and forty years old with an open sore across his chin and needle tracks down the insides of his arms. He sometimes comes to stay overnight, especially if the weather is bad or if someone moves onto his current sleeping spot in the graveyard. Not because they might be dangerous, but because Spud doesn't want to be tempted to knife them. He's a mixed blessing here. He can keep thieves out. But he also is one himself.

'Many of the beggars earned more than me,' says Greg. 'You'd be surprised how much a beggar can take.' He looks at Spud. 'Oh, I'm not suggesting it's easy. It's really hard. But you often get a reasonable amount.'

I look at Spud, thinking of my fiver. Spud looks at the carpet.

'Then there's the sex workers,' Greg continues. 'They used to make fun of me. I usually only got about twenty quid in an entire day, but it took them just half an hour to earn that. Then they'd go and score and be back in no time at all to do it all over again. Brutal turnover, of course. I always used to hold out until I'd got it up to a nice round number. Sometimes, it was only a tenner. Enough for a couple of brews and a bit of food.'

'You want pancakes?' I say. 'It's Pancake Day.'

'Course I do. With coffee. Spud, you want a pancake?'

'Sure.'

'It's Lent now,' I say, 'or it will be tomorrow.'

'So?'

'Well, what are you going to give up?' I ask them. 'You have to give something up for Lent and, frankly, I've never come across a pair of people who had so many options there.' I glare at Spud. 'I mean, heroin, fentanyl, crack, weed, alcohol, cigarettes. Need I go on?'

'Ketamine,' says Spud.

'Yep. We can add that to the list,' I say. 'So what's it to be?'

'Yeah, come on,' Greg says. 'What you giving up then, Spud?'

Spud doesn't hesitate. 'Chocolate,' he says.

11

It all seems perfectly manageable

Mr Radbert wakes like a sleepy brown bear coming out of hibernation. Chrissy has to hold him upright while I fasten the sling that gets clipped to the hoist. Mr Radbert grunts, eyes closed, as the metal arms lift him to a standing slump on the wheeled platform. Like a circus animal made to balance on its hind legs, he does his best to straighten up, eyes still closed and nose sniffing the air as I pull him through to the bathroom. The hoist is no match for the carpet that's become so wrinkled it's like manoeuvring over corrugated iron. Chrissy pushes as I pull us over the worst of the damage. 'Prepare for landing,' I say, and Mr Radbert nods, eyes still closed, as I lower him onto the shower chair. 'Mr Radbert?'

'Uh?'

'I'm going to make it good and cold today.'

His eyes pop wide. 'No, no, no!'

'But it'll really wake you up.'

Mr Radbert begins to laugh from somewhere down in his big belly. 'Whoo-hoo-hoo! Don't you go shrinking my equipment.' Wagging a finger at me he fails to keep a straight face, his enormous grin filled with perfect white teeth – all his own. Another attribute that he likes to show off about. 'You know my equipment is the biggest and the best!'

'Mr Radbert!' I say, affecting a shocked face. 'And you with such delicate little feet. Who knew?'

As I'm doing the showering, Chrissy changes the bedlinen, gets the breakfast things ready and dispenses medications.

Cycling gets you fit when you do it for miles almost every day. And when you're busy, you don't eat so much. Getting fit and getting thin give you more energy. But you're not as energetic as she is. She wears long false eyelashes, has dark, glossy hair, short but well-manicured nails. She puts on lipstick and a puffer jacket of the sort your children wear. She laughs loudly and flirts with some of the male customers. Not all of them, though. Just the ones who like it.

You're pleased whenever her name turns up on your rota. Things go smoothly when she's around. She never tries to avoid doing the writing up and knows how to puzzle together two half-sized, daytime catheter bags when the chemist didn't deliver enough full-sized, night-time ones. She folds and hangs the washing properly, so outfits are easy to find. Everything is fresh and clean when she has been.

He asks how old you are. You tell him he shouldn't be asking women their ages. He hoots, 'I bet you're only twenty-one! Whoo-hoo-hoo!'

You look sternly at him. 'I'm more than double that.'

And she says, 'That's nothing, I'll be sixty this year.'

You stop and stare. 'No way.'

'Way,' she says.

You tell her you'd not have put her at a day over fifty.

'It's all this caring,' she giggles. 'Makes you younger. Must be good for you.'

And you think, good God, perhaps she's right.

I'm drying the old bear's feet, claws long from an overdue chiropodist appointment, when Chrissy appears at the bathroom door with a clean outfit and a large red plunger. It's mine. My next customer has a slow-draining sink, so I've brought the plunger with me to try to clear it.

'See what Kate's brought,' says Chrissy.

Mr Radbert looks up. 'What the hell is that?'

'It's for clearing blockages.' Chrissy is deadpan. Mr Radbert raises an eyebrow, but Chrissy keeps her serious face on. 'I think it's for your constipation.' I squeeze my lips together to stop myself giggling. Chrissy takes two steps toward Mr Radbert, brandishing the plunger.

'No, no, no!'

Chrissy and I erupt and Mr Radbert looks from one of us to the other. He begins to laugh. His shoulders shake. He cries with it. 'You're not getting near me. Take away the red thing. Don't torture me with it!' And he laughs so loud he farts.

'See? It's working,' weeps Chrissy. 'It's good for your bowels!'

'Whoo-hoo-hoo!' shrieks Mr Radbert. 'Quick, I need a poo! I really do!'

I dry Mr Radbert while Chrissy re-hoists him off the shower chair and onto the toilet. 'Don't take too long, Mr Radbert,' she says, waggling the plunger.

It takes both of us to put on the incontinence pad, one standing either side of our bear. It would be nigh on impossible to do it alone. Mr Radbert's ursine girth is too large, the room too cramped and the sling, all buckles and clips, gets in the way. Thirty minutes into the visit, Mr Radbert's fully dressed and Chrissy bids us goodbye. In my remaining half-hour, I clean Mr Radbert's teeth, cook his breakfast, assist him to eat, oil his scalp and give him his medications. I wash up, put on the radio station that he likes, ensure that water and snacks are within reach and tidy the bathroom.

'See you later, Mr Radbert.'

'With Chrissy?'

'Dream team,' I say, and he puts his good thumb up and grins.

Later in the day, I get a text from the office. It is brutal. With immediate effect, Mr Radbert will no longer receive two carers for his morning call. Social services deem that the work can be done by just one. I am dumbfounded.

My next morning with the sleepy bear is tough. It takes some doing to balance him upright, put on the sling and attach it to the hoist on my own. We don't say much as we struggle over the carpet and through the showering. I'm too busy working out how I'm going to get the incontinence pad on, and Mr Radbert misses Chrissy's jokes.

The carers who can do this call single-handedly are few. It's exhausting and stressful even when things go smoothly and at Mr Radbert's house, they often don't. Sometimes the bed is wet, sometimes medications haven't been delivered, sometimes there are no catheter sets left. One day, the hoist breaks down and Mr Radbert has to be bed-washed.

Bed-washing a drowsy bear, made grizzly by not being able to have a shower, is a monster job. It's ridiculous. I heave the bed into the middle of the small room and scurry from one cramped side to the other, first to strip the bed, then back and forth with soapy water, a towel and cream. I'm little as a mouse, squeezing through the small spaces between bed and wall. God knows how any of the bigger carers manage it. At each stage, on either side, the little mouse sweats as it holds up the big bear so he can be washed, dried and creamed all over, and have his skin checked.

After the wash, I make the bed underneath Mr Radbert with some difficulty and slide one half of an incontinence pad as far as it'll go under one side of his big, flat-to-the-bed body, before scuttling to the other side to roll and lift him with one hand while reaching for the end of the pad beneath him with the other. Infuriatingly, he slips back onto it before I can pull it clear. My hand is almost squashed under Mr Radbert's bottom and the Velcro fasteners get ripped clean off on that side. I squeak. Mr Radbert frowns. I repair my smile, plump up my patience and go through the whole process again to extricate the broken pad and fit a fresh one.

Then I just have to put the trousers on. Trousers. Imagine what it's like for a mouse to get a pair of trousers onto a bear lying immobile on its back in a bed. No, really. Imagine it. Please. Yes. It's like that. I think of my mother-in-law. Intensely practical, she ran an old people's day centre until retirement. She saved my marriage by taking my three toddlers for the odd week's holiday. They returned shrieking about trips to McDonald's and visits to Woolworths to choose any toy they liked from saved-up pocket money. She's a goddess, my mother-in-law. She would not be beaten by this bed-wash. She'd deal with it. Practically, with no intention of giving up. And so do I but, nevertheless, the sixty minutes I'm paid for take me more than an hour and a half to finish.

Just as I'm leaving, the office, equally concerned about the heavy workload, call me to ask if we'd mind an occupational therapist coming at some point in the near future. Just to see how things are going. I am euphoric. The OT will see it is impossible to cope.

The day the OT is due, I'm at Mr Radbert's house ten minutes early. I sit looking out of the window. Eventually, she hops, crowlike in her black jacket, up the path to the front door.

Mr Radbert and I go through our routine under the beady eyes of the OT. Every now and then she squawks a question at Mr Radbert which he struggles to answer because of his growing dementia. I ask Mr Radbert if he minds me answering to speed things up, and he growls, 'Please, Kate, thanks, Kate,' so I do. The questions include *Are you able to walk?* and *Can you stand unaided?*

The OT isn't paying much attention to our struggle as her head is bowed over her clipboard, so I call attention to the difficulty I'm having in holding Mr Radbert up while attaching the sling. The OT suggests turning the hoist face on. I don't think this is possible because the room is so small and ask if she could show me. She doesn't. I battle on, determined to demonstrate that I am a good carer who does not put customers into danger, gets the job done efficiently, is sensitive to Mr Radbert's dignity and works hygienically. We make it into the bathroom and get through the shower with the OT continuing to ask questions about whether Mr Radbert goes shopping independently and if he can dress himself. When it's over and I'm my usual hot, ragged, post-sleepy-bear-showering self, I haul the hoist past the OT in her neat white shirt into the living room.

'Well, I'll be off now,' she says.

'But I thought you would stay to the end. So you can see how long it takes?'

'I'm just here for the hoisting. I'm happy with that.'

I realize, with horror, that I have made a dreadful mistake. My tiny, murine brain has been terribly stupid. I have done the job too bloody well. I have made it look possible. I could kick myself. I wasn't the person who should have entertained the OT after all. It should have been one of the carers who can't do it. Someone new. Someone who'd have cried.

'Can't you see, though, that we need an extra pair of hands?' I say. 'I mean, there's only fifteen minutes left to do all of the breakfast and give medications and clear up. And to clean Mr Radbert's teeth. And the bed's wet. It isn't possible to do it in an hour on your own.'

'I'm only here for the hoisting,' she says again. 'And it all seems perfectly manageable.'

'This is a good day!' I'm almost shouting now. 'Sometimes things are broken and without another pair of hands, it's murder.' I calm my voice down. 'Sorry. I'm afraid there'll be an accident.' I put a comforting hand on Mr Radbert's shoulder to reassure him that this likely event is unlikely.

'I'll see –' she turns to the door – 'if we can give you an extra fifteen minutes.' And with that, she puts away her clipboard and soars off.

We are paid barely the minimum wage, and a lot less if you factor in virtually unpaid travel time. Chrissy used to earn around five pounds for the half-hour she worked with us to make this visit safe and pleasant.

But five pounds, it seems, is too high a cost for keeping a vulnerable person safe and comfortable in their own home. It's simply too much to pay for taking decent care of a bear.

12.

Rockets

Just when you're relaxing into working again, in this job where you think there are no possible catastrophes to worry about, it happens.

He's an odd character. He pushes the boundaries. Boundaries are important. Yours are broader than most but they still exist. One day, he wants to find out if you're strong enough to pick him up. That's ridiculous, you tell him, but he cannot let it go and you bicker about it all through the washing and the cleaning and the lunch until it's time for you to leave and then he sighs, stands up from the bed, pushes the walking frame away and holds out his arms, as he so often does, for a hug goodbye. You are entirely unprepared for what's about to happen.

Just as you put your arms loosely around him, he collapses his legs, his entire weight is plunged down onto your shoulders through his armpits, his chin hits the top of your head and his normally bent-over neck is thrust violently upwards. A crack echoes through the room like the snapping of a trodden branch and it feels as though someone has hit you on the skull with a hammer. He is shaken, you are shaken, you sit next to him on the bed feeling ill. And angry.

He apologizes, tells you how loud it was inside his head. You're thinking how loud it was outside his silly head. He must have broken something. Surely bones can't make a noise like that and still be fine. He must be bleeding internally. Up near his brain. Perhaps he'll have a stroke. Jesus, he might die in his sleep. You make *him get up, sit down, get up and walk about the room, raising and lowering his arms. You ring the doctor. You're still feeling horrified when you leave.*

Afterwards, you call your colleagues when you know they'll be with him to check he isn't displaying adverse effects from a fractured vertebra just below the brain that does his fractured thinking. Your mind returns to the hospital where you once worked. You feel as though you are back in that place again, unable to sleep, ringing the ward staff to check you've not accidentally written the wrong number, prescribed the wrong fluids, that they've checked the tube site to make sure it's not inside a lung. You thought you could leave this behind by taking a simpler job, but it's come with you. You think, if he dies and I'm found negligent for crossing that boundary with a hug, then I will simply have to go to jail.

And for a fortnight at least, you actually believe this is going to happen.

Sometimes, I conduct little surveys among my customers. I call it Question of the Day. I once asked, *What's the nearest you've ever come to total disaster and got away with it?* The answers to that told me that everyone has a close call of some kind locked away with the skeletons in their closets. These near misses consisted mostly of lapses of memory that left babies in prams in launderettes or chip pans combusting or car doors unlocked with seatbelt-less toddlers inside, but some were even more dramatic. Risks taken for love or money that involved guns in the dark or jumping from a great height into the mighty Thames.

Usually, though, I keep it simple and just ask people things like where they were born. The answers to that question illustrate the diversity of my city. 'Bethnal Green,' 'St Lucia,' 'I don't know,' 'Turkey,' 'Glasgow,' 'Accra,' 'Oxford,' 'Jamaica,' 'Dublin' and 'Just up the street, at number twenty-nine.'

Once I asked what everyone had dreamed the previous night. The answers to that told me that many people don't remember, but when they do the dreams are often full of worry.

'Nothing.'

'That I was alone on an island and everyone else was on another island calling to me across the water.'

'Nothing.'

'That I had a lot of kittens and I was trying to keep them in a room but they kept getting out.'

'That I was running up an escalator but I couldn't get to the top where everyone else had disappeared.'

'Nothing.'

'That I was talking to you and then I woke up and you weren't here and I felt upset. Can you really not give me your phone number?'

Question of the Day today is, *What's the first thing you can ever remember?*

I meet my husband in the kitchen. He's been called to an early meeting and is making cereal and toast. 'What's the first thing you can ever remember?' I ask him.

He stares at me. 'You're serious? You're busy doing this job for months on end and looking after Greg and when we finally speak all you want to know about is the first thing I can ever remember?'

'It's my Question of the Day.' I risk leaning in and giving him a peck on the cheek.

'Sometimes it's all a bit much, Kate,' he says.

His sigh makes me feel guilty. 'I'm sorry,' I say. 'But Greg needs help. You know as well as I do that it won't last for ever.'

'The amount of time you're spending on him it will.' He reddens. 'God. I'm sorry. I didn't mean that.'

'I know you didn't,' I tell him. 'I know it's too much. But I can't abandon it all now. I just can't.'

He sighs. Smiles. Sort of. 'What's the first thing I ever remember? I remember lying in a cot and looking up at the lampshade and I think I must have been delirious. Had a temperature or something. Because the lampshade seemed to be getting bigger and bigger and bigger.'

'Thanks,' I say, 'and I don't just mean for answering my Question of the Day.'

I head to my first call. 'What's the first thing you can ever remember, Margaret?'

'Leaving the house in darkness as a siren went off, and going to an air-raid shelter off the high road with my mum and dad and falling asleep there,' she says.

Later, Julie has to ask Maureen because Maureen responds to Julie better than she responds to any of us other carers. Julie and Maureen have a bond. 'Kate wants to know what's the first thing you can ever remember?' Julie asks her.

Maureen doesn't hesitate. 'Hearing my friends calling me Donkey because I was born with too many sets of teeth and the dentist took out the behind ones instead of the in-front ones, so my choppers stuck right out.'

'What about you, Jules?' I ask.

'Being in the kitchen of a house and all the surfaces being really high up and running through a door into a living room where my dad and brothers are play-fighting on the floor and my mother scooping me into her arms,' she says.

I ask Bridget while I'm cutting her hair. I've cut it several times now. It looked great at first but has developed into a bouncy grey bowl because I'm not brave enough to attempt to layer it. She's like a gnarly, crooked matchstick with a big grey match head on it. Bridget's first memory is of breaking the engine from her brother's train set while he was at school and her brother returning to hit her over the head with his cricket bat. William's first memory is of his grandfather telling him about meeting a ghost on a wild and stormy Scottish night. Alice's is extraordinary. Being packed onto a handcart in the middle of the night surrounded by her family's possessions and fleeing their home due to unpaid rent.

Not everyone can tell me what their first memory is.

In the part of my borough that is most gentrified, one house contains a secret. The properties along this street are tall and plastered white. They have expensive blinds behind the restored wooden shutters of their neatly painted sash windows. Each has a flight of steps up to a front door beyond a grand porch, above which is a motif of the bold face of a man who, with his wild plasterwork hair, looks like Neptune. They are not timid, these houses. People strolling in front of them have affluent accents. The area is being taken out of the hands of those who can no longer afford to pay their rent or continue to refuse to sell, and brought into the hands of those able to replace broken fences with original Victorian cast-iron railings and paint their front doors in heritage colours. It seems that everyone who lives in the street has gone up in the world now. Everyone except for one person.

Number forty-eight is a little grubbier than its neighbours. It doesn't have those fashionable blinds. Instead, it has net curtains that have become grey. There are dead flies on the windowsills beyond them. The door is as big as all the others, but the paint is peeling. On the rare visits that I am asked to make here, I use the key safe to let myself in. The cavernous hall smells musty and I can hear all the sounds of the street through the draughty sash windows. The carpet is worn bare to the wood beneath. I've never been inside any of the rooms on the ground floor or the basement below it. The secret is upstairs. I ascend to the attic where there are three rooms. The toilet and the little kitchenette are not used by the occupant of this place. Instead, we visit them to warm puréed foods and fetch water for washing and make tea thickened to a specific consistency with powder before we give it with the aid of a spouted beaker.

There's a bed and a chest of drawers in the biggest attic room. The bed is a nest of wood-brown blankets and shawls the colour of clay and pillows in loose beige pillowcases. In the bed is a tiny creature. Without being told, I would not know its gender. It's like a little insect in a cocoon. The tiniest woman I have ever seen. Born before the inception of antibiotics when life expectancy for women was around half her current years, she has now reached a remarkable age. Lena came to London as a child on a boat, aeroplane travel not becoming commonplace until she was in her twenties. I cannot imagine the changes that this woman has seen. Cannot fathom that she was alive before the accessibility of the motor car, the telephone, the television. Her life is amazing but now she has gone back to babyhood. A creature in a burrow of cloth, spoon-fed, humming, gibbering, hugging a rag doll and old, so very old. A little walnut of a woman.

On top of the chest of drawers there is a pile of washing. The last carer here did not put it away. Perhaps she ran out of time or became distracted by Lena's chirping. I take the clothing piece by piece and fold it into the drawers. It consists only of nightgowns and shawls. Below the clothing are fossil-grey towels that I fold and store in the large bottom drawer. As the pile of clean washing shrinks, a photograph becomes visible pinned to the wall above the chest. It is of a young woman in a checked dress. She is standing in a park, smiling into the sun, looking out from under the hand she has raised to shade her eyes. The dress is plain but fitted and her figure is neat, the breasts pert and the legs slim under her skirt. Black-and-white Lena is wearing flat leather sandals. She has long curly hair and she is laughing into the camera held by someone whose shadow ends at her feet. The shadow is square-shouldered and wears a hat.

I look from our Lena to this Lena and marvel that the pretty girl in the photograph had no idea that she would, one day, end up in this attic room, cared for by me. Did she ever wonder what getting old would be like? Sometimes, when I wash and change her, she screams and when I feed her she purrs, but most of the time she chatters in a language I cannot understand. It may not even be a shared language. It might just be Lena's Language. I'd love to have Lena's first memory to add to my collection, but I'm not sure she's even aware I'm real. The memory would undoubtedly be of a rural existence that has been romanticized but which would have been hard. Her father was perhaps a farmer, a shepherd or a ploughman, her mother maybe a weaver or a lacemaker. Whatever it is, I can't have it.

Having been asked what her earliest memory was, Margaret has been prompted to dig out a handful of photographs. She wonders if I'd be interested. Absolutely, I am. Here are Margaret and her aunt in 1960s fashion, all big buttons, short hemlines and minuscule waists. Margaret in her twenties at the seaside in a very modest bathing suit. Margaret giggling with her teenage pals. Margaret talking to her school friends Edith and Lottie in the back garden during the war. All black-and-white, of course. Finally. Gorgeously. Delightfully. A toddler. Being led by an older girl down the high street. The toddler has a frilly dress and a bonnet tied with a ribbon under her chin. I can see the ribbon is satin. Her eyes sparkle so wide at the camera that they have sent her cheekbones high on her gorgeous face. But it's the mouth I notice. It's a cute one. Plump lips, dimples, beaming smile. Margaret's mouth. I look from baby Margaret to my Margaret and it thrills me that they're the same person. My lovely Margaret aged eighty-five was once this infant. I try to convince myself that I and my children will likely one day be elderly.

'By the way, what's the first thing you can ever remember?' I ask Greg when I finally get to the flat to make sure he eats something.

'My mum bringing a baby home and being told it was my sister. I don't think I liked that very much. Why? What's yours?'

'Sitting on my grandma's lap and watching a rocket being launched on a black-and-white telly.'

'I remember that,' Greg says. 'My mum came outside and got me in to see. She thought I was the only one old enough to appreciate it, so it was just me who watched that rocket go up with her.'

Everyone was once a child and, as I leave Greg's home to go back to mine, it seems incredible that he and I were once sitting in suburban living rooms at the same time in different parts of the country, marvelling at that rocket going up. And that one day, more than forty years later, we would have met and become friends and that I would nurse him here.

13.

I can pick them up in handfuls

Seeing inside people's houses fascinates you. Finding out whether they're empty or crammed full of junk. Old-fashioned or modern. Pristinely clean or covered in dust and muck and cobwebs. Streets used to be nothing other than mundane rows of similar houses. Now, you wonder what's behind each door. You never really thought about that before. You visualize all those homes with their roofs removed as though they were an enormous architect's mock-up of a housing estate. You imagine being a giant standing over them like a tourist in a model village and peering inside.

Of course, you can't really do that, but what you do get to do is take the keys of the houses of strangers and open them up. At first it felt like trespassing to be inside them. Or spying. Seeing how fat or thin people have been in the clothing through which you rummage for a change of outfit. Discovering what treats someone buys to eat while you assemble meals from ingredients in kitchen cupboards. Seeing what TV shows people like. Hearing what kind of music they play.

You're mindful that these homes do not belong to you, that it's a privilege to be accepted into them, that there are rules inside to be respected, behaviours to be maintained, confidences to be upheld. But when you're a carer, little is hidden from you, and you are never trespassing. Instead, you are a trusted member of the household. Witness to all the home improvements, the breakdowns, the new purchases, the blots on the landscape. In on all the secrets and the guilty pleasures. It's kind of fun.

'One of my customers filled her freezer with video cassettes,' I say to my husband one night as I dig in ours for frozen peas to add to the portion of shepherd's pie he has saved for me.

'There's something in that,' he replies. 'Running a freezer empty is expensive. You should keep a freezer fullish.'

Later, I tell Greg, 'She won't let me rub moisturizer anywhere except behind her knees.'

'Someone told me that's an acupressure point,' says Greg, 'good for mobility.'

I begin looking for truth in Ina's schizophrenic idiosyncrasies. Turning the television to the wall because it is bad for curious brains and, as she has pointed out, her brain is very curious. Boiling lemons and eating them whole to cure a cold. Rubbing crumbled aspirin on herself to prevent cancer. There remain few I can't trace back to at least a shred of good, albeit distorted, reason. Putting clocks on the floor to deter rodents is one of them. Stepping over a clock that's missing its hands and around the single bed, I straighten a cushion on the sofa and find seeds of purple wheat. 'Ina, is this what I think it is?'

'Rat poison. It's for the insects.'

'I haven't seen any.'

'Come out at night. Millions.'

Ina's body is big from its high-sugar, low-fibre diet and mottled with chocolate moles over her smooth brown skin. Stripped for a shower, it shows no sign of bites or scratches. As I wash Ina, she chats about her mother. Mrs Munoz, though long dead, remains Ina's source of strength and inspiration. 'Mother taught me to cook,' she says. 'Cooking's good for you. And she said trust in the Lord. I don't trust Him a lot. But I trust Him more than doctors. This medication's too much, missus.' She drools and slurs from its side effects. 'Mother liked to paint as well.'

'Maybe you've got her talent,' I say. 'You could go to painting classes. You'd enjoy it. Get out of the flat. Meet people.'

'Oh no, missus. Benjamin took me to an art class once. At The Hub. Do you know it?'

The Hub is a local mental health project for older people. Ina would be perfect for it. 'What happened?'

'I wasn't any good, missus. Benjamin said it wasn't worth taking me.'

Ina's brother Benjamin comes once a week to deliver shopping bought according to a list Ina dictates to me, and then reads to him over the phone at a time of his choosing.

While Ina dries off, I refuse entry to Jimmy, one of several parasites who call in to steal tobacco or make phone calls. I help Ina into her uniform of blouse, polyester skirt with elasticated waist and slippers with the backs trodden down. 'Don't let those people in,' I say.

'They're friends, missus. Can't keep 'em out. They just throw stones at the windows.' She shuffles into the sitting room, with its green walls and closed floral curtains glowing orange from the brightness of the day outside. The toilet brush holder in one corner is filled with plastic flowers, permanently blooming neon.

'Call the police then.' I open her curtains the permitted four inches and a slim shaft of light hits the pine laminate flooring, like a sunbeam coming through a forest canopy. It does little to brighten the bedsitting room, but gives it the feel of a staged, shady, woodland clearing. I haven't yet swept, so tobacco dropped during the night dusts the room like sprinklings of dry earth. Put down some fake snow, spray the flowers white and you'd have a cheap Santa's grotto. Ina could dress up in a beard and sit, rotund in red, in the arm-chair. Everyone welcome. Spongers and leeches included.

'I don't think that would be wise, missus. They wouldn't like it.'

'The police?'

'No, my friends.'

'They're not friends. They're pests.'

Delivering Ina's breakfast, I tackle the rat poison again. 'If you get it on your hands, you'll roll it into your cigarettes. I think it's more likely to kill *you* than these insects you're going on about.'

Ina puts down her mug of sweet tea and starts to chuckle. 'And my friends,' she says. She spits into giggles that rapidly become uncontrollable. 'Don't want to give you a headache, missus,' she snorts, heavy shoulders shaking and saliva flying everywhere, 'but when you come, we'll all be dead. Me in the chair and my friends on the bed. Like a film. A whodun-nit. You'll be Miss Marples!' Her laughter is raucous, mouth wide, crinkled eyes wet. It's beautiful. We're in fits, holding each other, weeping with it, and I have to wait until I can breathe properly to call the office and report Ina's fear of infestation as she nods along.

We don't laugh again for a long time. Ina puts fly spray, rat poison, razor blades and mousetraps on the shopping list.

'For the insects?'

'They're horrible, missus. I can pick them up in handfuls.'

There's plenty of wildlife in Greg's flat at the top of his building. He throws things at mice that run through his sit-ting room. Pigeons nesting in the rafters coo and scratch loud enough to keep me awake on the nights that I stay here now.

The nights when Greg is frightened. When we step outside onto the balcony we are at the same height as the topmost branches of a tree. A squirrel lives in the tree. It's probably several squirrels, really, but we like to think it's only the one and we call it Simon. Sometimes Simon leaps onto the balcony railing but he never comes inside. We know he gets up into the roof space though, because the pigeons become a frenzy of screeching. None of these creatures annoys me. But the moth caterpillars that live at different points of the same life cycle, upside down above us, do. Sized from pin to matchstick, some crawl across the ceiling past the bare bulb, others dangle and spin from invisible strings. When one drops into my hair one day, I take a broom to the ceiling.

'Oh, Kate,' Greg says, 'they're only trying to scratch a living. Just like you and me and the mice.'

I shake the broom out through the balcony door. Four floors below, the yard is metres deep in junk thrown from the windows of all the other flats in the building. Chairs, boxes, clothing, bags, cartons and big, empty cans the colour of batter that used to contain palm oil. A Fortnum & Mason's hamper lies, incongruously, on top of it all. 'They'll find plenty of places to sleep down there,' I say.

Greg says, 'I once lived in a hostel. It was a horrible place. I'd just been given the key, signed to say I'd be a good boy and let myself into my room. It was a dingy joint. Filthy bed-linen. Dirty windows. Peeling paint all over. I sat down on the bed and wondered how the fuck it had come to this. Then I saw the fridge in the corner. That perked me up. I went out, bought some brews and smuggled them back in. But when I opened the fridge door . . .' He winced at the memory.

'What?'

'The fuckers poured out. I spent the whole evening killing them.'

'Killing what?'

'Cockroaches. Millions.'

Back at Ina's, I take the covers off the bed all the way down to the mattress, pull the mattress buttons away from their holes to check underneath, take the seat cushions off the sofa, clothes out of the wardrobe and food out of the cupboards. I move the television, inspect Ina's skin again. 'It's not that I don't believe you,' I say, 'but I can't find any. No eggs. No droppings. Not even a dead one.'

'They don't come out in daytime,' she says gloomily.

Two days later, I find her sleeping on a blanket on the floor. A giant-sized Gretel in the wood. 'They were falling from the ceiling,' she insists, and I think of her climbing about trying to swat shadows and hallucinations concocted from swirls of peeling Artex.

'Why don't you sleep on the sofa?' I ask her. 'The floor's hard and cold.'

'Sofa's crawling with them.'

'I don't see any.'

'In the night. Handfuls.'

The following week both the sofa and the bed have gone. 'Council took them. They were heaving.'

'But surely they'd have told us,' I say. 'Are you sure it was the council that came?'

The bedsitting room is oddly big without the bed and the sofa in it. 'They get in my mouth,' says Ina as she rolls cigarettes. 'I saw a film once with insects coming out of someone's mouth. It's like that. In my mouth. And ears. In handfuls.'

'That was a horror film,' I say. 'Insects aren't coming in or out of your mouth. I'm not saying I don't believe they're here. It's just I haven't seen any. But I know they wouldn't be running in or out of your mouth. Hundred per cent.'

Ina sighs into her lap. 'Don't want to give you a headache, missus, but they are.' The words soak her navy skirt.

Next visit, expecting Eeyore, I get Tigger. Ina doesn't just press the intercom entry button, she comes down the stairs and right out to meet me. Her big skirt rocks and sways down the hallway, like a jolly ship. 'You can't clean, missus, not for two weeks. Pest control said so.'

'Pest control?'

'Sprayed everything.'

It's been bucketing down inside the sitting room. Puddles everywhere and dripping like a rainforest.

'They just left?'

'They said not to go inside for two hours.'

I step quickly back out and shut the door. We sit in the tiny yellow kitchen and I call the office. No one has let them know what's happened. The office ask whether Ina isn't just imagining the infestation. No other carers have seen a bug either. I tell them I don't know. 'The telly can't stay on the floor in here, Ina,' I say, 'it might get broken. And I think we should take the bin out of the sink. It isn't hygienic. You could get sick and that would make me sad.'

Two days later, Ina has a new bed and a replacement sofa, her bedlinen carefully folded into piles on top of it. The duvet is naked. 'I didn't sleep in the bed yet. Can you make it proper for me?'

'Sure.'

I put the duvet in the duvet cover and lift the pile of blankets from the sofa. My stomach lurches. Half a dozen bedbugs the size of my little fingernails wobble over the fabric, looking for cover. I reach out, pick one off, squash it. My blue glove is stained violet. I fetch a safety pin, stab three of the bugs on it and wrap it in a tissue. Red comes through the paper in patches.

'Ina,' I shout. 'I've seen them.'

'You have?' She is delighted.

'I think they're crawling out of somewhere to die. I'm sorry. It's just that I didn't see any. Not even one.'

'Ah, yes, missus,' she says, 'I understand.'

I make hot chocolate with extra sugar, go and buy tobacco to save Ina the trouble, and get a new lighter as well.

'How much for the lighter, missus?'

'Nothing. It's a present.'

'Aww, missus,' she says, flicking it and watching it flare.

Two weeks later, Eeyore's back. 'They're in the bed.'

'But the bed's only just arrived. Are you sure?'

'Mother never bought second-hand, missus,' she says sadly.

When I lift the blankets from the bed, a couple of bugs scurry for the darkness of the corner seams. 'Right,' I say. 'We're not having this. Help me move it.' And we slide the bed into the middle of the room. Behind it, a bit of the laminate flooring doesn't quite reach the wall and when I run a table knife down the crack, bedbugs tumble out.

'Watch the bit of wood,' shouts Ina, 'it's loose.'

The wooden panel on the wall, six inches square, was painted over when the bedroom was decorated. It's the same green as the walls, wedged on top of the skirting board behind an electric cable. I pull it up. Underneath is a square of bare white with a hole in the middle of it. The hole is dark and dusty and cobwebby. Inside there is a slight, but sinister, movement. If I were to reach in, I could probably pick them up in handfuls.

Bedbugs take a long time to eradicate, but Ina and I are a hit squad now. I bring a vacuum cleaner and take care to dispose of the bag properly. Ina washes clothing and cushions on anti-allergy 60, her new favourite setting. We ring pest control and force them to respray. Benjamin buzzes the intercom but leaves the shopping at the front door. Ina doesn't mind. 'He's better off outside, missus, he's in cahoots with them doctors, you know.'

When the bedbugs come out to die, I hate them. They remind me of my lack of belief in Ina. 'I wish I'd listened more,' I say to Itzie. 'I'm always going to assume people are telling the truth from now on, even if what they're saying sounds impossible. You know that keeping a freezer full is good for energy efficiency, don't you? And the vitamin C in lemons can shorten a cold? And that too much television isn't good for children and those with curious brains? And that aspirin is possibly protective against lung cancer?'

'But there's no reason to put clocks on the floor,' says Itzie.

Later, at Greg's, I'm flipping through one of those gadget catalogues that sell all the things you didn't know you needed. There are milk frothers and heated clothes airers and electric apple corers. 'Wow,' I say, 'you can get something called a teabag rest. And moulds to make chocolate pine cones. We could've done that last Christmas.' He will never do that now I think, suddenly distraught inside.

'Anything for mice, in there?'

'Hmm –' I turn to the pest control bit – 'there's spider catchers and moth traps.'

'Leave them out of it.'

'Oh my God. There's a rodent deterrent. It's electronic. Circular. And you know what? It looks a bit like when Ina takes the hands off her clocks. I think she was trying to keep mice out.'

'Do they work?'

'At Ina's. Don't be stupid. They're clocks.'

'No, the ones in your catalogue there. I think we should try one,' he says, just as a cigarette lighter flies past my ear into the kitchen sending a mouse fleeing for cover under the oven.

14.

Alcohol

We female carers can care for both men and women but male carers can only care for men. Most of my customers are women and most of my visits are single-carer calls so I don't see male carers often but when I do, I like them. There aren't many. There's Kenny with his silly jokes, and John, a struggling musician in his other life, and Danny who's really into fitness. And there's Andrew. All the male carers are young, but Andrew is the youngest.

I first met Andrew at Mr Radbert's. He'd just been given his first regular customers, Mr Turner, Lucy and Michael. Mr Turner was an elderly man, Lucy was his black-and-white cat and Michael was an alcoholic in a filthy navy puffer coat from which he pulled cans, half-eaten sandwiches, letters, broken phones and tobacco tins full of dog ends. According to Andrew, Mr Turner was one big smile, Lucy was one big purr and Michael was one big grumbling misery. Michael lived alone in a flat that contained nothing but a bed, a telly on the floor and black bin liners full of clothes. He found it difficult to walk because, he'd told Andrew, his leg brace had gone missing.

'What's wrong with his leg?'

'He says someone drove into him and his foot got squashed between the car and a post box.'

'Ouch. That sounds traumatic.'

'Yeah, but Bernard says it's just massively overgrown

toenails. Bernard lives next door. Michael said Bernard robbed him. I can't believe Bernard did that though. He's always trying to help Michael and Michael's stuff isn't worth nicking anyway. I'm going to try to get the leg brace back. Sometimes Michael's gone AWOL and when I find him it takes for ever to get him home because he can only walk on the sides of his feet.'

'Do you mind me asking why you're doing this job?' I'd said.

'I was going to go to university,' Andrew told me, 'but I changed my mind. I thought while I was deciding what else to do that I'd do something useful. Something meaningful. Learn about life.'

Turns out Andrew lives near me. We both cycle and we finish at the same time on Thursdays, so I meet him most weeks pedalling home. Soon, he'd been given his third regular. Pete. Another alcoholic. Pete couldn't go out to buy alcohol because of his right ankle. He had a history of gang affiliation, homelessness and getting really high on the railway embankment. Late one night he had fallen down the embankment and fractured his ankle. Being so high, it'd taken him a while to realize he'd broken it so he'd spent some time hobbling around and making things worse until he'd fallen again. Now he had a broken wrist to go with the broken ankle.

'I knew Pete'd be problematic,' said Andrew, 'because I met Danny and Sheila at Mr Turner's and they'd already refused to go back to him. The office said, "He's got a certain privilege that we allow him, but he's really friendly."'

'Is he?'

'I like him, yeah. He's a bit crude but clever enough to talk about science and politics. And he loves dogs. He had a dog when he was little, but he didn't get it from a pet shop or a dog breeder. He got it from a man in the market with a cage full of them. Pete wants me to buy him another dog now. For company. But I just buy the booze. That's the privilege. I hate it. But Pete needs lager to take his meds with.'

'He should only take meds with water.'

'Well, unfortunately he only drinks lager. I told the office and I pour him water, but he's taken them like that every day for ever and he's not dead yet, is he? Watching him wake up is like seeing someone pulled from the grave, though.'

'Boy,' I said, 'you sure are learning about life, aren't you?'

'I'll be honest,' Andrew said, 'it's a bit depressing sometimes.'

'How's Michael?'

'Tricky. He took the coat off the other day. Underneath he's not big at all. He's a little bent stick. Me and Bernard brought him a sofa in. And a coffee table to put the telly on. Bernard found them in a recycling place. But Bernard's odd too. His flat's a bit hoardy and he's quite intense.'

'Well, it's good Michael's got Bernard. Actually, it's good *you've* got Bernard.'

'Oh, they're no longer speaking to one another,' said Andrew. 'While we were shifting the sofa, Bernard said, "Michael, I don't appreciate you telling Andrew I nicked all your stuff. You know the council took it that time you went walkabout." Michael hit Bernard so Bernard reported him to the social worker. The social worker's like the teacher. Me and Bernard are just the supply teachers. Michael can get nasty or fool about with us, but when the real teacher comes he has to behave.'

'Leg brace?'

'The PT said ask the OT and the OT said ask the GP and the GP said ask the hospital so I'm taking him next Thursday.'

I have my own alcoholic. Stevie. Except Stevie isn't a proper alcoholic. He's a *recovering* alcoholic. That is to say that some time ago, having had one of his legs amputated, Stevie inadvertently agreed with a doctor to give up drinking in order to save the other. Now no one is allowed to buy alcohol for Stevie, so Stevie pleads with us to get it and swings in and out of hospital according to how successfully he has persuaded other people to do so. Despite the pleading, I'm generally pleased to see him. He has a sharp, dark wit and entertains me with the stories that lie behind his various scars.

'What's that one?'

'A knife. Get us some brandy.'

'My God. You could've lost your eye.'

'The other bloke came off worse. Please, Kate.'

'No. What's that one?'

'Fell off a roof running from the Old Bill. Get us some brandy.'

'No. My God, you could've broken your neck.'

'I just broke my arm. See this finger?'

I inspect his middle finger which is rigid. 'It won't bend. Is that from when you fell off the roof?'

He raises his hand in front of my face, middle finger still sticking up. 'No, it won't bend because you won't buy me any fucking brandy, eejit.'

I meet Andrew as I'm turning off the main road.

'How was the hospital?' I ask.

'They gave me two hours but it took four. Twenty quid for four hours with Michael is no joke. I'm knackered. You know what? I don't think there ever was a leg brace. I think Michael invented it. Him and the nurse looked at me like I was mad and it wasn't until we'd got home, miles from the hospital, that Michael told me he'd run out of medications.

So we had to go through the whole journey there and back all over again.'

'Oh God. How's Pete?'

'Miserable. I feel so sorry for him. I hate buying the alcohol, but mostly I hate him asking me for a cat.'

'A cat?'

'He says a cat'll do if he can't have a dog. He's so lonely. I want to get him a cat.'

'You can't do that.'

'Why not? He'd get one himself if he could.'

'Who'd look after it?'

'The carers can feed a cat, can't they?'

'God, Andrew,' I say. 'Don't get him one. Imagine if Sheila turned up and there was a bloody cat in there. Or Jen.'

'I don't think Jen would mind.'

'But Sheila.'

'Sheila won't even bloody go to Pete!' yells Andrew. And then, in a quieter voice, 'Sorry, it's just that it's all so dismal.'

On my next visit to Stevie, I hear nothing when I open the door. Occasionally, when I get to a visit, the customer is absent. They might have been taken out by relatives or simply decided to go out by themselves. And sometimes the office call me just before I'm about to arrive to tell me that the customer is not there. Usually because they have become acutely unwell and gone into hospital. If the absence is less than twenty-four hours before my visit is due, I still get paid for the call. There's always a small part of me that welcomes this. Especially on busy days. It's hard to admit it. I feel guilty for being even a little bit glad about it in some small pocket of my brain, but I am. Just as all the carers are. We might kid ourselves we're not, and of course we're pleased when the customer returns, but we all definitely feel a tiny bit glad about having a brief, unexpected, paid gap in the day. We might be carers but we're none of us saints.

It's not unusual for Stevie to be silent because he's often sleeping when I arrive to help him out of bed, give him a shower, dress him, cream his remaining leg, hoist him into his chair in the sitting room and give him breakfast and meds. More often than not, he refuses to get up. This is something of a blessing because getting him through all that takes longer than the hour I'm given to do it. But today, Stevie's bed is empty. I call the office. He's in hospital. I have to turn up for the next visit even though he's absent because we're not allowed to abandon the care plan until social services have formally suspended it. I unlock Stevie's flat, shout inside just in case, close and lock the door again.

Stevie's neighbour opens his own door. 'Stop buying him alcohol.'

'We don't.'

'Oh, don't give me that,' he says, looking at me with disgust.

'I wish someone would just tell me what the point is,' says Andrew. 'I mean, Michael doesn't want me there. He doesn't give a toss whether he has furniture or not. You know what happened today? I found his medications in one of the bin bags. I had to dispose of them. Michael's furious.'

'Why? Were they out of date?'

'It was impossible to tell if they were out of bloody date. They were just loose. Hundreds of little round white tablets in amongst the clothes.'

'Oh, right. And Pete?'

'Pete only wants us to get the drink and the drink's murdering him so I don't see the point of that either, to be honest. Unless he got the bloody cat he's always on about.

Then it might feel like something had changed but otherwise, it's all going in the same pointless direction.'

'Andrew!'

'Oh God, I'm sorry. It's just that it's all so grim. When I'm getting Michael home I have to carry the bag of cans and he's falling over and I'm pulling him up again. The way people look at me. As if to say, why aren't you helping him? Or, why *are* you helping him?'

A fortnight passes before Stevie's on my list again. He always comes out of hospital so much better than when he went in. You can see what a good-looking guy he is underneath his addiction. His remaining leg has become normal size without the fluid that accumulates in it and he's a nice healthy pink. He gets up on the morning call, eats a decent breakfast, drinks milky, sugary coffee and doesn't start smoking until he's in the sitting room. But soon the flat closes in on him. The sense of humour that I find so entertaining is, ironically, absent without the alcohol I hate so much. In the end, it all starts again.

'Get me brandy, Kate.'

'Don't be ridiculous. You're doing so well.'

'Fuck you. Call yourself a carer. What do you care? You're shite.' He starts to stay in bed all day again, refusing to change his clothes. I wash his face and hands, pull his pants down and his T-shirt up so I can keep his middle clean, and roll his trouser leg up to cream the leg.

'The only thing that'll matter to either of them is if I can get Pete the cat,' Andrew says again as we're cycling back one evening. 'He says he's going to top himself without one.'

'No,' I say. 'The office will go mad. You'd probably get the sack.'

Andrew looks at me as though I've told him there's a good chance he's going to win the EuroMillions.

'Really,' I say. 'Don't.'

Stevie's chant starts the minute I get in the door. 'I'll get up if you get me brandy.'

'Not doing it.'

We go through the bed-washing-Stevie-while-Stevie's-still-dressed routine and I leave him, cursing, in the bed.

Next morning, he's on fine form. 'If you won't go and get it, I'll go myself.' He pulls his leg over the edge of the bed with his hands. Gets a bit caught up in the duvet. Nearly falls reaching for crutches. Having ignored him in the hope that he'll come to his senses, I put a shoe on to prevent his sock slipping on the floor and hoist him, protesting, into the chair.

'I won't be here at teatime,' he growls. 'I'll be gone to the fucking shop.'

Contrary to expectations, he *is* there at teatime. Just not in the chair. Waiting in the hall for me to open the door he cannot manage with each hand over a crutch. 'Going to the shop,' he says, moving into the doorway to prevent the door from closing, and blocking my entry.

'I'm going to call the office.'

'Fuck the office.'

With one hand steadying Stevie's wobbling form to make sure he doesn't topple, I call the office with the other. They tell me that if he's determined to go outside there's nothing I can do. 'He's got capacity.'

'He'll never get back in again safely.'

'He's got capacity.'

I step aside and the flat door closes behind the teetering mountain that is Stevie reeling down the concrete walkway to the main entrance, the sound of his sliding footstep and banging crutches booming off the walls. I follow. Stevie whips one crutch up and his entire weight falls onto my frame as he slams it on the big square button that opens the main door. The door swings wide. Stevie hops gawkily outside and manages to stagger a few more steps to a bench on the grass in front of the building. He slumps onto it and stares across the grass at the shops on the main road.

'What do we do now?'

'Just go. I'll be all right. Someone'll help me.'

Reluctantly, I go on to my next calls but when I'm done, I cycle madly back. There's a big shape outside sitting on the bench again, shivering in the dark. A blue plastic carrier bag is now lying at its feet beside a pair of crutches.

'You made it then.'

'Thanks for coming back, Kate. Help me in.'

Stevie can only manage himself. I carry the blue plastic bag and steer him straight. As we're making our way down the hall, I wonder which of us will break the most if he falls. At the front door I fumble the key in the lock with one hand while holding the bag and ensuring Stevie is properly propped up with the other.

The door across the hall opens. The neighbour peers out. Looks at me with the bag in my hand.

'Liar,' he says.

15.

Duppy

At seven o'clock in the evening I stand, aghast, at Mr Radbert's bedroom door, staring at his bed.

I started at seven this morning, at Margaret's house. I enjoy getting Margaret up and washed. Nothing ever goes wrong at her house. Nothing goes wrong at Veronica's either. She was my next call. Then I went across the borough to Lorna and from her to Bridget, to fix her lunch. After Bridget, I went to Ina and then back to Veronica. From Veronica to Stevie, from Stevie back to Lorna and, finally, I've ended up with Mr Radbert.

I love Mr Radbert, but Mr Radbert's house is not like Margaret's. There's every chance that something will go wrong in it. Sheila told me it's a duppy. I told her duppy don't exist. I'm a scientist, but Sheila's a superstitious Jamaican woman. Superstitious Jamaicans believe in duppy. Duppy got the TV remote control once at Mr Radbert's, in the days before social services said the visit had to be done by just one carer. Sheila had put it on the bedside table before we'd hoisted Mr Radbert into bed. I'd tucked him in. 'Sheila,' I'd said, when she'd returned with a glass of water, 'where's the remote?'

'On the table.'

'Not any more.'

'You know what?' I'd whispered, as we searched under the chair, behind the curtains, in the wardrobe.

'What?'

'Duppy!' I'd hissed.

I hadn't been fully prepared for the reaction I got. Sheila screamed and leaped from the room in one backward bound. She's a large woman and she was at least six feet from the door. Mr Radbert had sat bolt upright, among his mismatched pillows, brown eyes wide. 'There's no such thing as duppy, Mr Radbert,' I told him. 'You're just going to have to have an early night. I'm sure the remote will turn up tomorrow.' Sheila was still standing in the hall hopping from foot to foot in her bright blue plastic shoe covers. 'Chicken,' I said.

On this Sunday evening toward the end of my weekend shift I'd found Mr Radbert, wheelchair-bound, in the middle of the sitting room resplendent in a ghost-white satin suit, black tie, polished shoes and woolly beanie hat. Everything looked normal. All the lights were on.

'Wow. You look great. Been to church? Want a cup of tea?' I put the kettle on. The kettle didn't boil. I tried the microwave, the toaster. Lifeless. 'Your plugs aren't working,' I said.

'Oh God. I need the toilet.'

I wondered how much power was left in the hoist that had been plugged into its impotent socket all afternoon. Thankfully, the arms had enough power to raise and lower, but the legs of it wouldn't widen to fit around the wheelchair.

'Oh God.' He was looking so far down at the floor, his spectacles had slipped to the end of his nose.

I pushed them up in front of his eyes again. 'I'm sure I can still get you onto it.' I changed Mr Radbert into a nightshirt, buckled the sling around his waist and put his useless left hand over the bar of the dying hoist standing just a little too far in front of him. I lifted his heavy feet out onto the footplate. It was easy to pull the red nylon loop on the left side of the sling onto the left hook of the hoist, but the right loop wouldn't reach. 'Can you grab the hoist with your good hand and pull?' I said. He got his fingertips to it. Mr Radbert weighs over a hundred kilos by my reckoning. He pulled the bar and I pulled the loop. To distract myself from the agony of my hands, I lost myself in their anatomy. The carpal joints were bent like bird's feet, the metacarpals prominent against my white skin. Down the insides of my screeching wrists, the tendons looked like those elastic bungees people use to strap bags onto a trolley when they've taken too much stuff camping. I was so fascinated that, when the loop suddenly slipped on, I nearly lost my thumb. 'Good God, we've done it,' I said, massaging the blood back into my fingers.

'I knew you would, Kate. Thank God. I need the toilet. This is all Micky Donagh's fault.'

I pushed the hoist toward the bathroom. It stopped dead. The carpet had come away again into a big fold. I sighed, went behind the hoist, hauled us over the hummock, went back to the front, pushed. We got into the bathroom, but the hoist wouldn't fit close up to the toilet with its legs closed.

'That bloody Micky Donagh,' said Mr Radbert again. 'All my money gone. And my car. And my electric wheelchair. And now this.'

'He can't have done this. He isn't even here.'

'He has. He's got it in for me. I'm going to fuck his wife.'

'For goodness' sake, Mr Radbert,' I said, 'you can't be talking like that. Keep still, while I get your trousers off.' I reached one hand around the front of the hoist for the control pad and the other around the back for the sling. I pressed the button to lower the hoist at the same time as pulling the sling out over the toilet until he landed on it. 'There, we've done it. Micky Donagh or no Micky Donagh. Now, just relax.' I rubbed his back. 'I'm going to get a catheter bag.'

There were no catheter bags. They had entirely vanished. I thought of my last two customers, waiting. I thought of my dinner. I thought of my bed. I screamed on the inside of my head. Mr Radbert howled like a banshee.

'Now what's wrong?'

'It's stuck.' There were tears coming down his face.

'Relax, I'll hoist you up a bit. Maybe that'll help.'

Again, I pressed the control pad with one hand, while holding the sling out over the toilet with the other. I continued screaming inside my head. My arms screamed back. Mr Radbert screamed out loud, 'Fuck Micky Donaaaaaaaaargh!'

'You can't blame Micky Donagh for your constipation.'

'He's a bastard. He wants to turn me into a white man.'

'For goodness' sake,' I said, 'I'm going to put you down again. Just relax. You'll have another stroke at this rate. Think of something nice. Like your car.'

'Black Beamer. I want to go back to St Lucia. Far away from Micky Donagh.'

'Of course you do.'

'Did you get that replacement licence?'

'No, Mr Radbert,' I said. 'I haven't quite had time for that yet.'

'Get it tomorrow, yeah? Hey, Kate, I've done it!'

'Thank God for that, where's the toilet roll? Oh hell, there's no toilet roll?'

I pushed the spectacles back up the nose again, picked up the blue plastic bowl, squirted soap in it and took it to the kitchen where the hot water tap actually works. After I'd washed and dried him, I had a little battle to get an incontinence pad around Mr Radbert's massive belly. Tried to fasten it, failed, thought of my dinner, tried again, sweated a couple of buckets, failed, thought of my bed, tried again, thought of a glass of wine and succeeded. 'My God,' I said. 'I think we've done it.'

'I knew you would, Kate. Fuck Micky Donagh.'

'We're all God's children, Mr Radbert. Think about the car instead.'

'Oh yeah.'

'I'll just make sure the bed's been made,' I said. 'Hold on,' and I sauntered, victorious, to the bedroom, took one look at the bed and shrieked.

And here I am, standing with my mouth open, wanting to weep. The mechanical bed is levitating far from the floor and is now, powerless, at the height of Mr Radbert's waist. There is no way Mr Radbert will be able to sit down onto it like that. 'Bloody duppy,' I think, flopping into the armchair. I close my eyes. Then I reprimand myself. I want my dinner, I tell myself. I do not believe in duppy. And I head back to the bathroom.

'Houston, we got a problem. Who was on this morning?' I pushed the spectacles up the nose again.

'Dunno.'

'It was Shelly, wasn't it?'

'That tall one? With the big—'

'Never mind those. She's forgotten to lower the bed and now I can't make it go down. There's no power to the plug.'

'Oh God. Fuck you, Micky Donaaaaaaaaargh! I'm going to fuck your wife AND your daughter, you bastaaaa—'

I put my hand right over his mouth. 'For God's sake, shut up. Someone'll call the police in a minute. Think about your car.'

'Mmm . . . mmm . . . sha . . .' he mumbles through my fingers.

'Yes. St Lucia. Think about St Lucia.' I take my hand away.

'OK. But Micky Donagh took all my mon—'

'Stop! Just stay calm and listen. We've got two choices. We can phone for an ambulance, but we'll have to wait hours, because we're a non-urgent call.'

'No!'

'I agree. So, shall I try to get you into bed?'

'Yes. Do that, Kate.'

I labour the hoist back over the hillocky carpet to the bedroom, and slide its legs under the bed. 'You'll have to stand as tall as you can.'

'I am.'

'Taller!' I pull Mr Radbert's big, padded bottom up and push the mattress down as flat as possible. 'Right up on your toes with your good foot. Now. Push down really hard.'

'I can't do it.'

'Think of Micky Donagh.'

'Fuck Micky Donaaaaaaaaaargh!' and he pushes down so forcefully he almost jumps off the hoist at the very same time that I flatten the mattress. His bottom is suddenly three inches onto the bed, feet dangling. I dive down and grab the feet to stop him sliding off again. Holding his weight with just one hand, I reach for the loops of the sling with the other. 'Don't slip. Put your right hand on the bloody bed!' Some of the weight is taken off me. I peel the right sling loop off the hoist. 'You OK up there?' He nods. I pray. Sweat. And long for Margaret's house. Think of the glass of wine. Peel the other loop away. We are flying with no safety net. I reach my right hand under my tired, holding-up-the-legs left hand, release the brakes of the hoist and painfully finger-shove it away from the bed.

'For God's sake don't let go of the bed.' On a count of three I heave the legs up with all the strength I can muster. 'My God, we've done it.' I sit down heavily in the armchair and realize my next call is long overdue.

'I knew you would, Kate.'

I'm glad to get to Veronica again and, finally, back to Margaret where there is no duppy and everything almost always goes completely smoothly and when it doesn't there is a sensible explanation and a perfectly safe way out of it.

'You all right? Had a good day?'

'Bloody hell, Margaret,' I say, 'I'm absolutely shattered.'

'You going up to see your friend?'

'Yeah. I'll see you again first thing tomorrow.'

'Honestly, by the time you get home it won't be worth going to your own bed. You might as well just come back here tonight. You can have the spare room.'

'I'm going to have a big glass of wine.'

'Good for you.'

I go out into the fading summer evening, and rummage in my pocket for Margaret's key so I can put it back into her key safe. My fingers play with metal. My heart sinks. There are two keys in my pocket.

At half past nine, more than fourteen hours since I started this morning, I'm angry with the people I pass in restaurants and bars, happily having dinner or drinks as I trek back to Mr Radbert's house, his key rattling in my pocket. I spit the same phrase over and over. 'There's no such thing as duppy, there's no such thing as duppy, there's no such thing as duppy . . .'

'I hate to say it, Kate,' Greg grins, when I finally make it up to the flat, 'but I do love it when you look knackered. It always makes me feel so much better, mate.'

16.

Feet

Ray Davies is singing about morphine. Greg is face down on the coffee table. The ashtray, invisible, must be somewhere underneath his barnet. Most of his hair is solidly matted into the shape of an upturned flowerpot underneath the purple headscarf, but some escapes in wild black and greying strands that cover much of the table. I stand in the doorway half-wondering if I should worry whether he's still breathing or not. After a few minutes, his voice emanates from the top of his head. 'It's fucking cold.'

'No, it's not. It's a lovely day. It's warm in here.'

'Hear that guitar? That's John Martyn. Born in Surrey but his daddy was a Scotsman. Me and my sister, we loved watching him on the telly. Cracking songwriter. I was going to write a new song today. But you stole my pen.'

'It's on the table, next to your ear. What's the matter with you?'

'My feet are horrible. You look at them. I can't. I had to cut my socks off.' He lies back on the sofa and puts his legs up on the opposite arm. 'See,' he says, careful not to so much as glance at them, 'you're shocked now, aren't you?'

'Actually,' I say, 'I'm not. I see feet like those all the time now.'

The feet in my days often start with Margaret. 'Sleep well?' I ask before helping her legs swing out of bed and onto the floor in front of a waiting walking frame. I'm used to her feet now. On the end of slender, purplish calves, some of the toes sit almost at right angles to the foot, pointing away from Margaret and out to the opposite corners of the room. They want nothing to do with her. The toenails are thickly ridged. It is as though several nails of slightly different sizes have grown on top of one another. I have forty-five minutes to get Margaret up, washed, dressed and breakfasted, but some days her feet entirely refuse to be part of the team. When she tries to stand they scream and then I have to fetch everything needed for an impromptu bed-wash. It's often not until we've finished that Margaret's feet become just cooperative enough to allow her to get to her armchair.

I only saw Lou once but I remember his feet. They were hugely plump. Not with lipid, but with water. Like two pale pink shiny balloons patched with angry red and blotches of blue and green. Big bulging feet on puffy legs, with Lou's toes like balls arranged in order of size from golf to marble. Fatima taught me how to wash and cream feet like this so that the stretched skin does not split and allow bacteria inside that can cause an infection. The scarlet patches on Lou's feet were sore, and the mottled parts had darker lines in them like veins in blue cheese. When I pressed my finger gently into the flesh, it left an indent as though I had pressed on a bag of sand. Every now and then his skin looked extra shiny, and then sweaty, before clear liquid oozed out and came together in a bubble that swelled and fell when it was heavy enough.

'Look at it, I can squeeze it out. You try,' Lou had said.

Ever so gently, I'd pinched Lou's leg and my fingers got wet. If I were him I'd have been on the phone for an ambulance day and night, but he winced about his flat unperturbed, cheerfully awaiting his next appointment with the foot clinic.

Lorna has tiny, perfect feet. She needs help to dress, and she certainly can't bend down to reach her toes. They are always beautifully manicured, the toenails painted a fashionable blue. This is a little mark of friendship. It tells me that Lorna has people who call on her and give her a bit of attention.

She isn't that old. Not much older than you. She's educated too. And funny and warm and immobile. Goes between bed and chair and bathroom with the aid of a hoist. She tells you about her life before she became ill and how she was tiny then. You silently doubt this is possible. She is overweight. But then she points out a photograph of herself as she was, in her dancing days as she calls them. In those dancing days she's a size eight at most and visibly strong and supple and full of movement.

Now her entertainment comes not from dancing but from reading and phone calls and visitors and television. The reading takes more concentration than the illness can give it really. The visitors are lovely but she tires quickly so they can't be with her long. But the television, well, television's easy, isn't it, and when it's not it sends you to sleep? And isn't MasterChef brilliant? And did you see Doctor Who last week? And can you not wait until Strictly comes back? And doesn't the park always look beautiful? And don't you just love people-watching and won't you be impressed with her front garden when spring arrives? She's carefully picked the flowers that friends have planted for her. Friends who come and make things run more smoothly. The flowers are all pink with green foliage. Carnations and peonies and dahlias and tulips and roses and lupins and all of them pink.

And you think to yourself, silently of course, Jesus, there but for the grace of God go I. What have I to be scared about? What have I to be cross about? What have I to feel sorry about? And you suddenly adore this woman and her stoicism and her love of life and you want to be one of those people who help make her life run more smoothly and you realize that being her carer is exactly that.

Eddie's feet were poorly kept. I helped him shower on the first of his morning calls. He could barely see as far as his feet. They were dry and flaky, toenails curving over the ends of his toes like the hooves of a neglected donkey just admitted to a sanctuary. This was a little mark of isolation. It told me that Eddie had no one to call on him and give him a bit of attention. I called the office to let them know that his feet needed some.

Bridget's feet are completely hidden. She wears an extraordinarily clashing variety of mismatched clothing that is changed on a weekly basis. She usually has on a flowery blouse underneath one of a variety of brightly coloured cardigans, black jogging bottoms splattered in something unidentifiable and maroon slippers over the top of beige compression stockings. Bridget won't remove her clothes at all without firm prompting. It's a long visit, an hour and a half to get her washed, changed into fresh clothes, do her shopping, load and unload the washing machine, give her some companionship and take off the stockings that have been on for seven days so I can clean and inspect her feet. Our conversation always goes something like this.

'How's your friend? Must I really wash my hair?'

'He's as well as can be expected. Yes.'

'Why?'

'It smells and if we wash it, it won't smell.'

'Do I have to change *all* the clothes?'

'Yes.'

'Can't we just not do it? Will you tell the office?'

'Bridget, I don't care about the office. Think how smart you'll look when we've finished.'

'Would you say I'm nice-looking?'

'Yes. Hey! I asked Maggs about that wheelchair. She's going to help get you one.'

'Never mind that. Am I going to get gangrene?'

'On your feet?'

'Yes.'

'Not if we take off the stockings and look after them.'

I have to rummage on the floor to struggle to compile a complete change of outfit under Bridget's suspicious stare. Her top half washed and changed, I sit down on the floor in front of her and brace myself for the job ahead, Bridget still chatting nineteen to the dozen.

'Is diabetes curable?'

'Afraid not. Can you feel my hands down here on your legs?'

'Yes.'

'Then you're managing it well and you don't need to worry.'

'Will I go blind?'

'I shouldn't think so.'

'Will I get cancer? Like your friend.'

'My friend smokes. And drinks. Do you smoke?'

'No.'

'Drink?'

'No.'

'There you are then. I doubt you'll get it.'

'Will I get Alzheimer's? That's dementia, you know.'

'I know. I don't think you'll get it.'

'Do you watch those fly-on-the-wall medical documentaries on the television at all?'

'No, Bridget, I don't.'

When I pull Bridget's jogging bottoms up to her knees so I can get to her stockings, a great cloud of dry skin erupts into the stuffy room. I'm always so amazed at its density that I inhale quite a lot of it before remembering not to breathe. The dust settles into my hair like a bad case of dandruff and speckles the brown lino floor. Bridget's compression stockings are unbelievably tight. It's like peeling shrink-wrapped English cucumbers. Scarlet shins give way to ankles around which it is challenging to manoeuvre the stockings but, after that, they whoosh off so quick that Bridget usually nearly comes off the bed with the force of it. Her feet are real shockers.

'Are they dead?'

'No, they look great,' I lie.

They are white, with areas of large, dry, greenish scales over deep yellow crevices around the base of toes that have no gaps between them. The toes and feet look as though they have all melted together or been modelled by a child. Crude plasticine feet with four slits at the ends to make five square-sided toes. I have to look between the toes to make sure they are not fungal and to dry them thoroughly. This takes some doing. The sides of the toes are absolutely flat to one another and the inner sides of each big toe are like a cross-section of well-seared tuna, with a paler border surrounding a slightly darker red centre. Mercifully, it always appears normal. For Bridget.

Sometimes the shock is in absence. Zainab's feet looked innocent enough in red ankle socks. She was bedbound and non-English-speaking, so it was difficult to find a rapport. The bridge was in gestures and smiles, a thumbs-up when the pad change was complete, miming eating to ask if she enjoyed her meal. Despite the gaps between us, we were jolly together. It was easy to be cheerful in Zainab's home, with children and grandchildren surrounding her and Bollywood songs on repeat. The smallest child got placed in

Zainab's high-sided medical bed as though they were both in the same playpen, the toddler quickly removed when it discovered my bowl of soapy water at the bottom of the mattress. I whipped Zainab's socks off and was momentarily flabbergasted. She had beautiful skin the colour of polished pine, and her thin shins ended in shiny brown, amputated foot stumps that looked a bit like table legs.

Now, still standing in Greg's flat, I look over to the sofa at his feet. 'Well?' Greg says. 'That's shocked you, hasn't it?'

His feet are huge, the toes all puffy. He has tried to take off the joggers. This ought to be easy. Greg has never carried much weight, but now his legs are stick thin and the baggy jogging bottoms are baggier than ever. Despite this new bagginess, however, he cannot possibly pull them over the big, bare, clawed feet sticking out at the bottom. I push the joggers up to his skinny knees, get a bowl of warm soapy water and wash them. He complains.

'Just leave it.'

'I can't, we need to look after them. We need to ring the doctor tomorrow.'

'Fucksake, there's no point ringing him. I don't want the doctor. You're putting cream on?'

'Yes,' I say, 'I'm a professional now. I know about these things. The skin will stretch and split, see? Then you could get an infection.'

'I don't care.'

'I'm doing it.'

'Fucksake, Kate. You're being ridiculous. Leave me alone. I don't care about infections. I don't care about anything. Nothing fucking matters.'

'I can't listen to you any more without a large Bloody Mary,' I say.

It's like whispering the word 'sweeties' to a four-year-old.

He sits bolt upright. Grins. 'Neither can I. Make it blue label, though, yeah? It's been a hell of a day already.'

'I ought to make you drink more water and eat more food. Then I'd be doing a proper job.'

'Get the Bloody Marys instead,' he says, 'because that's what I call caring.'

17.
Families

'Nan?' Suzie says. 'They've made a series about the Royal Family. I can get it on the telly for you. You'd love it.'

'Oh! She's absolutely right,' I say, 'you really would.'

Margaret looks at me. Smiles. Then looks at Suzie. 'Maybe . . .'

Suzie grins. 'Great. You can watch an episode tonight.' She picks up the TV remote control.

Margaret reaches out. Removes the control from Suzie's hand. 'Not today, though,' she says. 'Maybe tomorrow. Or next week. And don't go nicking any more of my bananas.'

I catch Suzie's eye, shrug and grin. In her twenties, she lives with her grandmother and does a great job of looking out for her, a constant presence between the visits and telephone calls from the rest of Margaret's lovely family. Checking she's comfortable every night after we've gone. Repositioning the pillows, fetching tea in the day if she's not at work, cooking Sunday lunch, getting the paper. Suzie doesn't bicker back. Her patience is steadfast. I've never once seen her lose it. Margaret adores her really, and trusts her more than anyone. Theirs is a lovely relationship.

Mr Radbert is proud of his children. 'How come I've never seen them?' I ask him.

'They live back home. In St Lucia.'

He tells me their names. 'Kate, you must help me get

some money together for Christmas. They might come visit me and I should have something to give them.'

'Christmas is months away, silly. But of course I will.'

When I get to Bridget, she has something new to show me. We're excited and nervous about it at the same time. I unfold it and she circles it warily for a few minutes, occasionally touching it with her fingertips as though it might wake up and bite.

'They said if I broke it or lost it, I'd never get another.'

'We won't break it or lose it.'

'People will laugh at me.'

'It's not like that now. No one will laugh. I think you'll enjoy it.'

It's more difficult to get it down the concrete stairwell of Bridget's building than I had hoped. A bit heavier and more unwieldy than I'd expected. Bridget comes down one step at a time, best foot forward, one hand on the stair rail and the other on the wall, holding everyone up and chatting madly. At the bottom it takes some doing to hold the heavy main door open, lug the wheelchair out of the building and help her down the three front steps without anything to hold on to.

'Supermarket, yes?' I say, the office having suggested that I take Bridget shopping with me now.

'What about the hairdresser?'

'Hairdresser? You used to go to a hairdresser?'

'Of course! Why shouldn't I have gone to a hairdresser occasionally?'

'My God. But good idea. When did you last see her?'

'Oh. Must be ten years ago.'

It's thrilling to be outside together. Bridget's mood, that of an inmate fresh out of prison, is infectious. She points out anything she recognizes and this is mostly everything we encounter. More animated than I've ever seen her, she stamps her feet on the footplates of the wheelchair and the walking stick almost decapitates several people until I confiscate it. She constantly screeches at me to stop so she can look more closely at the bench she once sat out on, the café she was thrown out of, the Methodist church where she once sang hymns. We are beside ourselves with the discovery that the tree root that once tripped her up and led to her shattered hip and need for carers is still there. I'm hoping the hairdresser's salon won't be gone. I've never seen one round here, but Bridget directs me around a corner into a road that I have not been down before. A woman is smoking outside a doorway a few doors down. As we get closer she shields her eyes with one hand and squints.

'Good heavens!' the hairdresser shouts. 'Come in, my lovely!' She pulls the door wide.

'My God, you remember her?'

'Of course! What a character.' She shakes her head sadly at Bridget. 'Always in a spot of bother, weren't you, madam? I thought something terrible must have happened.'

Bridget is delighted to be recognized and the pair of them exchange ten-year-old news while Bridget's hair is cut with her still sitting in the wheelchair she's now so pleased with.

'Who on earth's been chopping your hair though?' the hairdresser says, shaking her head. 'They've done a terrible job. You looked ridiculous, I'm afraid.'

When the hairdresser's finished, Bridget's face looks longer and fresher than normal. She can't raise her head up enough to see in the mirror properly. 'Would you say I look attractive?'

'Absolutely!' And it's true. With her hair properly trimmed, I can see Bridget's fine bone structure. She looks younger now.

Bridget beckons to me. I put my ear to her mouth. 'It's ten pounds,' she whispers. 'Not a penny more.'

'That was ages ago though.'

'Ten pounds, yes?' Bridget says to the hairdresser firmly.

The hairdresser grins. 'Of course! Ten pounds!' Then they bid one another goodbye like long-lost sisters. In reality, Bridget has a brother rather than a sister but, like the rest of her family before him, this brother appears to have discarded Bridget as soon as possible. Bridget knows that, although she wasn't invited to the wedding, Alan was married and is likely to have had children, so she probably has nephews or nieces somewhere in London with their own kids by now. I've asked Bridget if she'd like me to try to find these family members but she resists it. Having suffered the agony of rejection once, she does not wish to risk repeating it.

William is always in and out of hospital. He's been in a week this time, calls cancelled. Today my visit is back on. I let myself in and walk through to the lounge to find William, disorientated in his chair, still wearing the regulation hospital pyjamas. An elderly couple are sitting opposite him. It's never occurred to me to think how old William's children must be. They've waited for me, even though it's late.

'We can't find his falls alarm. Have left his dinner on the side. Can you help him with it?'

'Of course,' I say. They look exhausted. 'You should get home. William will be fine.'

William's son and his wife get up stiffly. He walking with a stick, she still looking for the missing falls alarm.

They told you that he used to love to garden. You're no gardener. Especially not flowers. You've never really seen the point of growing them. Vegetables maybe. At least they're useful. You ask him about gardening and he tells you that he hasn't done that since his wife was alive. Before he moved into this flat. Not vegetables. Flowers. When he talks about flowers, he makes them sound like every favourite thing you ever lost and wished you could find again, so the next time you're due to wheel him out to the shops you arrive five minutes early, take a detour through the local park and sit, him in the wheelchair and you on a bench, in front of the municipal flower bed. Sitting there with him, you notice the sound of laughter, the sharpness of shadows, the susurration of the trees, how the wind-blown birds look like so many crooked stitches in the sky.

The outing becomes a regular part of your time together until the day the lift breaks down. You feel relieved not to be put to the effort of finding his outdoor clothes and getting him into the wheelchair on that day. But when you get back he looks so miserable that it makes you feel guilty for feeling that way. The next week the lift is still broken. You help him to the balcony door, open it and look out together at bits of rubbish, a broken chair and several pots of dry dirt and dead twigs. He tells you he especially likes the scent of roses and the colour of geraniums. You remind him that roses take ages but maybe geraniums are possible.

The next week you plant geraniums and over the weeks the geraniums blossom and even though he's almost blind he can see them because they are so bright, he's right, the colour is amazing, you never noticed that before when geraniums were just things in pots lining the front doorstep that were a bother to water. But now, now, when you examine them together, geraniums have become exquisite. Miraculous.

A lack of evidence of my customers' families is common and I find it painful. I would love to see some pictures of their earlier lives. Bridget, especially, frustrates me. I have so many photographs of me and my children. There is no fear that if and when they marry there will be any shortage of silly photographs to show at their weddings. I've spent a good bit of time trying to find a picture of Bridget in the belongings that clutter her flat. The nearest I've got is a picture of her mother in a long dress at some formal dinner. Bridget's mother died long before the age that Bridget is now but Bridget looks very like her so I sort of know what she must have looked like at the age of fifty-two. It is the closest I will get to a photograph of Bridget before we at the care agency knew her.

I once asked Ina if she had a picture of herself as a youngster. 'No, missus, but I have a picture of my mother,' she'd said. 'It's in the wardrobe.'

'Oh, of course! Can I see?' I'd started rummaging underneath all the clothes before she'd even answered me.

It was still there amongst the unopened toiletries, chocolate, tobacco and pens just as I'd remembered. An A4 envelope. Stiff with the piece of card inside that had the photograph printed on it. It was a picture of a woman in a formal pose in a professional photography studio. She was wearing a long skirt, smart shoes and a plain white shirt. Her hair was intricately pinned up on top of her head and looked rather beautiful, but I could not see her face at all. It was entirely missing.

All the black-and-white ink of the portrait had been kissed away just there.

I wonder a lot about Greg's family. I worry about what they'd think of the job I'm doing. I never stop him smoking, nor insist he goes to hospital. When he didn't want to continue with the chemotherapy, I didn't force him. It isn't possible to make Greg do anything he doesn't want to do, but I hope his family know this.

'Greg?' I say cautiously. 'Is your mother still alive?'

'Me dad is.'

'When was the last time you spoke to him?'

'We speak quite often actually,' he says. 'At least once a fortnight.'

'Does he know?'

'He was the first person I called,' Greg says, 'from the hospital. The doctor was brutal. He just said, "Sorry, it's lung cancer. It's terminal." I was reeling. Didn't know which way was up. And then I met Sadie on my way out. Lives on the estate. Known her years. Always stopped for a chat when she was on her way home with the shopping. Anyway, she saw I was upset, and I told her what had happened. Straight off the bat Sadie reaches into her pocket, pulls out a tenner, puts it into my hand and says, "Call your dad."'

'Why aren't you with him?'

'I can't make him put up with me,' he says. 'I love me dad but I've caused him no end of trouble, Kate. And he lives in a little Scottish town. If I went and lived there I'd embarrass him.'

'But you're his son.'

'Look at me. You think I could go and live in the countryside?'

'I dream of the countryside sometimes,' I say. 'A nice pub, no traffic, birdsong.'

'For goodness' sake, girl,' he says, 'you wouldn't last a week without an all-night corner shop.'

18.

Vegas

Janey's been with the agency four years but as is the norm, she is paid no higher a rate than someone who started yesterday. She works around forty hours a week to earn enough to live on but, if you include travelling time, it's a lot more hours than that. Today, she's excited.

'There's another agency. You should come with me. It pays better.'

'How much more?'

'Fifty pence an hour more.'

I'm tempted. I'd like that extra fifty pence an hour. But I'd miss my regular customers.

She's in her eighties and has recently had a stroke that prevents her getting in the shower until it's been adapted. That'll be months away. It's not the same being washed at the bedside. She never feels completely clean when her feet don't get properly wet. Doesn't feel fresh. She's fed up. She no longer chats to you the way she used to before her stroke. She doesn't smile a real smile.

You give her the medications and while her lunch is in the microwave you fetch a bowl of water, take off her slippers and socks and put her feet in it. 'Ah, that's lovely,' she tells you. 'Refreshing.' She's eating her lunch when the doorbell rings. The neighbour comes in, sees the feet in the bowl.

'Toe-riffic,' the neighbour says and the two of them giggle. You take the feet from the bowl and dry them.

'Why don't penguins get married?' You raise your eyebrows.

'They get cold feet,' she says.

'Unless,' says the neighbour, 'they're sole mates.' And they're off again.

'Lovely,' she repeats, as you put her socks and slippers back on.

And you think what a difference small things make round here and how sweet it is to do them.

Janey leaves. The agency loses all her goodwill and skills, and her customers lose a friend as well as one of the best carers they could have. Everyone is sad. Two other carers go with Janey but, not having her experience, they're a bit easier to lose. Andrew isn't one of them, but he is equally despondent. Since he can only work with male customers, he doesn't have enough hours to earn more than four or five hundred pounds a month and Michael and Pete are wearing him out for it. He's looking for a different job. All the carers are fond of him, and Michael, Pete, Mr Turner and Andrew's few other customers are getting good care from such a youthful soul. As a young man, he's also a breath of fresh air in this world where male customers see mostly older women. They'd be far worse off without him.

'You know what? If I do leave, I'm getting Pete that cat before I go.'

'Don't.'

'Who's to stop me?'

People tell me I cannot grumble, that I've chosen to do this and I'm overqualified for it – and perhaps I am, but I also know I'm doing the job well and that this work is important and takes skill. I'm not expecting to earn a fortune by any means, but I don't feel valued at all when I can no longer easily afford the bigger things I used to be able to buy. Not just the luxuries but the ones I need. A repair for my cracked phone screen. A paid service for my bike. I'm grateful that my husband earns a decent income, that we have a house and that, although my children cannot easily afford to move out of that house, they are old enough to work to support themselves independently. Even so, sometimes I get fed up.

'You know how much I get paid, Margaret?' I can't help it. She looks puzzled. 'About six quid an hour today,' I say, 'if you count the travelling I'll have to put in.'

'Get you brandy?' I say to Stevie. 'You're lucky you can afford bloody brandy.'

'Honestly, it's probably a good thing I don't get much holiday allowance, because I certainly can't afford to go on one,' I say to Veronica Rose.

At Mrs Gibson's I'm still moaning and when Itzie and I are done, I continue in the lift on the way down. 'It's just not on. It's not fair. I mean, we work so hard. Our job is definitely important. I know people who spend their days publicizing teabags and organizing weddings and managing art galleries. They're not more critical than us, are they? They earn loads more, Itzie. Loads. It's criminal.'

I wait for Itzie to agree but she says nothing.

'I can't even afford to buy a new pair of boots,' I continue. 'Actually, now that the charity shops have increased their prices because people with money have turned second-hand into vintage, I can barely afford to buy someone else's old boots. I thought charity shops were for people who need stuff on the cheap.'

Still Itzie says nothing.

'Vintage!' I spit. 'What is that, exactly? It's just a made-up thing. Vintage. Ugh.'

Itzie's eyes silence me as the lift reaches the bottom of the building. 'Kate,' she says. 'You have a house to live in, you have food to eat, you have friends who love you, you have a healthy family, you can run and you can dance. You do not have to sit in a tower block dependent on others or lie waiting every morning until someone comes to hoist you out of bed or be lonely all day and then all of the night. Be happy. You have everything. Everything. Ever . . . ree . . . thing.'

I never moan out loud again.

A few weeks later, I recognize Janey across a busy road. I shout and hurry to try to get through the traffic quick enough to catch up with her.

'How are you? How's it going?'

'No good.' I realize she was trying to avoid me so she wouldn't have to have this conversation.

'No good. But why?'

'I don't earn half as much as I did. I get about six hundred a month.'

'But what about the extra fifty pence?'

'They keep a high number of carers on,' Janey says. 'So when one of us gets sick they can still cover the customers really easily.'

'And?' I'm still confused.

'Well, the office are all right because they don't have to stress about sudden absences. And the customers are all right because they always get their care on time. But –' she looks miserable and embarrassed – 'there aren't enough hours to go round. I hadn't thought of that. You just can't win, can you?'

Andrew says the same thing when I next see him. 'You just can't win, can you?' He and the other carers who go to Mr Turner have raised concerns about his worsening condition. Mr Turner and social services have decided that he'll have to go into a nursing home. 'So now I've got one less customer and even less money,' Andrew says.

He looks so despairing that something inside me snaps.

'You know what?' I say. 'Let's get that cat. For Pete. If you really think it'll make a difference. I'll help you find one.'

'You will?'

'You'd better not tell the office it was us.'

'Promise.'

Initially, I ask my neighbours and friends if they know of any cat that needs a home with a lonely, animal-loving man who is, I say, rather unusual but just a bit down on his luck. He would give it a lovely home, I assure them, but, for reasons I can't go into, we cannot buy one for him. I just need to sort of come across one. No one knows of any unwanted pet cats, but I hear of a feral one that's been terrorizing the local moggies. I spend several cold late nights walking the streets looking for it. A feral cat sounds perfect for feral Pete. They'd probably get on wonderfully. They could compare battle scars. But, without a single sighting of the monster, I am forced to put the request for a cat out to the other carers.

Carers don't question your common sense. They trust you and they trust to the moment. Even though I know this, I am unprepared for the speed at which things now happen. A cat materializes in seconds. Pauline has one that she has adopted from a customer. She's done it several times before because she can't bear anyone to go through the agony of having their pets put down when they have to go into nursing homes. The latest adoptee has been confined to her bedroom because it doesn't agree with Pauline's other cats. 'Please,' she says, 'take this one. It's a lovely little thing but five cats are a bit much.'

At Pauline's house, it's feline madness. There are litter trays all over the place, fences and gates cordoning off routes that separate the resident cats from the latest cat refugee. Cat litter has spilled down the stairs and there are three separate feeding stations in different parts of the house. 'My

God,' I say, accidentally paddling in another bowl of water by the sofa, 'I'm surprised you didn't just get rid of it without telling him.'

'Oh, I couldn't do that,' Pauline says, 'he just loved that cat. It's a house cat so they were very close. He said he wasn't going anywhere unless he knew she would be looked after. I promised him she'd be really happy.'

We go to the top room to look at the cat. It does not look happy. A patch of fur is missing from one of its haunches. Its ears are flat, its eyes are wide, its whiskers are drooping, and it emits a constant, growly meow. It appears to have a severe case of post-traumatic stress disorder. I pack the little old black-and-white, shaken-up thing into my cat basket and arrange to meet Andrew at Pete's house. Pete, Andrew says, is beside himself with excitement. Abruptly, I become anxious now about what I have done. The cat is a bundle of nerves crapping everywhere. Pete is a heroin-addicted, gang-affiliated alcoholic. The office are going to sack everyone in sight.

At the door, Andrew is beaming. I take the cat basket, covered in a blanket, through to Pete's room. I've brought a litter tray and cat litter with me that Pauline donated and bowls given by Julie along with some cat food from Kenny. A man with a shock of black hair and bright blue eyes is sitting on a bed in shorts and a striped rugby shirt, with a plastered foot and a matching plaster cast on his left arm. He has a can of lager in one hand of the sort that is so strong I've never before seen anyone actually drinking it, and a lit cigarette in the other. He looks up. I open the door of the cat basket and whip the blanket away like a magician.

Andrew squeaks, snorts and then tightly closes his lips.

The little black-and-white cat springs out and hides under the sofa. Everyone holds their breath. Pete puts his fag out.

I assemble the cat litter tray in the hall and when I return the cat creeps into the open, sniffing at the air. Andrew stares at it with his hand over his mouth.

Pete begins to cry.

'Oh, she's beautiful,' he says. 'Thanks a lot, love. Thanks, Andrew, mate. Mate, you've no idea how happy I am. Come on now,' he says to the cat.

'Oh,' I say, 'I forgot to ask what she's called.'

Andrew squeaks again and then shuts up.

The cat does the unthinkable and jumps onto Pete's lap where it becomes one big purr. It's lovely to see them there, this unlikely couple. I no longer care about who's going to feed her because it's clear that the benefit of putting them together is perfectly mutual. Everyone will be able to see that. It's obvious.

'Doesn't matter,' Pete says, 'I already know what I'm going to call her. I'm going to call her Vegas.' Andrew snorts and leaves the room.

'That's nice,' I say. 'I'd better go.'

'Thanks again,' Pete says.

Andrew's waiting at the door. 'What the hell's wrong with you?' I say.

He can barely speak. 'Vegas,' he says, 'is a terrible name.'

'Oh, leave him alone. He can call it what he likes.'

'No, I mean it's a terrible name for Lucy.'

'Lucy?'

'It's Mr Turner's cat.'

'Wow,' I say. 'I guess sometimes you do win after all, eh?'

19.

Till death do us part

Diabetes has taken some bits of Mr Andino's feet and dementia some bits of his brain. Greek television is being broadcast from beside his bed on one side of the lounge. Mrs Andino's armchair is on the other, separated physically and psychologically by piles of wipes, nappies and barrier creams that lie on a smoked-glass coffee table between them. Magazines, pointless now, are relegated to the floor.

'Hello, Mr Andino.'

'Yes, yes, yes,' he growls.

John guards Mr Andino's hands while I check the pad. Clean and completely dry.

'Yes, yes, yes.'

'Mr Andino should drink more,' I say. Mrs Andino shrugs. John gets fresh water.

'This blister pack of medications is out of date, is there a new one?' John asks. Mrs Andino shrugs, pushing the medications back at him. 'I'll phone the office,' he says.

Having stepped within reach of Mr Andino's hands, I remove them from my bottom and try to put them on the bed. Like two similarly charged magnetic fields, the bed and the hands repel one another. I remain polar opposite for the hands. I look at Mrs Andino. She shrugs.

'Yes, yes, yes,' growls Mr Andino.

'No.' I say it gently, but it feels harsh. I fetch moisturizer and massage Mr Andino's toeless feet. He smiles. It's not until I turn that the punch hits my left side. I am just far enough from him not to be winded.

'Yes, yes, yes,' he growls.

'I'm fine,' I say to John. I look at Mrs Andino and think how little she must have anticipated this version of her husband. And how he wouldn't recognize himself. 'Doesn't matter, not his fault. You OK?' I say. She takes my hand and squeezes. We shrug.

Many other elderly couples cope with caring for one another on their own until things fail. At the Jacksons' house, my notes tell me that Mrs Jackson's husband will let me in. I use the key safe when no one answers the door. She nods hello from her bed. The room is silent. No television, no radio. Just a skeletal woman within white walls, the window behind her.

'I thought Mr Jackson would let me in.'

'He fell in the kitchen. Yesterday. A stroke. He's in hospital. The family are there.'

'I'm so sorry,' I say, taking her hand. 'It must be a dreadful shock.'

Her skin is smooth, her eyes clear, her silver hair silken over the pillow. She is a beautiful, elderly angel.

'Can you be taken to see him?' I ask.

'No. He may die. If he lives, he won't come home again. They think he won't know me now anyway,' she says.

Other couples are still soldiering on quite cheerfully. Mr and Mrs Seddon appear on my rota without warning. They live in a well-kept house, with immaculately trimmed shrubs and flowers standing to attention down the garden path. I ring the bell at nine in the morning. An upper window opens and an authoritative voice booms down, 'Door's open!'

I go inside and through a kitchen into a living room and up the carpeted stairs. Three rooms come off the landing at the top. A bedroom, a bathroom and a small study in which Mr Seddon is attending to paperwork. 'And you are?' he says, peering at me over his glasses.

'Kate,' I say, 'carer.'

'Bedroom!'

In the room next door, Mrs Seddon's thin body is entirely shrouded. Only the very top of her head is visible, wispy grey above the sheet. I return to the study.

'Forgive me asking,' I say, 'but is it all right to wake her? She's sound asleep. I'm so sorry to ask but, as I've not met her before—'

'How,' says Mr Seddon, firmly, 'are you going to shower her if you don't wake her?' I have been reprimanded.

I go back to the bedroom and lift the sheet from my new customer's face. 'Hello, Mrs Seddon.' Put my hand on a bony shoulder, say, 'Good morning.' Nothing. Gently nudge, run my hand over her cheek. 'Time for your shower.' She opens her eyes. Closes them. 'I'm Kate,' I try, cheerfully. Nothing. I stroke her arm. Squeeze it. She opens her eyes again. Closes them again. I feel stumped, but thinking about how Mr Seddon must be able to hear me failing to do my job intimidates me into sweeping the sheet from Mrs Seddon's shoulders and taking both her hands. Mercifully, she sits up. 'Yes,' she says, 'aaaaaaah,' and rises like a phantom in her full-length white nightgown.

'Yes, aaaaaaah,' I reply, 'shall we go?' and we walk slowly out of the bedroom, me backwards, and into the bathroom.

Mrs Seddon is as thin as string and I don't know how well she can sit or stand unaided. She appears so fragile that I'm honestly afraid the force of the shower will crush her, but she enjoys it. She hums and takes the flannel when I offer it, and I do the bits she cannot reach and we sing, 'Yes, aaaaaaah.' Then I dress her, and we go back to the study like two naughty children.

Mr Seddon tuts, 'Could do better. Her hair's all sticking up.' We retreat to the bedroom and find a hairbrush before further inspection. 'Breakfast!' Mr Seddon booms, dismissing us downstairs. I sit his wife at the dining table in the kitchen, serve her cereal and put the kettle on.

Mr Seddon is pleased with the cup of tea I take up to the study. 'Oh, cheers. Are you with us all day?'

'My rota says until eleven.'

'Not good enough, I'm afraid. We're due to go out at ten. Won't be back until one o'clock. We'll need you with us till then.'

Today, this is my last call until my mid-afternoon visits begin. The gap is a nice, long, three-hour break that I look forward to every week. A break I use to go home, have a cup of tea and some lunch, and do some cleaning. I don't really want to work through to the evening without it, but I think of Mrs Seddon missing her outing. 'I suppose I could—'

'Jolly good.'

I ring the office to let them know and they agree to pay the extra time. 'Where are we going?' I ask, expecting it to be the hospital as usual.

'Cycling.'

'Cycling?'

'Cycling.'

'What, with pedals?'

'Of course with pedals. It's very good. Mrs S just loves cycling.'

Back downstairs, Mrs Seddon has finished breakfast. 'Yes, aaaaaaah,' she says.

'Yes, aaaaaaah,' I reply. 'We need to get your coat on. Mr Seddon says we're going cycling.'

Mrs Seddon stares at me. I smile back over the empty cereal bowl and imagine her before she was unwell. Her husband's footsteps are muffled by carpet and the noise of a passing car is faint through closed windows. Her blue eyes become locked on mine in this hush. Her expression is unchanging. I continue to smile. We do not blink. I think our breathing has become synchronized. And then a shot is released into the quiet. 'He's a clever one, isn't he?' says Mrs Seddon, loud and with clarity. I jump. A candle blown small by wind was briefly bright in stillness.

I am shocked. It is magical. I want it to happen again. 'Mrs Seddon? Cycling?'

But all is dark once more. 'Yes, aaaaaaah.' No further thoughts are immediately coded in this shrunken brain, to jump the missing gaps in chains of neurons and escape the mouth. It was not, in fact, a candle flickering. Just one of many single, stray, verbal fireworks which erupt occasionally and unexpectedly at the end of a lifelong, coordinated display.

I'm surprised at how immobile Mr Seddon is when he finally leaves the study. He uses crutches. 'I hope you can cycle. We had one girl come who'd never cycled in her life. Palbhi, I think her name was. Sometimes we have Laura. She's a great cyclist. Mrs S just loves it when Laura comes cycling.'

'Well, I do it all the time,' I say.

'Excellent. Good girl.'

'Do you mind me asking what you and Mrs Seddon used to do?' I ask cautiously.

'Police officers!' barks Mr Seddon briskly.

There is a complex bit of manoeuvring to get Mrs Seddon's wheelchair and Mr Seddon's crutches in the cab and then we're off. The sun is warm through the windows. I offer the water I packed in my bag to Mrs Seddon while her husband shouts at the driver, 'You know where we're going?'

'Park?'

'Cycling.'

'Oh yeah?'

'Do you know where the cycling is?'

'The park's a big place, sir.'

'It's near the Mortimer Road entrance, close to the football pitches, you know them?'

'Your directions say Pelham Road.'

'It's not Pelham Road. We tried that last time. It's near the pitches. And the kiddies' playground.'

We drive around the roads surrounding the park for some time, finding no clues as to where we should be. The sun is scorching through the windows now. Mr Seddon fans himself with the sheet of paper containing the useless directions, Mrs Seddon finishes off my water, and I'm beginning to doubt the cycling exists. We must surely be looking in vain for some mythical bicycle with magic pedals. Finally, in the absence of further information, the cab pulls up on an empty side road between a housing estate and the green of the park. The driver sighs. Again.

'Oh, never mind,' calls Mr Seddon cheerfully, 'we'll find it.' And he gets out and sits on a low wall, still flapping the directions about.

The driver and I extract Mrs Seddon and her wheelchair. 'Yes, aaaaaaah.' I wheel her over to Mr Seddon. 'Can I look at those directions?'

'Oh, they're all wrong,' he grins.

'Can I look at them anyway?' He passes me the piece of paper. 'Pelham Road' is written on it, partly crossed through, next to a square with a line labelled 'Mortimer Road' and the words 'Changing Rooms'. 'Football pitches,' he says, stabbing at the paper as the sound of the taxi's engine disappears into the distance. I wonder how I got here, trapped by poor cognition, immobility and my own naivety, and silently rehearse explaining the importance of autonomy and capacity to the police. Then I get a grip on myself. 'Right,' I say. 'I'll go into the park and find out where the cycling is then. You'll be all right for a couple of minutes?'

'Off you go!' barks Mr Seddon.

I sprint into the park trying not to imagine muggers menacing the housing estate. After running full pelt until I can barely breathe, I see a group in the distance. They are wheeled. A group of people on big trikes or bikes that are somehow bolted side by side in pairs. Some able-bodied and some with impaired mobility. 'Oh, thank God,' I say, 'Mr and Mrs Seddon are stranded.'

'Brilliant!' says a woman in lycra with a clipboard. 'Kev! Myra! Go pick up Mr and Mrs Seddon, please.' Two of the side-by-side bicycles make their way out of the park and I run alongside, sweating buckets. No wonder Palbhi wasn't very keen.

'Terrific!' shouts Mr Seddon and immediately climbs up onto Myra's side-by-side bicycle. 'Let's go!' I help strap Mrs Seddon next to Kev. When I next look up, Mr Seddon and Myra are out of sight.

Mrs Seddon hasn't said anything, but looks content. 'Are you too hot?' I check, adjusting her coat. I put each of her feet on a pedal. Kev pulls away carefully and muscle memory urges Mrs Seddon's feet into action. She smiles, frowns, smiles as each of her feet push down in turn. The bike moves slowly into the park and over a concrete path through the green of the trees. I watch them disappearing before thinking she should not be without me in case she becomes unhappy. 'I'm taking a trike!' I scream.

The trike is hefty and difficult to steer and for a few minutes I am less steady than Mrs Seddon, desperately trying to catch up whilst going slower than I have ever ridden before. When I get level with Kev and Mrs Seddon, I shout, 'Everything all right, Mrs Seddon?' She looks at me but doesn't smile. Instead, she raises an eyebrow as though I am a wayward teenager who has infringed the law.

There is a shout from far away. Mr Seddon is a speck but fast approaching, one hand waving madly and the other on Myra's thigh. 'Hellooooo!' he screams. 'Isn't this great? How are you getting on?' As he bursts upon us, he grabs the handlebars from Myra and, cutting me up, forces a spin right around Mrs Seddon who is still proceeding sedately. Mrs Seddon looks up, startled.

'Isn't this fantastic?' Mr Seddon shrieks again, snorting with so much laughter he can barely get his words out. Now he has one arm around Myra's shoulder. Fortunately, Myra is smiling. 'See?' grins Mr Seddon. 'Mrs S just loves cycling!' And before taking Myra on another lap of the park, he bloody winks at me.

You are impressed by these marriages measured in gold and diamond and sapphire. Even in platinum. A friend of yours once said how lucky you were to have met your husband because it was obviously so easy for you to be together. You were an automatic, perfect fit.

You'd been cross with her for saying that because it wasn't always easy. You laughed a lot, but you still had to work at it as you brought up the children and played to your strengths and he was the best of dads and you thought you did pretty well as a mum. Now, here you are, three schools, a couple of universities, eight cats, around twenty-five holidays, hundreds of parties and countless ups and downs later. And you've not even reached pearl.

20.

The Second Otis Redding

'I'm famous, you know,' says Mr Radbert.

'Really?'

'Singer.'

'Oh yeah?'

'Soul singer. I was known as the Second Otis Redding.'

'Why don't I ever hear you sing then?'

Mr Radbert looks scornful. 'I can't sing now. Not like then. The girls loved me. My God, those girls, whoo-hoo-hoo!'

'We should put Otis Redding on in here,' I say. 'You've got a stereo. Is it working?'

'Of course it's working,' he says indignantly. 'No CDs, though,' sadly.

'I'll get some.'

'Oh yeah. Like you'll phone the DVLA . . .'

'I will. I absolutely will.'

'You're all talk, you are,' shouts Mr Radbert, as I'm closing the door behind me and starting out for Maureen's house.

The curtains are closed in Maureen's room, but they're no match for the brightness of the day. It's noisy too. Her brother Paddy's playing the radio in the kitchen of the flat. The Bangles urge Maureen to walk like an Egyptian. Maureen can't even walk like a Londoner. Maureen's getting upset that we're not Julie, Chrissy's getting cross and time's running on. 'For goodness' sake, Maureen,' says Chrissy, 'we haven't got all day.' She presses the button on the control pad that tilts the head of the bed down flat again.

Maureen shrieks, 'It's too low. Sit me up, sit me up. Julie!'

'We're not sitting you up again. Not till we're finished.'

I take Maureen's hand. 'Maureen,' I say, 'do you like cats or dogs best?'

'Dogs.'

'You ever owned one?' Chrissy is taking down the jogging bottoms.

'A dog called Buster.'

'A boy dog? What colour?' Chrissy removes the pad and begins to clean.

'Staffie. What's she doing? Julie!'

'Julie'll be back tonight. Chrissy's just changing the pad. Then I can give you tea and biscuits. How does that sound? Did you go to school round here? What was your favourite lesson?'

Paddy puts his head in the door. 'Sports,' he says. 'Isn't that right, Maureen?'

'Yeah, 'specially football.'

'Tell her,' says Paddy. But Maureen has become coy.

'She was a right tomboy,' says Paddy. 'Better than me at running and batting and football. Always up trees. I was more into drawing,' he grins. 'I was the arty one. But she – never mind she was a girl – she was always outside running around, hanging out with boys playing football. And once she was up Croydon way, the only girl playing with a group of boys in a park. She was brilliant at it, ain't that right, Maureen?' But Maureen just grins as Chrissy pulls up the joggers. 'She was brilliant,' Paddy repeats, 'and someone saw her and asked her where she lived. That night, they knocked on our door. Two people actually. And they wanted to talk about the boy they'd seen playing football that afternoon. They said they'd watched him for a good long time and that they'd decided there and then to offer him a place in the junior squad. Well, my ma called for me,' Paddy said. 'And Ma said these men are wanting you. But,' said Paddy, 'I hadn't been playing football.'

'Maureen!' I say. 'Good God, woman. You been signed for Crystal Palace?'

'I wasn't allowed,' said Maureen. 'When they found out I was a girl.'

I go home for lunch and then force my son to come out with me to search in every charity shop we can find for an Otis Redding CD. We don't have much luck. I'm disappointed. I'd thought it would be easy. After two hours my son is bored: 'We're not going to find any. Nor any reggae either.'

'What about Bob Dylan?' I say. 'Perhaps Mr Radbert will like that. There's a Bob Dylan greatest hits package here.'

'If Mr Radbert wants Otis Redding,' says my son, 'I don't think you should buy Bob Dylan.'

I'm agreeing with him when I realize there is a middle-aged man standing next to us. The man is staring down at me with something like pity on his pudgy pink face.

'I think you should know,' he says with a smug and self-satisfied smile, 'that a compilation LP will not be Bob Dylan's best album.'

I suddenly feel very, very tired. Tired of spending my break looking for Mr Radbert's CD. Tired of having to go up to Greg's flat every spare minute. Tired of missing meals and getting skinnier than I'd ever even wished to be. Tired of feeling guilty about avoiding my home life. Tired of being unable to spend my free time doing and buying things for me.

I remain squatting, unmoving, for a few seconds tuning in

to the awareness that my temper is coming to the boil. When it begins to steam, I stand up.

'Clearly,' I say to the man, 'it is not Bob Dylan's best album. Do you seriously think I don't know that a greatest hits package is not Bob Dylan's best fucking album?'

We leave the shop.

'God, Mum,' says my son, 'there was no need to be like that. He was just trying to be helpful.'

'No,' I say, 'he wasn't.'

'You don't know that. Maybe he was just being nice.'

My son goes home and I go up to Greg's to make him some food. I tell him about how the man in the shop thought he'd educate me on what a good Bob Dylan album was. Greg doesn't say, 'He was just trying to be helpful,' or 'Maybe he was just being nice.' Greg says, 'What a patronizing git, Kate. He was probably just trying to chat you up,' and begins rummaging through the hundreds of cassettes and CDs that litter the flat. Eventually, as I'm presenting scrambled eggs he says, 'I don't really like Otis Redding. Except his version of "Satisfaction". That's on the live album I have. Your customer can't have that. But he can have this.'

It's a double CD of Otis Redding's greatest hits.

Before I can take this homage to Mr Radbert's earlier musical genius to the Second Otis Redding, I have to get to Patrick. He's the last person I'd expect to have any surprises in his history.

Patrick's dementia's getting worse. I find him fast asleep in bed. When I wake him, he's of the opinion that it's six in the morning, not six in the evening. I have an hour to fast-forward through an entire Patrick day, tire him out and convince him that it's night-time so that he'll be willing to be helped back into bed again. Patrick dresses, comes downstairs to the kitchen and loads his breakfast tray with a banana and a bowl into which he drops a handful of branflakes. He takes the milk jug from the fridge and puts it onto an exact spot on the tray next to his empty medication dosette box. The dosette box consists of seven individual lidded compartments, but Patrick doesn't use it for his medications.

I take his tray through to the dining room. He sits at the table and lifts the lid from the third compartment of the dosette box. Feels and counts the opened compartments from left to right. 'Monday . . . Tuesday . . . Wednesday,' he says. 'It's Wednesday?'

'Yes.'

'Is that bin day?'

'No. That's Thursday.'

Next Patrick tells me, as he always does, that he takes Lansoprazole because once when he was visiting his sister-in-law he'd developed some discomfort in his chest. His sister-in-law had immediately driven him to the local doctor and this doctor had diagnosed reflux. It isn't a particularly interesting story, but Patrick doesn't tell me about it because it's interesting. He tells me about it because it is the hook on which he strings the conversations of his day. The medication dosette box and this story are part of a system Patrick has put in place to maintain control over his unravelling brain. That he has overslept today is evidence of this system beginning to break down.

The next key landmark of his life that needs to be told is the story of how Patrick met his second wife. The one he loved the best. Not the first one with whom he'd had a baby that died in early childhood. He has stopped mentioning the baby and the destruction this loss rendered to that first marriage. Forgetting this tragedy ought perhaps to be a blessing. But I don't think it is.

There are three storeys in Patrick's house. I've often

wondered what's on the top floor that I don't go to. I've always assumed it was just another bedroom. After breakfast, I lead the way up to the second-floor sitting room.

'What are you doing?' Patrick shouts as usual, this too being part of the system. 'You're in the way of the light. I can't see the stairs with you there. You'll make me fall, stupid.'

You used to be frightened by anger, hated people shouting at you. He once made you cry, screaming and swearing while you cleared up the cup you hadn't broken and the tea you hadn't spilled. He didn't notice because he's almost blind. You just let the tears run down while the bullying illness raged at you and your non-existent ineptitude.

But now you no longer cry when he or anyone else gets angry. Well, rarely, anyway. Only if you're feeling exceptionally fragile. You've learned that anger isn't usually a primary emotion. It's not aimed at you. It's not really aimed at anyone. It's just covering things up. Things like fear, pain, frustration, anxiety or embarrassment.

I go into the sitting room with a pear and a bottle of water, but Patrick doesn't follow me. It appears that another part of his system has broken down. He walks right past the doorway and continues upstairs to the top floor. The floor I've never seen. I follow him. It's dusty up here. Patrick goes to the landing window. Looks out over the street. 'I can see someone moving.'

'It's your neighbour.' My voice is a bit short. I'm worrying that this extra floor is equalling extra, unpaid time.

'It is? I can only see the shadow. I can hardly see anything now. It's dreadful. What day is it?'

'Wednesday.'

'Bin day?'

'No, that's tomorrow.'

Patrick steps off the landing and into the only room here at the top. It's a storeroom-cum-office. He clicks on the light. 'I think this used to be a bedroom,' he says. 'I think it was the room my sister-in-law stayed in on the night my wife died. My wife was in hospital and Felicity was staying. She lived in . . . Oh God, I can't remember where she lived. She got me to the doctor, you know. And he diagnosed me with reflux. That's why I take . . .'

'I know,' I sigh.

'Felicity stayed in this room. It's not a bedroom now, of course, it's a study. But I kept the chest of drawers.' He opens a drawer and looks inside. 'What am I doing?'

'We were taking your pear to the sitting room.'

'Then why have you brought me up here?'

I look around the room now filled with discarded objects from a long life. There are lots of papers and folded linen. A table in the middle is draped with an old-fashioned embroidered tablecloth, hiding a filing cabinet that Patrick no longer opens.

'What day is it?'

'Wednesday.'

'Bin day?'

'No.'

There are boxes of papers here, and photographs. Some of them are stuck on a big sheet of card pinned on one wall. It's a collage of Patrick's life. 'What's this?' I say, stepping closer to it.

'I think someone made it when I retired,' he says.

The photographs are all of Patrick at different ages and in different situations. Someone has put it together as a commemoration. I can see Patrick as a mischievous-looking boy, as a teenager in shorts and deck shoes, smart in a suit at a desk, getting married in a registry office to a smiling woman with permed hair and a twinset, the type of woman who would attend meetings of the Women's Institute. Patrick raising a toast, smiling up from some writing he's doing, another of him in an open-necked shirt behind a stall at a church fete, another of him sitting at a different desk under which someone has written 'Salesman of the Year'.

The last photograph is of Patrick in front of workmates, glass of fizz in hand, about to begin his retirement, but the picture that catches my eye is not glossy, it is a newspaper cutting. It shows Patrick being embraced by the smiling, permed woman while a senior police officer stands along-side them. I read the headline over and over. I cannot take it in. Cannot tally the man in front of me with the event in the newspaper report. 'My God,' I say, 'you foiled a robbery? You must have been a hero, Patrick.'

Patrick steps toward the picture of him with his work-mates. Traces his fingers over it. 'I had a presentation. They gave me something. I can't remember what.'

'But this,' I say, pointing to the cutting, 'Patrick, this is extraordinary. Weren't you scared?'

He points to the smiling, permed woman. 'I think that's Betty.' I hold my breath. 'But I can't remember what it was all about. What day is it?'

That night, at Mr Radbert's, I whip out the CD.

'Oh!' Mr Radbert shouts. 'I eat my hats!'

We put the stereo on and Mr Radbert urges me to turn the volume full up. We sing at the tops of our voices. Mr Radbert knows every word. He shrieks and squeals, his beanie hat fallen to the floor, and I take his hands and we dance, we shout, we sweat, me jumping and him in the wheelchair moving from side to side, the drab of his flat faded away in the glory of it all.

We weep, we belt out tune after tune ridiculously badly

and sway through the ballads, Mr Radbert's perfect white teeth on full display as he croons, and I think, Jesus, I wish I'd known this soul in another life, how much fun we could've had, this silly man and me. At last we stop, breathless, more with excitement than activity. 'Whoo-hoo-hoo!' Mr Radbert yells, his glasses in his lap. I admit to him that it wasn't me who gave him the music, it was my friend.

Mr Radbert is incredulous. 'You tell that friend of yours he made me so happy. You make me love you both. I can't walk, but the music makes me dance in my mind.'

'He loved it,' I tell Greg. 'I boogied the Second Otis Redding all the way to bed. Why on earth don't you ever sleep in a bloody bed? The reason your feet are bad is because you stay there on that sofa all the time. Your feet swell up because they're always at the bottom of you. Can't you at least put them up on the coffee table?'

'I'm used to sleeping in odd places,' says Greg. 'I spent most of my working days sleeping in a drum booth.'

'What the hell are you on about?'

'I was a drummer. The guitar came later. When you're making records, you often end up having to sleep late in odd places. I can sleep anywhere, mate.'

'A drummer?'

'Yes. Back in the day. I've got a gold record somewhere.'

I want to know what record.

'It was a long time ago.'

'And.'

'It's not relevant, Kate. It was a long time ago. I don't want to think about it.'

At home, I look him up on the internet and marvel that no one knew a thing about it when he was playing guitar out on the street.

21

You'd sure better marry your soulmate

The smell of unwell is a telling odour, diagnostic in its pecu-
liarity. Diabetes smells fruity and sweet, poorly kept feet like
potatoes left in an airless container to rot, while dialysis is
metallically meaty, the odour going straight to taste, like a
coin in your mouth.

Diverted from my normal patch to cover for a colleague,
the only details I have for the customer are that she is female,
bedbound and non-English-speaking. The smell comes out
to meet me while I'm still walking in from the street to be
greeted by my co-worker and the customer's elderly husband. I know this smell from hospital wards. It is the smell
given off when you turn a dead fish over on the beach and
find the underside rotting, combined with the stink of horse
manure and the sweet-sickly reek of a baby's full nappy. This
smell has a colour. The colour is ochre tinged with dark
green. This smell has a noise. The noise is the indignant hum
of a bluebottle on its back. This is the smell of clostridium
difficile diarrhoea. C. diff for short, but never, ever sweet.

I try to close the curtains but the husband forbids me. It is
bright with sunshine flooding in from the windows and
garish with plastic flowers on shiny furniture covered in lacy
cloths. The floor is hard pink lino. A huge mirror with a gilt
frame reflects the horror right back, just in case you were
hoping to turn the other cheek. Catching Val's eye, I understand that shock is visible on my face. Taking a deep breath,

I recompose my features into a friendly mask. 'Do you know this lady?' I ask Val calmly.

'I do.'

My relief is huge. 'Well, you'll have to lead,' I say. 'I don't know where to begin.'

All my senses are telling my brain to get my body to leave the area, have a hot shower and boil-wash my clothes. Instead, I go briskly to the opposite side of the bed trying to look as though I see this every day of the week. I tell myself bacteria cannot fly. Val exudes an air of control. I exude an air of calm. The husband exudes an air of fear. The woman, bare of blankets and lying on a sheet, exudes slimy yellow liquid.

She is contorted, short but heavily built and somehow formless from the waist down. The legs are like those sewn onto a home-made rag doll by a child who knows nothing of anatomy, but has simply added two stuffed worms to a pouch of body and allowed them to randomly tangle. The skin of the woman is pale greenish pink, and filmed in sweat. I think of a whelk. Squirming. Then I stop myself thinking of that.

The room is hot. Airless. Someone has folded hundreds of pieces of kitchen roll into four-inch squares and stacked them carefully into a tower more than a foot high on a chest of drawers next to the bed. The woman takes one, coughs up into it and throws it into a black bin liner on the floor.

Even though I have not yet touched the woman, I feel I have inhaled her.

I think she is angry. I put a hand on her shoulder, but she doesn't respond. Her hair is long, greasy and grey, her eyes grey too. She shouts at her husband, stout and olive-skinned in pink shirt and grey trousers with sharp creases down the front, his black shoes so shiny the underside of the bed is reflected in them. Diarrhoea has seeped out of the incontinence pad and made a puddle underneath. I look at Val. 'Is it always like this?'

'I've not seen it this bad before,' she says. 'They wanted to cancel the calls, but the office refused. Thank God.' She undoes the pad and tries to lift the pelvis toward me, in the direction the knees seem to be mostly facing. The woman shrieks. I lean across and, gently as I can, try to roll her so that we have half a hope of getting to the pad underneath. It is not possible. The legs and pelvis move as one unwieldy lump and it feels as though something might snap unexpectedly if moved the wrong way.

'Take the sheet off the bed so we can wrap everything in it,' I say. We slip it down from the top of the bed behind the woman's head, past her shoulders. It comes to an abrupt stop at the base of her spine. We pull it up from the bottom of the bed, behind her ankles, past her knees. It comes to an abrupt stop at the top of her thighs. With the flood partially contained, we try again to lift her pelvis from the bed.

We are murmuring to the woman in between speaking to one another. Soothing words, kind words, calming words. Words she cannot understand. She says only, 'Tamam, tamam,' over and over. 'Enough, enough,' I think. I want to comfort her. Val takes the woman's hands tenderly and places them on the bed rail in front of me. She leans over and pushes gently down on them, indicating that the woman should help us by lifting herself. By some miracle it works. The woman raises her body enough for me to be able to hold her pelvis and buttocks off the bed. Val swoops up the filthy sheet and soiled pad, separates them, ties the bedlinen into one plastic bag and the rubbish in another, whips off her latex gloves and dons a new pair. In seconds. It's impressive.

'Don't let her go,' Val says and begins to wipe and wipe and wipe. Then she washes with warm soapy water. Then it's my turn.

I help the woman turn herself toward Val, so I can clean her left side. I wipe. The stuff is like jelly. It slides over the cloth. I have to scoop as much as swab. I wash. I say soothing words. We check for bed sores. We cream. We disinfect the bed. We lay the pelvis flat again and separate the feet and legs enough to be able to clean between them at the front. We wash. We dry. We put on a fresh pad. The woman furies all the way through. The husband trembles next to me, unresponsive to our request for fresh bedcovers, unmoving, until Val shouts, 'Sheets, sheets!' and, verbally slapped, he jumps and beetles into another room, re-emerging with linen. We lay clean sheets over and under her. We soothe. We spread a soft blanket on top. The woman curses and moans. 'Tamam, tamam.'

My hands feel wet through my gloves. I know this can't be so, but still I hope I have no broken skin. I will never bite my nails again. I will eat my dinner holding my knife and fork at the very ends and will not have any bread. I will drink water from a mug with a handle instead of a glass.

Val and I go into the bathroom to wash in the hottest water we can bear. We use the bath taps because the husband is busy in the sink, rinsing contaminated flannels. We say, 'You must use a washing machine.' Puzzled, he frowns at us, readying the medications.

Administration of medications involves applying the five rights. You check that the right medication is being given in the right dose, via the right route to the right patient at the right time. This is usually easy. Most customers only have two or three tablets at a visit and they're obvious. The distinct, round blue finasteride with

F stamped on it, the pink repaglinide, the peachy, oval simvastatin or the half-red, half-clear capsule within which you can see tightly packed pancreatic lipase enzymes. Easy to count and easy to identify. But her medications are nine tablets deep and consist of tiny round white pills that all look the same. It takes a magnifying glass to read the minuscule letters and numbers stamped on them.

Counting them onto a clean, dry saucer with a clean, dry spoon using clean, dry, gloved hands, you discover there are eleven instead of the nine on your list. You silently swear and begin to separate them out, tally them against the list and manage to identify the first three. She screams. You go to comfort her, return to the plate, change your gloves, start again. Look at the clock. Get as far as four this time. Comfort her, change your gloves, start again, the desire to trust the pharmacist and just give the bloody tablets jabbering in your head. Stop again. Adjust the pillow. Think of the time. Start again. Keep your kind face on. Turn back to the scream and knock the plate. Watch the whole lot falling to the floor as you dash to the bed. Spend ten minutes finding them on the lino. Pick up the fragments of the plate. Wrap the contaminated tablets in tissue and shove them back into the blister pack so the next carer knows they haven't been given twice. Ring the office, pop out a fresh set of medications. Curse in your head. Start again.

Finally, you discover that the pharmacist has run out of full doses of two of the tablets and has given two half-doses of each instead. My God. You may not be a saint, but this job sure takes the patience of one. You'd normally have shouted, berated and torn your hair out, but here, where you are screamed at not by people but by the pain, confusion and frustration of illness, you've learned to be tolerant. Calm. Composed.

Outside, it seems impossible that normal life is continuing. The sun shines, music plays, people pass arm in arm, laughing. I phone the office to advise of the need for infection control and for a doctor to come and for swabs to be taken. I ask that social services urgently review the entire situation. I confirm that calls cannot be safely refused.

'My God,' I say to Val, 'you did that so well. I had no idea how we would manage. You are brilliant. That's the worst I've ever seen. The worst.' Although I've not met Val before today, the intensity of the experience we have shared bonds us in some odd way. Relationships with co-workers are like this. Even though you don't spend a long time growing them, friendships develop suddenly in this environment. We swap telephone numbers as I often do with my colleagues.

'Makes you think,' Val says as she types my number into her phone, 'you'd sure better marry your soulmate, don't you?' We hug and head off in opposite directions to complete the day's calls.

At home, I cannot shake the smell from my nose. I can't work out if it's pure memory or if, somehow, it still actually exists inside my nostrils. It lingers until I go to bed where I lie down next to my husband and remember what Val said. I am certain that I married my soulmate and that he married his. There is no doubt in my mind about this. I'm just not quite sure if those two soulmates who met all those years ago are the same people as the two who are lying in bed together now. But I hope so. I nudge him. 'Hey. You OK?'

'Huh?'

'I do love you, you know,' I say. 'Whatever happens, I'll always love you.'

'Me too you,' he mumbles sleepily.

Greg had once said, 'If only we'd met years ago, Kate, we could have been together.'

'That,' I'd told him, 'would have been a disaster. You'd have driven me bonkers never coming home and smoking the place out. You wouldn't have even lasted this long, mate.'

A week later I find him weak. In pain. I titrate morphine and dole it out. Know I can't go home tonight. Force him to put his feet up on the arm of the sofa. Tuck a blanket around him. Make my bed on the comfy chair. When I wake he's sitting upright, trying to light a cigarette.

'Why?' I say. 'It looks so painful.'

He doesn't answer. I don't think he can. He's barely awake. More like dreaming. I join him on the sofa wrapped in my own blanket. Pour myself a whisky. Stroke his knee. Put my arm around his skeletal shoulder. Slump back, doze off. He's still bolt upright when I next wake, face tilted to the ceiling, gasping at the air like a landed fish. I open the balcony door. Look out into the blackness. The cold air always made a difference before, but not tonight. He continues to sit, chin up toward the ceiling, gasping.

'Is it time to call for an ambulance?' He shakes his head. 'You're sure?'

He is. Just sits, gasping, and me beside him holding his hand. I wonder if he'll die tonight. He seems delirious. Begins talking. To whom I cannot tell. I rub his back. Melt menthol to try to clear his tubes and make the breathing easier. Eventually, he nods off. His breathing develops a strange arrhythmia, steady for a minute or so and then jumpy and groaning. People breathe differently toward the ends of their lives, and I wonder if this is happening now. In the dark, the two of us alone, I become convinced of it. Idiot that I am. I nod off again.

When I next wake up, he's still in distress. 'Ambulance?'

'No.'

I look about the room at our ridiculous existence. Caring for him is both the same and quite different to caring for my customers. I would be unable, in this situation, to deny them an ambulance, but they'd have been transported into the arms of the hospice long before now. My customers' pain management is supplied by the pharmacist, his by anything that comes through the unlockable door. From the very beginning it seemed pointless to try to deny him the familiar habits of a lifetime. It is autonomy in the extreme. If it weren't for the support of his doctor, I would be scared to death. As it is, I am only ever half-scared to death.

'Please?'

'No.'

He becomes more and more agitated. Twitching. Panting. Takes my hand and holds on tight. Then, toward dawn, he wants the toilet. Is panicky for it. We should have gone earlier. Those wretched 'should's.

I fetch the commode, not for him to use. It's too late for that. Instead, I drive him sitting on it the short distance to the doorless bathroom where I do the thing he'd been dreading. The thing I'd once thought I could never do. I make him clean.

'I'm sorry, Kate.'

'It doesn't matter,' I say. 'It's much worse for you than it is for me.'

And this is so.

22.

Flying ant day

None of my customers has much of an appetite and they're all refusing to drink any more than their usual, mostly pitiful, amounts. Except, of course, the alcoholics who should be doing exactly the opposite. I'm not too worried about Margaret in the basement where her house is coolest, but Veronica's room upstairs is already stifling by nine o'clock. It's no joke wearing gloves and an apron in the heat when you're doing physical work. Sweat runs down my back.

Downstairs, Mr Rose has both back and front doors open. He stands in the kitchen between them, fanning himself with the plastic lid of an empty ice-cream tub that he's washed out and filled with soil. A keen gardener, he's planting cuttings in it.

'When they come good, you can take one home,' he says. 'Boy, it's a hot one already.'

'Beautiful,' I say. 'Like Ghana!'

'In Ghana you got the river and the sea, though. Not like here.'

'I don't care, I love it,' I say.

'On a day like this you need him river,' he says, still fanning himself as he flops down onto the chair that isn't quite behind him. I grab his elbow and steer him into it only just in time to stop him tumbling to the floor. 'Boy, it make you weak, the sun when it like this,' he says, still fanning away. 'Unless you in him river.'

The summer air feels good on my skin when I'm cycling. I've been wearing a halter top and twenty or thirty minutes between visits has given me a good bit of colour on my arms and my back, but not long enough to burn. Until today. Today, I packed a cotton shirt and I'm already wearing it by ten o'clock. I welcome the cool of the concrete stairwell in Ina's building. Up on the second floor, someone has beaten me to the oven that is Ina's flat and left two bottles of mineral water on the coffee table.

'That lady from the office came, missus.'

'Maggs. But you didn't drink any?'

'I'm not keen on water, missus, but even so I've been drinking it non-stop.' She picks up one of the bottles and standing up from the sofa she steps toward me to hold it in front of my face. The amount that's missing wouldn't fill an eggcup. 'See, missus,' Ina says, swaying even more than she normally does. I open the windows but leave the curtains closed in an effort to keep out the blazing sun.

'You need to drink more than that. What about a cup of tea?'

'Maggs says it's a bit hot for tea, missus.'

'Tea is much better than nothing at all,' I say as Ina falls heavily backwards onto the arm of the sofa. I dash forward to slide her securely into the seat of it. She agrees to drink tea while I run to the corner shop. That's when I first notice them. Crawling from cracks in the pavement, their neatly folded wings like tiny shards of Perspex.

'What about this?' I say when I get back, fanning myself with Ina's catalogue of ready meals. 'It might make it easier to drink those bottles of water.' She allows me to flavour them orange and I put the bottle of squash in my bag thinking it might come in useful for other customers today.

Heat radiates from the pavement. They're crawling, wings wide now, or drifting through the still air, all the way from Ina's to Bridget's house. The water fairy's been there as well but the bottles of water remain untouched.

I pull the squash from my bag. 'God, it's hot. You want a bit of flavour in those?'

'I had two cups of coffee already.'

'Have another.'

'What is it?' Bridget points at one of them making its way across the floor.

I step on it. 'Never mind that. Have some orange squash.'

'I don't really like water. Or squash. I like Sprite. But Maggs said . . .' For the second time this morning, I run to the shop.

'Anything will do as long as it's wet,' I say when I get back, perspiring like a fountain, with three Sprites. 'Doesn't have to be water.' I shake my hair and several of them fall out of it. 'My God, they're everywhere now.' They tangle themselves on the worktop.

'This weather,' Bridget says, 'is going on for ever.'

'It's too warm for working, really. But I'm getting a tan.'

'You are?' Unable to bend her head upward on her frozen neck, Bridget tilts her body back to look at my face. She's like a cartoon character doing a gravity-defying backward lean and just as I realize she's going over, I shove the wooden chair behind her. She sits unexpectedly elegantly.

'You look nice,' Bridget says seriously. 'Tell me honestly now. Would you say I looked nice?'

'Of course you do,' I tell her.

By the time I've cycled home my clothes are wringing

wet with sweat. They tumble out of my clothing as I strip off in the bathroom. Crawl over the floor. I stand on a bulbous abdomen and it bursts under my bare foot. The phone rings. I answer it naked. Maggs doesn't even begin to apologize. She just says, 'Help.'

'I'm about to hop in the shower.' I feel something tickling my neck, slap it away.

'Mr Seddon just called. Mrs Seddon's falling off her chair. She's not yet reached the floor so if someone can come quickly he won't have to have the ambulance out.'

I swear, shove my clothes back on and hurtle to the Seddons' house. Mrs Seddon is looking surprised, halfway between the seat of her armchair and the carpet. Mr Seddon has one of his crutches propped underneath her skinny backside, the end of it wedged against the base of the sideboard. Sweat is pouring off him. Even under Mrs Seddon's scant weight, Mr Seddon's crutch is threatening to snap and he's purple with the effort of holding it. 'Good girl,' he yells as I come through. Mrs Seddon looks ever more startled. The crutch is ever more slightly bending in the middle. 'Pull her up!' Mr Seddon booms.

I notice them floating in through the open windows.

Mrs Seddon's only wearing a vest. Her shoulders look about as strong as gnats' legs. I scan the room for something to use as a sling, frantically considering taking down one of the curtains. My arms tickle. I slap them. The crutch bends. I look optimistically at all the cushions, wonder if there's time to run upstairs for a sheet. Mrs Seddon slips an inch down the sloping crutch. I squash one that's walking down my nose. She squeaks. Mr Seddon yelps. I shriek and whip off my tunic. Slipping the blue fabric under the top of Mrs Seddon's thighs, I bend my knees and heave her up into the chair again, she looking furious and Mr Seddon helping with his trusty crutch.

'Good girl!' Mr Seddon yells. 'How long are you with us?'

'I'm not. I'm only here because they called me about Mrs S sliding out of the chair,' I say, clapping my hands into the air twice over to kill two of them.

'Not good enough, I'm afraid! We all need an ice cream,' and he rummages in his wallet for a twenty-pound note. 'The nearest shop's on Charner Road,' he says. 'Get one for yourself.'

They swarm in their trillions now, regurgitated from every crack and crevice, drifting lazily through the windless afternoon in droves into my face, up my nose and suddenly in my eye. I stop and pick black legs from my tear ducts, eyes streaming. Back at the Seddons' I put the ice creams in the freezer for ten minutes to firm them up again and then we sit and eat them, me writing off my lunch break. 'Isn't this grand?' Mr Seddon says, licking his lips. 'See?' He winks. 'Mrs S just loves an ice cream!'

Today of all days, you don't need this unexpected, extra call. The gate is locked. You call the office. The office call her. The front door beyond the gate opens. She doesn't come out herself, just sticks out her head. 'Climb over.' You leap the fence, expecting her to be impressed, grateful, amused even. She simply disappears.

Inside, she's standing in the hall, young, but bald, and in pyjamas. 'You carers never do a good job,' she says flatly. You follow her into a sitting room. A boy aged around four sits on a cream leatherette sofa, staring at the television. 'Get to bed,' she shouts. He slides sullenly from the room. 'People think it's clean but it's not,' she says, wrinkling her nose and sweeping her arms wide to indicate the entire floor is tantamount to an open sewer. Seems a little sleepy underneath her ferocity. 'You carers don't know how to clean.'

Sod you, you think.

'Do it properly,' she snaps. 'Vacuum, wipe down with this, rinse with this, dry with this, then use a wet wipe. This room first then all of the rest.'

You begin vacuuming the only traces of dirt you can see. Crisp crumbs around the sofa. You work under her tutting, trying to remember in what order you were told to do things and with what while she tells you a little bit more about how fucking hopeless you and all the other carers are. You hold it together until you reach the wet-wipe stage in the hall. On all fours, hot, flustered, nose to the laminate, wiping the floor with a silly, damp square of perfumed polypropylene, you feel slapped. You want to scream at her. Tell her she's not worth ten bloody quid. You want her to know how it feels to be punished for something you didn't do. For the first time in a long time, you hate this job. It's a thankless, miserable job after all.

The clean flat soon looks cleaner than ever. 'Better,' she says, opening another cupboard containing soaps and creams. You follow her into the bathroom and she strips off. You tell yourself you just have to get through the next half-hour and then you can ring the office and tell them you're never coming here again. Deciding to do this makes it easier. 'What's your boy's name?'

'Robbie. He'll go to school in September.'

'He'll love that, I expect,' you tell her.

She stares at you, unsmiling. 'Actually,' she says, 'you just never know what's going to happen, do you?' She sighs. 'I'm waiting for my next round of chemo, I was supposed to go last month. It got cancelled. I could get an infection before it gets rescheduled and then it would be put off again.' She stares.

You look away. There's a picture on the wall of a young woman holding a newborn. They're both wrapped in a sheet. The baby is wrinkled and the woman is sweaty and they each have pale skin and full heads of wet, red hair. You massage moisturizer into the *dry patches of skin. You take the removed, still perfectly clean, pyjamas, put them in the machine. 'Morphine,' she says.*

It's in the fridge compartment where you'd put cheese, next to a sticky syringe and some little pots of flavoured fromage frais. 'There's not much left,' you say, tipping the bottle to one side so the syringe can reach the last of the liquid in the bottle.

'There's never enough,' she says sleepily. 'It's you fucking carers. Every week you knock the bottle over and spill the lot.'

You decide not to argue. You no longer feel you're the one being punished. You don't know the meaning of the word, you realize now. But you do know that you won't, after all, be calling the office to say you're never coming here again.

Out in the open again the swarming continues to Lorna's and back to Veronica's. I swat and twitch and wriggle and spit all the way to Mr Radbert's house. Mr Radbert's road is planted with trees. Grown enormously tall, some more than a century old, they arc over the street. It feels peaceful standing on the pavement beneath these graceful, leafy branches. Chaining my bike up outside, I realize a miracle has occurred in the place I'd least expect one to happen. There are none of them here at all. I stand for a few minutes, savouring the cooler air, revelling in the absence of those annoying tickles and thanking the Lord for the unexpected relief given by, of all people, Mr Radbert. I leave the shelter of the trees and approach his front door with some reluctance.

Inside, the hallway smells oddly lemony.

It takes me a moment to notice it. A trail of white powder running along the skirting board. The powder continues at least halfway up the architrave of Mr Radbert's inner front door but it's hard to see it there because it's covered in undulating black trails. Thick black strings, alive with shiny white, wobbling wings that reflect prisms of iridescent green and lilac under the light bulb of the hallway. Black legs, black heads, black thoraxes, black abdomens. Big black lines wobbling down the door frame, like living scrawls of marker pen, weaving, knitting, marching, pushing up out of the hall carpet, dribbling along the flock-papered walls like lumpy liquid, coalescing into puddles at my feet that crawl up my legs. I quickly become covered in them. They walk up my arms and into my sleeves, wriggle under my armpits. I squash them, swat them, spit them out and open the door.

Inside, they stream from the plughole in the sink, pour out from beneath the washing machine, launch themselves from the cracks around light fittings. Some are pushing themselves out of the electrical sockets. The air is full of them. Mr Radbert sits in his wheelchair in the middle of his sitting room, mouth tight shut, brown eyes blinking like crazy.

He looks like one of those Victorian photographs of beekeepers making bee beards.

23.

Fish and chips

Autumn begins to close in. Greg gets ever more sick, I get ever more tired and we both lose ever more weight. Some days I can barely open my eyes. In the morning, I drink coffee so strong that it's sticky. Great mugs of it before I leave. Don't bother with breakfast.

Margaret says, 'I'm worried about you, Kate, you look exhausted. Why don't you make yourself a coffee?' So I gulp down yet another.

At Veronica's, I have to sit down in the kitchen while I'm waiting for her porridge to thicken. After Veronica, I go on to Ina and can barely get through the visit. As I'm writing up my notes, I feel her gaze on me. I look up. 'What?'

'Eyes, missus.'

'My eyes? What about them?'

'Bags, missus.'

'Oh, cheers, Ina,' I say. 'I feel much better now.'

'Try peanut butter.'

'Oh, stop,' I say, 'you're making me hungry. Anyway, I already eat peanut butter. I love peanut butter but it doesn't really seem to be doing the trick, does it?'

'You don't eat it, missus. You put it on them.'

'Peanut butter?'

'Yes, missus. It's very good. It nearly blinded me though when I checked how my eyes were working after. The sun is awful strong. Do it inside.'

'You put peanut butter on your eye bags?'

'I used mud first. But later I thought of peanut butter. Peanut butter's like mud, missus.'

'Mud? On your eye bags?'

'No, peanut butter.'

'Mud, peanut butter and eye bags,' I muse. 'What can possibly connect mud, peanut butter and eye bags?'

Ina stares intently, 'Missus, I—'

'No. Don't tell me, don't tell me. Wait. Don't give me any clues. Ha! I've got it!'

'You have, missus?'

'Jesus, Ina!'

'I'm sorry, missus.'

'No, I mean Jesus is the missing link. He put mud on a blind man's eyes and when the man washed it off he could see again.'

'Ah yes, missus. That's right. But use peanut butter. And do it inside. You do the peanut butter and I've got some aspirin for your friend.' She goes to the wardrobe and rummages at the bottom. 'Here, take this. It'll be good for him. Just what he needs, missus.'

'It's a bit late for aspirin, I'm afraid.'

I finish with Ina at eleven and have time to run to Greg's flat. I put the little packet of aspirin that Ina gave me on top of the fridge next to the morphine and methadone bottles. The liquid morphine is clear, but the methadone is bright green. The same shade that a child might use to colour in a witch. The cupboard is bare except for a couple of slices of bread and some beans so I make those for Greg and head out for the lunchtime calls. Margaret forces me to eat a packet of crisps. Back at Veronica's, Mr Rose has found a deep-fat fryer at the bottom of a cupboard.

'Look at it. I forgot I'd bought it. Never used. Looks marvellous, doesn't it?'

'Marvellous,' I sigh.

'You don't need to make her a sandwich today, I thought I'd do some fish and chips.' As I'm toileting Veronica, I smell the fish frying and realize I haven't eaten a proper meal since yesterday lunchtime. I look at myself in the mirror while I'm waiting for her to finish. My uniform tunic's falling off me, but I love my new cheekbones. When I've seated Mrs Rose back in her chair I go downstairs to plate up her fish and chips. My mouth waters.

I travel on to Stevie and make him a bacon sandwich. It's torture. I snatch another bag of crisps from the shop and eat them as I'm cycling home, one hand holding the crisps against the handlebar and the other dipping in and out of the packet until they're gone. A failed dietitian eating crisps while riding a bicycle. Perhaps it's appropriate.

At home, I fall asleep and wake, groggily, at four o'clock.

The first of my evening calls is far away so I leave still without eating an actual meal and am especially thankful for the quarter-portion of shepherd's pie from the meal I split with William before running on to Mr Radbert. I'm not really up for Mr Radbert's usual ridiculousness today, but as it turns out he doesn't speak anyway. For the first time ever, he doesn't say a bean. He's almost suffocating with the effort of it, lips squeezed so tight together that they've lost all colour while the rest of his face has gone purple.

'Why are you so quiet?'

'I've got some wonderful news,' he squeaks.

'Well, you'd better tell me quickly. Otherwise it looks as though you'll pass out.'

'I'm savouring it. You're going to love it. I need the toilet first.' He squashes his lips steadfastly back together again.

'I'm surprised you're able to hold on the way you're

squeezing yourself like that. For God's sake, breathe,' I say as I'm hoisting him onto the toilet.

Even after all these months you still marvel that you're expected to hoist. You used to watch healthcare assistants hoisting in the hospital and think you could never do that. Not just the practical complexity of it but the taking charge of someone's dignity. Moving legs and arms to get them comfortably into the sling. Squashing breasts and bellies as little as possible.

His hoist is complicated but you've used it so often now that you could do it in your sleep. It's only when you have trainee carers with you that you remember how difficult it was at first. It's a standing hoist rather than a swinging hoist. Swinging hoists are tall, with an overhanging bar to which the sling containing the customer is attached. It's a bit like those grabber games in seaside amusement arcades with the customer as the prize. You don't like swinging hoists because you don't see them often. It doesn't matter that you grow unfamiliar with them during the long gaps between using them, you still have to do it. You're expected to maintain your expertise without practice. You always try to arrive early to a job with a swinging hoist and you take it slowly. Very slowly.

But the hoist you like least of all is a ceiling hoist. You've only ever met one of those. At Mrs Singh's house. A sling that carried your giggling cargo across a room along a track on the ceiling that looked about as robust as the one on your shower curtain. You were aghast at having to work out how to use it safely by yourself, at no notice at all. But you no longer thought that you couldn't do that. You just did it.

I wash my hands, go and get the medications ready and put the kettle on. I hear Mr Radbert humming and singing in the bathroom. 'What the hell are you so jolly about?' I yell.

'Get me off here first.'

I manoeuvre him onto the hoist, clean him up and change him into nightclothes. 'Tell me now.'

'Wait till I'm in bed. Whoo-hoo-hoo!'

'I can't wait any longer,' I say, as I unshackle him from the sling and heave his legs up onto the mattress.

He sits up, triumphant, in the bed. Starts snorting so much he can't speak. Puts his pyjama sleeve to his weeping eyes. Takes a deep breath. Exhales. Looks at me. 'Micky Donagh,' he says with forced calm, 'is dead.'

'What?'

'Dead!' Mr Radbert screams. 'Dead as a doorstep! Car accident. Sheila told me. Whoo-hoo-hoo!'

'Really?'

'Yes. This morning, as soon as I started talking about Micky Donagh, she just came out with it. She said, "Mr Radbert, I can't stand it any longer, I'm just going to have to tell you that Micky Donagh is dead." Whoo-hoo-hoo!'

It's a stroke of genius. Sheila's smarter than I gave her credit for. 'Well, I never,' I say happily. 'I just can't believe that's true.' He looks suspiciously at me. 'But of course it absolutely is,' I add. 'What luck. How?'

He grins again, 'I told you the man was an idiot. Dead! Took my car but couldn't even drive it properly. Dead as a doorway.'

'Wait,' I say, crossing my fingers behind my back. 'It was *your* car he was driving when he crashed? It must be a total write-off. Oh no. Now we'll never get it back. We'll have to abandon looking for it. That's just terrible.'

'No, no, no!' Mr Radbert shrieks. 'I went crazy until Sheila told me Micky Donagh was driving his own car when he crashed it into the wall.'

'Oh. Well, that's just wonderful,' I say sadly.

'I'll have a cup of tea, thanks,' Mr Radbert says and as I'm walking away he yells, 'Micky Donagh's dead as a doorbell! Let's have biscuits!'

I turn around, still a bit pissed off that Sheila was too chicken to lie to him that his car got totalled as well. 'Please,' I say, 'you can't speak ill of the dead.'

'I can if it's Micky Donagh,' he weeps. 'Whoo-hoo-hoo! Dead as a doormat!'

With no time to share Mr Radbert's biscuits, after another couple of calls I'm back with Margaret and then on to Veronica. Mr Rose is fetching cooking oil from the cupboard. My stomach is so empty now that it hurts. The aroma teases me as I'm hoisting Veronica from her chair, helping her to wash, tucking her into bed. My stomach sounds like a lion. Mr Rose, keen to use his new gadget as often as possible, is busy frying again. I wish I could stay here and eat whatever it is. 'That fryer sure is getting some use today,' I say to Veronica.

'He's a good man,' she smiles.

'He is.'

I have to wipe my drooling mouth on a tissue as I'm coming down the stairs. I shout goodbye into the kitchen as I'm putting on my coat. The dark outside looks cold.

'Wait!' Mr Rose shouts. 'Don't go yet.'

'What is it?' I'm famished and desperate to leave so I can try to grab some bread on the way to the flat.

He scoops something out of the oil in the fryer and drops it into a plastic container. Pops a lid on. 'Here,' he says, 'you look so tired, woman. Take these fish and chips for your dinner. I put a bit in for our friend as well. You tell him to hang in there.'

'God,' I say, 'thanks so much.'

*

At the flat, Marble's back. 'Kate,' he says, 'what's the richest country in the world?'

'It's America, I'm telling you,' Greg says. He looks weak but has perked up in response to Marble's daft and unexpected company.

'I reckon it's France,' says Marble.

'Nah,' says Greg. 'France isn't rich.'

'Germany then. They make them fridges in Germany.'

'Bosch,' says Greg. 'But actually everything gets made in China.'

'China then. China is big as well, right? China's the richest country.'

'Big doesn't matter, though,' Greg says. 'Look at Russia.'

'Russia's broke.'

'Exactly,' Greg is triumphant. 'See? It *is* America.'

'You forgot,' I say, draining the remainder of the cooking fat from Mr Rose's meal onto kitchen paper, 'about oil. Kuwait. Surely Kuwait's the richest country? You want some fish and chips?'

Marble eats almost two thirds of it. I manage about a third. Greg has two mouthfuls.

No one has Ina's aspirin.

24

Hard. But soft inside

The first sign of trouble is the ambulance, glowing yellow against the red brick of the low-rise flats along this road. I can't actually see from this distance that it's parked up next to the shabby front lawn of my mid-morning customer's block. I just know. The ambulance is a frequent visitor here. Occasionally, the customer gets loaded into it but, more often than not, they refuse to leave. I wonder which it will be today.

The key is missing from the key safe so I buzz the intercom and am let in by a strange voice. I'm daftly pleased not to have had to fiddle about to get the key. Until I clock the carnage. Blood is smeared along the floors in a flat empty of extras. No pictures, no lampshades, no cushions, no rugs. Just bare furniture and blood, drying to a black scab over blue lino. My customer is perched groggily on his bed in the sitting room, one eye bruising up nicely beneath his blonde fringe, dark stains down his tracksuit jacket. 'Stevie had another fall last night,' one of the two ambulance crew chirps. 'The District Nurse found him first thing this morning. He'd had a long lie on the floor as well. But he doesn't want to come to hospital. We've checked him out and patched him up. He's all yours.' Stevie signs a form saying he accepts the risks of staying with me instead of going with the experts, and the experts push their lifting equipment out of the flat. Abandoned, I wonder for a few seconds who's going to clean up all that blood before I realize it'll be me.

'Get me into bed,' Stevie says into the silence. 'I'm cold.'

He grunts as I lift the dead weight of his leg up onto the bed. The calf is swollen to three times its normal size. The leg is hard and grey like a pockmarked concrete bollard, and almost as big as my waist. When I've lugged it up, I balance Stevie in a sitting position with one hand and take off his tracksuit top and change his T-shirt with the other. I reposition the pillows. His teeth are chattering while I sweat.

'There's some bowls on the floor. Don't spill them,' he says.

'Bowls of what?'

'Piss.'

I call the office, tell them there's blood everywhere, make tea and give Stevie his meds. He has something else on his mind. 'I need brandy,' he says. 'Money's on the table in the sitting room.'

'Can't do that, Stevie.'

'Fags then.'

'I'll call the office but I think fags are OK.'

'And brandy. I won't tell them.'

'Doesn't matter, honey. I'm not buying alcohol.'

'Eejit.'

I take Stevie a cup of tea and a bowl of milk and cereal, and gather bloody clothing, overflowing ashtrays and a plate of half-eaten dinner on my return to the kitchen. I'm looking for bleach when I remember the bowls. Stevie is pleading with someone for brandy over the phone. I locate a china bowl full to its brim, carry it as steadily as I can to the toilet and nearly slip on a large clot in the middle of the bathroom floor looking exactly like someone dropped a dessertspoon of blackcurrant jam. I pour urine the colour of tangerine skins into the toilet bowl. First I let it trickle against the side and then I try tipping it directly into the pan. Neither method completely eliminates the splash and I spit into the sink. Just in case.

It's a crime scene in the bathroom. There are red hand-prints along the bath, up the pedestal to the top of the sink and over the toilet. The end of a mop handle is covered in them. A few isolated fingerprints are high up the wall. I puzzle over them like a detective before concluding that, using the mop as extra leverage, Stevie probably crawled in here during the night and spent some time trying to pull himself to his feet. He must have gotten upright for a few seconds and leaned on the tiles before falling again. In one corner, a jumper is folded into a gory pillow where he finally gave up trying.

'Fags,' shouts Stevie.

'Right you are, honey.'

Outside, life continues in its exquisite normality. It's so utterly perfect. A musical after a horror movie. Everyone is going about their business, chatting and smiling and mobile and clean. With their normal problems like running out of milk or not having change for the parking meter. I am reminded of a film I saw where the director had inserted a dance sequence into their story to emphasize how wonder-ful life is.

On my return to Stevie, he smokes in bed while I don two pairs of gloves and fill a bucket with water and bleach. I run the wet mop from the far end of the trail all the way to the bathroom to soften the black crust. I'm afraid the blood will flood the floor scarlet as it liquefies but the mop soaks it up nicely, the water in the bucket changing from salmon to berry to chocolate. Occasionally, pieces of blood break off and slide around, leaving a trail of watery red like cut rare steak on a dinner plate. When I try to pick them up, I find the blood fragments are actually little discs of jelly that slip between my fingers and fall back to the floor.

Finally, the job is done. I wash and dry my hands three times before I go back to Stevie's bedroom to collect his dirty breakfast plate and mug. He's pressing two tiny tablets out of their foil container with his giant-sized fingers, his mop of blonde hair falling thickly over his broken face as he concentrates, breathing heavily. There's a shaved patch on top of his head where it got glued back together, and a red-purple bruise thunders over the whole of his right cheek, below an eye now swollen closed.

'What are those?'

'Temazepam.'

No paracetamol required then, I think. 'I'm going to call the office and let them know, OK?'

'Very fond of calling the office, aren't you?' he smirks. And promptly falls asleep, lit cigarette in hand. I remove the cigarette, stub it out but leave it long in the ashtray within reach, tuck him in, make sure the bed is low and put a urine bottle close in so that he doesn't risk falling out of bed trying to reach one. Then I clean the dishes, top up the washing machine with bloodstained clothing, switch it on and leave for my next calls.

Your visits are rarely horror shows. Someone's neighbour has baked them a Victoria sponge and they wonder if you've time to share a piece. Another customer has had an unexpectedly smooth trip to hospital and wants to tell you about it. Yet another success-fully uses the toilet after being constipated for days, and you give each other a high five.

Sometimes you get secrets. Sometimes you get fed. Sometimes you get the giggles. And sometimes you even get taught about things you would otherwise have no knowledge of.

Every time he comes to the door, he almost fills the hall. It's not so much his size, but the angles of him. His pleading hands wrap themselves around one another at chin level with the elbows sticking out, both knees slightly bent as though he is sitting on an invisible bar stool, and the whole of him covered in an unzipped bottle-green coat worn like the carapace of some colossal insect. He's quite well-to-do but fallen on hard times in his very old age. He likes philosophizing and has a sophisticated vocabulary. He once explained that he loves classical music but doesn't have the means to listen to it any more. Especially the more obscure compositions. You told him it was possible to listen to anything nowadays by searching the internet. 'Internet,' he said, 'that's the World Wide Web, isn't it?' You asked him what he would listen to if he could listen to anything, and he said 'Sibelius' with a faraway look on his face. You took out your phone, searched for Sibelius, pressed play and held it out to him. He took it, held it to his ear and listened to 'The Oceanides' while you were cooking and cleaning, with a look of bliss on his face. Afterwards, you told him you didn't know anything much about classical music. You asked him where you should start. Your classical music education began, of course, with Bach. And now, every time you visit him you get set another beautiful piece of musical homework to listen to.

You've grown to love these calls. These quietly joyful, intimate connections.

At six thirty, I return to Stevie.

'Hello, it's Kate!' I shout as I step through the door.

'Get in here!' he yells over the sound of the television.

'You OK?' I say. 'My goodness, that's a corker of a shiner you've got now, Stevie. How're you feeling?' He's in the chair in the sitting room, festooned by damp washing unloaded during the lunchtime call. Sheets hang over doors, clothing over radiators and furniture. The smell of fag smoke is obliterated by the synthetically floral reek of fabric conditioner.

'Why did you tell the office the place was covered in blood?' he asks.

'I had to. I had to clear it up. They needed to know.'

He *is* a big guy. Waving a crutch. Red-purple eye furiously closed. Unscathed eye furiously open. I check I'm out of range of the crutch. The full urine bottle on the floor isn't.

'They rang the doctor.'

'So?' I dodge in, grab the bottle, duck the crutch and congratulate myself on the manoeuvre.

'So? Now I've had to argue against going to the surgery. To check I'm not bleeding into my brain or something. Very fond of calling the fucking office, aren't you?'

'I thought the ambulance people would have sorted that. What do you want for dinner?'

'Eggs, tomatoes. Toast.'

'Cup of tea?'

'Nah,' he says, putting a pint glass half-full of barely diluted brandy to his lips. 'I'm all right for tea, thanks.'

'How d'you want your eggs?'

'Hard. But soft inside.'

There's a photo on top of the fridge. I always look at it while the food is cooking, or the kettle is boiling. It features a different Stevie. He doesn't have crutches. He's pushing a little girl, a toddler, on a swing. I can see traces of the Stevie I know in the photograph, but I can never find traces of the photograph in the Stevie I know.

I take the dinner through and smash the boiled eggs open. Yolk dribbles out through their fractured shells. When Stevie bends forward over the plate, I eyeball the glued-up skin and write *Seems to be holding* in my notes. The news is being broadcast from the corner of the room.

'You see there was another shooting last night?' says Stevie.

'Poor kids,' I say, sitting down for a minute on the sofa. 'Poor mothers.' I wipe the coffee table clean, picking up and putting down the punctuations of Stevie's day as I do so. Loose change, packet of fags, med cup, sleeping tablets, lighter, bottle of brandy, TV remote, ashtray. Overflowing again.

'Bloody dangerous out there,' he says. 'You be careful.'

'I'll be fine. Don't you worry about that,' I say.

'Well, you take care anyway,' says Stevie, eggy spoon aloft in his good, right hand.

'Ah thanks, honey,' I say.

'You be careful.' His voice cracks a little. 'Really. Wouldn't want you getting hurt.'

Hard. But soft inside.

25.

No one closer

We dread pressure sores. Once they get established, they are stubborn. The office trains us to spot them by showing a slideshow of increasingly gruesome pictures in which skin turns from discoloured, to lumpy, to broken, to oozing, to bone. What's worse is that they generally appear in the most private of places.

After weeks of barely moving from his nest on the sofa, Greg has a pressure sore. His GP and I examine it together, Greg facing away from us, trousers round his knees, skinny bum like a baby elephant's saggy backside, protesting loudly because I had the audacity to call the doctor who *doesn't need to be bothered with all this malarkey, do you, doctor?*

The doctor thinks otherwise. There must be district nurses now. Greg doesn't want them, but the doctor is firm. 'You can't put this on to Kate as well. She's doing too much alone, helping you stay in this place where you want to be. She needs some help here.'

I love this doctor and want to agree but I can't join in. I'm giggling too much. 'Sorry.' They stare at me. Finally, I stop snorting with laughter and breathe. Wipe my eyes. 'Sorry,' I say again, 'it's just. Well, you know,' and I'm off again, 'district nurses . . .' snort, 'will . . .' snort, 'be . . .' snort, 'fucking hilarious. Good luck to the district nurses, then.'

'And,' says Dr Kott, trying and failing to maintain a

serious face, 'a medical bed. With an inflatable mattress to prevent any more pressure sores.'

'Oh. My. God,' I snort, weeping again. 'A medical bed. Double whammy. District nurses *and* a medical bed. Brilliant.'

Lorna hums Gershwin as I'm changing the pad. Today, as I sweep it away, my heart sinks. I stuff it angrily into a plastic bag for the bin and feel sick as I hoist her into the chair and remake the bed.

Lorna used to do one of the hotshot jobs. She's much cleverer than me. Over the months, as I've cared for her, I've learned about what it was like years ago being a woman employed in the managerial sector of a man's world. Sometimes we discuss ethics. Sometimes politics. Sometimes fashion. For a minute, I consider continuing with my extra-curricular education, so I don't have to be the person who has to spoil her day. But, of course, I can't do that. 'Listen,' I say, 'I'm afraid there was a little blood on the pad. I think you should tell the doctor.'

There aren't many customers who want to tell doctors things that might lead to a hospital job and Lorna certainly isn't one of them. 'Can't we just keep an eye on it?'

I think about having to look at the state of that pad every day. 'Let's report it. Right now.'

Mr Radbert hasn't been on my list for two weeks. When he returns from hospital he needs bed-washing while he recovers enough to get back in his wheelchair. As I'm washing him, I think I see something. It's in a difficult place. I lift and separate and pat dry. I lift and look again. The skin is a little discoloured. I roll Mr Radbert onto his right side, away from me, ask him to hold himself up and I pull his immobile left leg to a right angle so I can get a better view. I grab my phone, put on the little torch.

Mr Radbert usually wears a convene catheter. It's like a condom with a tube on the end. Like many of the most effective pieces of equipment we use, it's also one of the simplest. It gets attached to a bag that keeps Mr Radbert dry. In the hospital, it often gets removed because it takes a few minutes to change, a few minutes that busy ward staff often don't have. It's probably been removed during his stay and Mr Radbert has been living with a damp pad under his immobile body for a fortnight.

I lift and prod and peer, my face inches from the tiny patch of slightly pink skin in the dark skin around it. I cover it with barrier cream, roll Mr Radbert back onto a fresh pad, put on a new convene, fasten the pad over it, call the district nurses and, for the next few weeks, I know I will be inspecting the most private part of this man and that we will fight a little battle together to prevent it getting worse.

When I next call at Lorna's, the appointment has already materialized. 'It must be bad,' she says. 'Usually you have to wait for ever, don't you? I don't think I can go.'

'I'll come with you.'

'I need to be ready two hours before the appointment.'

'Two hours?'

'Hospital transport.'

'I'll take the afternoon off.'

A week later, I get Lorna ready for her afternoon appointment and we wait in the atrium of her building, me on the wooden stool and her in the wheelchair, with her best jacket draped over her shoulders, her most expensive handbag on her lap and her nicest shoes on. The ones that match the jacket. Eventually, an ambulance pulls up. Lorna sniffs. 'Don't worry,' I say, wheeling her outside. 'I'm with you.'

'Is this her?' The transport crew member looks at his watch.

'This is *Lorna*.'

'And you are?'

'Kate. Carer.'

'We'll take her from here.'

'You'll take *Lorna*.'

'Kate's coming too,' Lorna says, clutching her handbag tight.

'Afraid not,' the transport man says to me. 'You're not booked in.'

'I didn't know I had to do that,' says Lorna weepily.

I bend down. 'Don't worry, I can cycle up and meet you. Everything's going to be fine.'

I wait so long at the other end I'm afraid I'm pacing the walls of the wrong building. Hospital transport ambulances pull in and out again but none of them is hers. I'd like to phone her, but we're not allowed to exchange numbers with customers, so I just continue to wait until, eventually, I see her being pushed by a burly crew member toward the entrance. She hasn't noticed that her skirt has risen over her knees. I pull it down again and put her feet more securely onto the footplates of the wheelchair.

Anxious Lorna is loaded onto a hospital bed. She can do nothing to build the rapport that will soothe things along, so I make the small talk and jokes that tell Dr Lynn we are likeable, intelligent and cooperative. Lorna grimaces. Dr Lynn says, 'Hmmm, yes, there is something there, we can remove it.'

'Oh,' says Lorna, 'no.' And to me, 'Do you think I should?'

'Yes. Think of this evening. At home. When it'll all be over. Best get it done. Then we don't have to come back.' Her face is doubtful.

All the way through, Lorna and I look into one another's eyes, and I tell her how brilliantly she's doing and that it will soon be done and tears run down her face while Dr Lynn rummages. 'Not long now,' I say, 'nearly over. Everything is fine.'

The whole episode takes so long that I have to leave Lorna waiting for transport to get to the late-evening calls I didn't cancel. Then I go racing back to her building to check she's home and comfortable. By a delightful quirk of fate, the ambulance has just parked up. When the doors are opened, I stick my head in. She's looking down at her feet, so she doesn't see me yet.

'You know what I'm going to say, don't you?' I shout out to her. She looks up miserably. Raises one eyebrow.

'What time d'you call this?' I say.

She grins. 'Boy, am I pleased to see you, Kate.'

'We can manage from here,' I say to the transport crew.

'But there's just you. To hoist?'

'We do this all the time.'

'We would never hoist with just one person,' he says. 'In the hospital. It isn't safe to do that.'

'Well, I'm afraid out here, we're used to it,' I say. He looks at me as though I am insane.

'Oh, for goodness' sake,' says Lorna, recovering her normal, feisty spark. 'How on earth do you think I ever get out of bed? We're fine, thanks.' I feel proud of us.

Inside, I make a cup of tea and think there is no one closer than this. The occupational therapists come with their advice and equipment and they go, leaving us carers to help people learn how to use it. The physiotherapists come with their exercise plans, leaving us to find ways to fit them into our customers' lives and encourage these people to do them. The dietitians come with their meal plans and supplement drinks and leave us to make and serve them. The doctors diagnose and instruct the pharmacy to dispense medications and leave us to prompt and administer them. The nurses wrap dressings and bandages and leave us to make sure everything remains clean and intact. We advocate, help others see what is needed and, perhaps more importantly, what is *wanted* and, when things go wrong, it is the care worker who works through everything and helps pick up any broken pieces. This is a curse because it's tough and largely unrecognized.

But it is also a blessing.

Being as close as this to someone is a uniquely precious place to be. It is a place where secrets are revealed and fears are shared and outrageous jokes are made that could not be told to anyone else. It is a coalface of human experience. A place where feeling comes thick and fast. Raw and beautiful.

That night at Greg's flat, I'm trying to turn a corner shop ready meal into a gourmet roast chicken dinner. I add seasoning to gravy, swap the tablespoon of mushy veg for newly steamed greens and throw pallid cubes of pre-cooked potato into a hot frying pan to crisp them up. The stuffing isn't robust enough to survive a makeover, but the end result is pretty good, nonetheless. I'm garnishing it. Garnishing. Anything to make him eat.

'Hey, Kate?'

'Yeah?' I turn to look at him. George Harrison is singing from the CD player.

'If not for you.'

It takes me by surprise. 'Oh, go on.'

'You're the best friend I ever had.'

'You just want my roast chicken dinner.'

'I love you, Kate.'

It melts me, this thing he's never been able to say before and will never say again.

Two days later the medical bed arrives and is fitted by two

burlies. It has a control pad and a pump-up mattress so Greg can lie on air and not get any more pressure sores. I switch it on.

'What's that?' Greg's sharp ear hears everything. The pathetic ringtone of his brick phone beneath Roberta Flack singing at full volume. Dealers talking in the car park outside above the sound of the kettle coming to the boil inside. Sex workers sneaking customers through the closed but broken entrance door, three floors down.

'It's the bed.'

'Why's it making that racket?'

'It's inflating itself.'

'There's no way that can stay on, it's deafening,' says this studio musician with such sensitive ears.

'It's nothing. I can hardly hear it.'

'It's a pneumatic fucking drill. Turn it off.'

The bed never gets switched on again. Greg complains when I sit on it and it exhales the scant remnants of air left inside from its one, brief, half-inflation. It continues to do this long after it's switched off. There is so little air left in it, I wonder how this is possible.

So little air.

You live here now, your toothbrush in the bathroom is proof of it. Your family are upset at having had to be temporarily given up by you. You hope you have not been permanently given up by them in return. You and Greg have dinner together. One meal shared, him eating his tiny portion. You eat pudding too, you little couple. Full-fat yoghurt with berries that you like or ice cream that you don't but if you eat it he will have a spoonful long after it has become melted to a drink like one of the dietitian's vanilla shakes that you gave up trying to make him take centuries ago. Always he has a brew and you a gin and tonic ready mixed from a can that is expensive but who would want to go so far as to buy a bottle and admit that every day is a drinking day now? You wash up, tidy the kitchen and pack the frame of the hospital bed with duvets to soften its metal ribs on the off chance that he might actually decide to sleep in it.

It seems impossible that, outside, those he once knew best are going on with their own lives, people he saw daily but will never see again. The cab drivers and controllers, the supermarket security guards and trolley boys, Sadie, Spud, Smitten, the guys at the kebab shop, the grannies, the kids and the shoppers, his father, the woman who sells doughnuts in the market. Marble. It's inconceivable that somewhere, out there in a different version of life, Marble is still talking shit in his blue polyester tracksuit, and cleaning windows really badly.

The night was already long before you knew it had become twice the length of the day and full of too much time for thinking. You plough through it together, the dawn taking ever longer to arrive. You've learned to sleep at the drop of a hat and anywhere. In the armchair, your feet sticking out over one arm, neck hanging back so that when you wake up all the blood is in your head. On one of the hard kitchen chairs or with your head wedged under Greg's chin to stop his face smashing down onto the coffee table. Standing bent over the wheeled commode chair waiting the eternity it takes for him to get on it to be pushed through and sat over the toilet. With the telly at full volume, showing some classic comedy or a trashy American show about pawnbrokers. Or with the DVD playing film noir or the cassette blasting Ry Cooder or the CD pumping out one of the Bobbys, Womack or Dylan, or the minidisc playing one of the Terrys, Callier or Reid; or some old demos he made forty years ago of a band who went on to better or worse things.

But Greg, though exhausted, can never sleep more than twenty minutes at a stretch.

26.

Bridget's evening out

'I sent away the man who came about the smart meter,' Bridget told me. 'I don't think I need a smart meter after all.'

I was disappointed. 'But I have one. I think you'd love it. It's brilliant. I never have to read the meter again. It does it all for you. It even tells the time. And the date. It's fantastic.'

'Well, I've cancelled it anyway,' Bridget continued blithely. 'Oh, and I cancelled that hospital appointment on Thursday as well. I can't go at half past five. It'll be dark.'

I didn't really mind about the smart meter but I was furious about the hospital appointment. A fortnight before, when I'd unwrapped Bridget's legs, we'd found that they'd swollen to twice their normal size.

'We'll have to call the GP.'

'What if he tells me I'm going to die?'

'If we call him, you'll be much less likely to die.'

When Dr Kelling visited, he'd been surprised. Not so much at the state of Bridget's legs as the state of Bridget's flat. Her home is the tattiest one of all my customers. I used to get angry with the council for allowing her to live in such squalor, but that was before the office tried to get them to take out the decaying bath and install a modern wet room. The council were pleased to be asked but every time someone came to measure up, Bridget decided she didn't want a wet room after all. She didn't even bother to pretend to allow me to get them to install central heating.

I'd given up on the smart meter, the shower room and the central heating, but I'd refused to give up on Dr Kelling. Bridget told me he had once paid a visit to the flat whilst he was out on his general rounds. He had never returned. Until I'd called him and asked that he turn up while I was there. Dr Kelling appeared anxious when I answered the door. I smiled reassuringly and made a bit of small talk about the weather, but he continued to look as though he'd been invited to have a cup of coffee in an asbestos mine. He had one hand in the open to carry his case but kept the other firmly in his pocket.

'Fasten the door, would you now?' Bridget shouted from the living room.

Dr Kelling looked aghast as I locked him securely inside with us, but soon began to relax. Every now and again he glanced around the room with something like wonder on his face. Bridget, ever keen to expand on her medical knowledge, had lots of questions for him about their health. Dr Kelling explained his own minor ailments whilst exploring the long list of Bridget's fears about the swollen legs. He refuted cancer and dementia and both dry and wet gangrene before declaring that Bridget was likely developing heart failure. Then Dr Kelling packed his case, and I escorted him back down the hall and unlocked the front door. He didn't leave immediately. He cleared his throat and held out a hand. I shook it. 'Well,' I said, 'bye then. Thanks very much.'

'I just want to say,' Dr Kelling began, 'that I have never, *ever* seen that woman looking so calm and clean.' I was delighted by this because, despite all our efforts, Bridget's home remains almost uninhabitable as far as I'm concerned, and she only changes her clothes once a week. 'If you could've seen her when we found her,' Dr Kelling continued. 'She was in a terrible state. And the flat . . . The toilet . . .

The slippers . . . The bed . . . Well, you and your colleagues are doing marvellously.'

I was feeling jolly as I went back to Bridget. She soon put paid to that.

'I'm going to die,' she wailed, wringing her hands.

'Don't be daft, you just need to have some furosemide, I expect.'

'But hospital. I'll never get through it,' she wept, as though Dr Kelling had sent her to Strangeways for a twenty-year stretch.

When it arrived, I also felt that the five-thirty appointment was a little late, but Bridget was so afraid of imminent death that I hadn't expected her to cancel it. When I called them back, they gave us one for six thirty because all the earlier ones had, by then, run out.

I don't think those responsible for scheduling heart failure clinics late in the evening in winter have ever taken a frail, elderly person in poor housing with extreme anxiety and a personality disorder to hospital. I do hope that one day they will.

The office tell me to go to Bridget for six and give me two hours for her call. I manage to swap my remaining evening customer in order to get to her at five thirty because I know it'll take at least half an hour to persuade her to go. Being so nervous, she's eaten nothing for dinner. While I'm wittering on about how easy and fascinating it's all going to be, I find an old scarf and a pristine pair of gloves that a well-meaning person once gave to Bridget. There are no shoes for her to change into, buying shoes for someone being more compli-cated than buying a scarf or gloves.

She stands for a minute, examining her gloved hands. 'Are they all right? Would you say I look pretty in them?'

'Certainly you do.'

Without you, she would be going alone. But she has you. Her companion. People need companionship. It isn't insignificant. It obliterates loneliness. And loneliness isn't being alone. You can be lonely in a crowd. You can be lonely in a city full of people. You can be lonely in a classroom. Being lonely is seeing something lovely, or thinking something interesting, or feeling frightened and not having anyone to share these things with. It makes you depressed. It makes you ill. Lack of companionship won't kill you as quickly as lack of air, but it is as essential as oxygen to the human spirit. Companionship is part of caring. But it is difficult to find the extra time to provide it. Carers so often have to care without giving companionship. To care without properly caring. Imagine a bus driver having to drive without properly driving. Or a cook having to cook without properly cooking. It's laughable. But carers so often have to care without properly caring. It's awful doing that.

We switch off the blower heaters but leave on the light. Bridget unlocks the door, we step outside, she locks it again, and then she unlocks it. She goes through this process twice more, while I begin to get wet from the drizzle coming in through the open balcony. Then she sways down the concrete corridor to the stairs while I lug my bag, the walking frame, the wheelchair, the walking stick and the wheelchair footplates down to the first landing. The wheelchair has tiny wheels that stick out underneath it at the back and I can't see them very well because, half the outside lights being broken, the stairwell is barely lit. Once I've smashed the little wheels into my shins a few times I run back up to Bridget who has decided to come down left foot first, that being the one on the longest leg. The journey, challenging in daylight, is hazardous in near darkness. I point the torch of my mobile phone at her feet and, as she's coming down, Bridget berates everyone except herself, God, me and Dr Kelling for putting her through this ordeal.

'Him next door. He doesn't help.'

'He's young. He's got a job to go to. He can't be worrying about you. Just concentrate on your feet.'

'Why can't the council fit a handrail, the bastards?'

'We could ask them to, but then they'll find out you're living somewhere that doesn't meet your needs. Actually, let's ask them.'

'No. Let's not. That woman that used to live downstairs. Mrs McDermott. She once told me I left a trail of destruction wherever I went. She was no help either, was she?'

'She was probably just fed up with you losing your temper.'

'She knew I didn't like living in this place but she never helped me to get out of here.'

'Why don't you let *me* help you get out of here?'

'Where would I go?'

'Somewhere with a bloody lift would be a start.'

Once we reach the main exit, it's just a matter of holding the heavy metal door open for Bridget with one hand while heaving all our baggage over the three steps down to the pavement and unfolding the wheelchair with the other. These last three steps are almost impossible. I always have to do the unthinkable at this point and support her weight while she descends them. In daylight, when she can see the steps, it's merely nerve-wracking. In the dark, it's a full-blown nightmare.

'Why don't they put a fucking ramp in?'

'Why don't you move to somewhere more suited to your needs?'

'I do wish you'd stop bletherin' on about that. It's terrible here but I'm used to it.'

By the time we finally make it outside, I'm no longer hoping the people who scheduled our late-evening appointment have to one day help their own elderly person do it, I'm hoping they have to *be* the elderly person themselves.

The taxi is late. Bridget, in slippered feet, is frozen. I crouch beside the wheelchair and put my arms around her to try to keep her warm. Wheel us under a tall thin bush growing optimistically from the litter in a nearby concrete planter. Lean right over her to take all the rain on my back. When he arrives, the taxi driver berates us for living in a place with a similar name to a road several streets away but is able to get the wheelchair into his cab without Bridget having to get out of it. Bridget is impressed.

'See? I told you it'd be all right,' I say.

'What's your name?' Bridget screeches at the driver. 'Can you pick us up after? I'm having a scan. Do you know Dr Kelling? Do you think I'm going to die?'

'I can't wait outside. Call us back when you've finished.'

The hospital feels closed and unfriendly. Lots of the lights are off and the receptionist is packing up. She directs us upstairs to a waiting room where the reception area is empty. Bridget needs the toilet, her bowels stretched to the limit by anxiety and a level of activity that they're not used to. I'm afraid that if we leave the area we'll get locked out. Bridget holds on while I put my head through several doors before finding a clinician and another patient being scanned. 'Sorry, have we got time for the toilet?'

The toilet, without a plastic seat raiser fitted to it, is too low for Bridget's frailty. She bumps down onto it uncomfortably and won't let me leave, preferring to suffer the indignity of having me watch her defecate than be left alone feeling so unstable. It's not until she's done that we discover there's no toilet paper left at this end of the day. I scrabble at the bottom of my bag for crumpled tissues and then struggle to help Bridget stand, wipe herself and pull up her pants and joggers without having anything much to hold on to.

Eventually, we make it back to the waiting area.

The radiographer beckons. I wheel Bridget into a room containing several long couches, curtains drawn around them, next to ultrasound machines. It's quiet in here. Only one couch is lit. It looks like an operating theatre.

'Am I going to die?'

'Don't be daft,' I say. 'Of course not.'

'Am I seriously ill? Critically ill? *Dangerously* ill?'

I look at the radiographer's badge. 'This is Rachel,' I tell Bridget.

After a little more encouragement and a couple of jokes, Rachel begins to understand the complexity that is Bridget. She is kind and answers her questions patiently. Like all the health professionals we meet, once she sees how intelligent and endearing Bridget is, she's charmed by her, but it takes me to convey this to her. Feeling protective and proud of Bridget, I undo her cardigan and the buttons on her shirt. Her skinny chest gets plastered with electrodes and she undergoes the procedure with twitchy good humour.

Heart scan done, Rachel disappears. I help Bridget back into the wheelchair and we emerge into the waiting room. I push the door. It doesn't open. I find the green 'let us out' button, press it, return to the wheelchair, pick up all our belongings and try to push us out of the door that has locked itself again. The silence of this normally busy area is stifling. I toddle back to the green button carrying all our belongings, push it again, drop the walking frame, pick it up, run back to the wheelchair and ram us at the door before it locks yet again. My shoulder is beginning to hurt like hell.

Back downstairs I ring the taxicab service. There's a long

wait for a new driver but eventually the cab deposits us back outside Bridget's building. It's nine o'clock, pitch dark and pouring. The cab scoots off while we struggle up the three front steps. Bridget manages to get the main door unlocked and I hold it open with one hand and pull the wheelchair and all our belongings up the steps with the other, my shoulder killing me now. A sinister-looking character appears out of the darkness. I recognize him from the hostel just up the street. In daytime he seems friendly but in the dark I'm jumpy. I just manage to get everything inside the door and slam it shut before he reaches it. He pushes his face, flat and distorted, against the glass on the other side. I calm my wits and lug everything back up behind Bridget again.

Inside, the flat is cold. We switch on the blower heaters. 'I wish you'd let them do the central heating.'

'How can they do that with all this stuff in here?'

'They're used to it. What are you having for dinner?'

'I can't eat.'

'You haven't had anything since lunchtime.' I make a sandwich and take it to her where she's sitting, exhausted, on the bed, next to a large plaster statue of the Virgin Mary standing on the bedside cabinet. I sit down beside her and put one arm around her shoulder, the Virgin Mary looking over both of us.

Next day, I find Bridget frantic. She can't get me inside quick enough. It doesn't seem to have anything to do with the heart scan.

'Help. It's terrible. I'm ruined. I'll be evicted!'

'What's the matter? Is it the legs? The neck? Is something leaking? Has the bath gone through the floor?'

'Get in here. I need you!'

'Calm down. It can't be that bad. Whatever it is, we'll sort it out together.'

'Seven thousand pounds!'

'Huh?'

'Electricity bill. Seven thousand pounds. Seven thou—'

'Stop! It can't be. I promise.'

'It is.'

'It can't be. Even with the blower heaters.'

'Seven thousand pounds,' she screeches. 'However will I pay it?'

I ring the electricity company, re-read the meter, give the electricity company a figure minus the extra several thousand that Bridget's short-sighted eyes had accidentally added, and the bill turns into four hundred and eighty-three pounds.

'It's been a terrible week. Nothing short of torture.'

'I know. But it's all right now.'

Then, the following week, she is more *jubilant* than I've ever seen her. I follow her down the hall. 'Calm down, you're going like a rocket. What on earth is it?'

'Look! It's wonderful.'

There is a little plastic box on top of the fridge. 'I love it. It's brilliant. I never have to read the meter again, it does it all for you. It even tells the time. And the date. It's fantastic!'

'Oh. So how about we tackle the central heating now?'

'I do wish you'd stop bletherin' on about that.'

27.
Travelling

One of my friends takes a journey by aeroplane, following the sun to get double the summers and none of the winters. It's fortunate that he's funny and kind because I would otherwise resent the images he unintentionally taunts me with as I trek through the rain, keeping people safe in exchange for job satisfaction and what counts as a minimum wage. He has seen so much of the world that it takes a lot to impress upon the warm privilege in which he lives. The sights and sounds that make the grade this time are extraordinary. The beauty of a dawn chorus at sunrise in the desert. The enormity of a bamboo forest in the vastness of the most extensive botanical garden I have never heard of. The ridiculousness of a model rooster bigger than my bathroom.

I travel within the country, limited from going further by lack of money and fear of environmental impact. Having worked through Christmas, in January my sister and I leave the city for a few short days to light fires, make soup and swim bravely for minutes in the freezing sea out where it is calm beyond the breakers. We haven't gone as far as my friend, but an English winter can still take my breath away. Deer plunging out of a frosty copse ahead of me as I walk alone at dawn. Hibernating ladybirds clustered in their hundreds against the stained-glass windows of an empty church. The infinite variety of shades of green among mosses and lichens growing in a dripping wood.

Ina travels within the boundaries of the borough on forays to the supermarket, the chemist, the doctor's surgery, and church on Sundays. These are far-flung places for a woman with her weight, gait and paranoia. She warns me of the perils that lie ahead before we contemplate leaving the safety of her flat to begin our quest for sucky sweets, Sellotape, tobacco and milk. We prepare for the journey. Select the shiny wooden walking stick over the metal one that can't be trusted not to carry some unbalancing charge it may have gained from being left too near the television. Close the curtains. Put on our coats.

'Money?'

'In here.' Ina pats her pocket.

'Keys?'

'In here.' Ina shakes one of her feet and then we're off on a lolloping hike to the end of the road, me keeping an eye on her shoe to make sure the keys don't fall out of it. Where my brain sees a quiet residential street, Ina's sees an eight-lane highway, the run-down corner shop almost inaccessible on the other side. She scratches her tightly curled grey hair and peers earnestly over her lensless glasses. Tuts and steps back from the kerb again. In the distance, a vehicle is approaching. The speed limit is twenty miles an hour, so we wait a good few minutes for it to pass. Next we are impeded by a far-off bicycle and yet another car. Then, a miracle. No visible traffic in either direction. I pull gently on Ina's free hand to slow her down so she doesn't fall over in her frantic haste to cross.

The shopkeeper is pleased to see us. 'More sticky tape, Ina? What *are* you doing with it all?'

When we're safely back in the flat Ina needs a cup of tea to recover, so I go to the kitchen, peel back the tape that now seals the cupboard closed and search among the glass jars of decanted cornflakes, pasta, flour, hot chocolate and curry powder for those that contain teabags and sugar. I peel the sticky tape from them, make a cup of tea for Ina and seal the jars back up again with fresh Sellotape.

Ina is free to bring back artefacts from her solo expeditions. The latest is a bent-up, wire-stemmed, red fabric rose that has been unwound, straightened and exhibited on the windowsill. Once she returned with a slice of tree trunk two feet in diameter and eight inches thick. I have no idea how Ina achieved this, but that she did so is a mark of her enthusiasm for home improvements. She rolled it into the sitting room so I could stand the television on it and over the next few days, we admired the raised picture with all the seriousness of a couple of interior designers.

Bridget travels within her flat. There is no lift and she lives four floors up with legs that are too infirm to manage the stairs alone. She has few visitors. The chiropodist calls every six months, and Mrs Flynn, an old acquaintance, visits on Bridget's birthday. Meals on Wheels have stopped coming because it was costing them thousands to serve Bridget and the other eleven people who still used their service. To this day, we wonder what happened to Douglas, our favourite delivery driver and human barometer. Sopping wet, well wrapped up or hot and sweaty depending on the weather, Douglas had a lovely smile. There is a view of green space from Bridget's living-room window, but Bridget doesn't care to look out of it because there are people in the green space enjoying themselves. She sometimes opens the front door and peers down onto the road instead. Bridget often tells me how much she hates gravity, and then we imagine what it would be like to be able to step out over the balcony and go for a mid-air walk. But while gravity and Bridget's impaired legs still exist, her travels are largely restricted to kitchen, living room, hall and bathroom; the time and frequency of her journeys dictated by constipation, hunger and what's on the telly.

Despite the limits of her surroundings, Bridget and I still find much to be fascinated by. We can become absorbed in junk mail, choosing which commemorative items we would send for if only we were mad enough to want any. The ripeness of fruit is of great interest, pears being edible only at one particular point of maturity, and bananas needing to be watched for the day they become so overripe that I must take them home and bring them back as cake. Crane flies gather on damp patches on the windowsill outside the kitchen. We study them to see how they communicate. Bridget is still certain they are speaking to one another. I think it's more about the legs. I once arrived to find her excited by a large moth that had got inside the flat. A matchbox-sized brown triangle that lived for a few days on the wall above her bed until we found it in the bath. Bridget hadn't been able to resist trying to find out if it could swim. She was upset that it was dead, so I said I'd go and make coffee to help her over her little bereavement. I'd only gone a couple of steps when she called me back. 'Hold on, I'll come with you,' as though I'd started out on a long afternoon stroll instead of a six-yard trot to the kitchen.

Tiny Annie travels within her room. Tiny Annie is hunched down to the level of her chest, the flannelette hump of her back rising up behind her head, her grey hair hanging in two plaits as thin as fraying shoelaces. The extent of her journeying is from bed to chair and back again via a standing hoist. Tiny Annie remains in full command of this small realm. I wash her at the bedside. Strip off her nightdress, lift her arms. She tells me to be sure to do under the pits, reprimands me for not doing her belly thoroughly enough and giggles when I inspect her feet. I help Tiny Annie dress, fetch teeth from their little pink plastic box on the bathroom windowsill and fit the smile into her face. Then, we travel via the hoist over a threadbare path to the armchair. A two-foot-wide trail worn hard and flat through wear, verges of untrodden, fluffy carpet either side of it.

How will you feel when you are in the world but no longer with the world? How will you feel when someone has to cook for you and their cooking is too soft or too hard or too salty or bland, but you have to be grateful and eat it anyway? How will you feel when you can't go and choose? When you can't catch a plane or even a train? When you will never go to the sea again? Never jump your way over the waves that crash on the shore. Will you mind, when that happens? How will it feel to always be caught in the breakers, ever struggling, unable to get to that calmer water? To never float freely again? Will you be as cheerful as her when that happens?

Tiny Annie's possessions are kept in plastic carrier bags, two of which are from well-loved department stores that stopped trading decades ago. The bags have to be placed carefully around her so that she can reach them. Knitting in one. Papers in another. Toiletries, make-up, books and stationery in others. One is full of dress patterns for garments that will never be made. Few intrusions happen here now – just the occasional appearance of the doctor, and birthday cards on Tiny Annie's special day. But the weekly delivery of food by her great-nephew is enough. We marvel over it. Put together little combinations. Before I leave, I make the bed. 'You are an excellent bed-maker,' she tells me. It pleases me, this praise for a small skill that is of such importance here.

*

Victoria inhabits a space three feet wide and six and a half feet long, next to a window in the room of a grand Georgian house that looks out onto its front garden and the street. In summer, the window is often open. Victoria's cat startles me when it soars through it onto the bed without warning. It never lands on Victoria or the plastic tubing running out from her nightdress. The cat has grey and white fur in leopard-skin patches with a dark dorsal stripe from head to tail. Victoria has pointed out the scarab shape over its green eyes and tells me it is an Egyptian Mau. The cat trills like a budgie, but Victoria's whisper is as quiet as the sound the sliding sheet makes when we reposition her. Through the seasons, we have charted the times of sunsets outside from winter to autumn, and the strength of light that travels over the floorboards. The sleeping cat curls tight against Victoria. It appreciates her bedbound constancy, her absence of physical movement, her almost-silence. She cannot stroke it, but it loves her. Victoria lies in one of three positions. Looking out at the path of thin rectangular brick tiles through overgrown flower beds. Looking up at the white ceiling. Looking into the basil-green walls, and polished wooden floor. The radio plays throughout.

I might once have thought that Victoria, immobile, no longer travels anywhere, but now I know this is entirely untrue. Here where nothing happens, but everything happens. As I care for her we talk and, as we talk, we travel through each other's minds, exploring what was, what is and what might have been. And that is almost the very furthest anyone can travel.

Greg's condition worsens enough for him to have to finally leave the flat and be taken into a hospice and then to hospital. I explain to the ward staff and the doctors that I am acting as his next of kin. They write this on his notes but, when I telephone, no one is willing to give me information. At the hospital we tell them again and point out my name written on his notes. Greg looks ridiculous in a hospital bed without his sunglasses or his headscarf. He feels trapped and claustrophobic and wants to be wheeled outside. The staff tell me he's making a fuss, that he's a nuisance. I try to explain that he spent most of his life on the street. Ask if he could be put next to the window. They tell me he's fine where he is, that he is troublesome. The next day I arrive to find the curtains drawn around his bed. They ask who I am. I explain, yet again. I'm told he had a seizure, and they are trying to intubate him. I ask why they didn't call me to let me know. We underline my name on the notes and I go through the curtains and calm him down, stop him screaming and struggling so that the procedure can become possible.

I'm crying when I meet Sheila in the street. 'My friend isn't making sense. He's so sleepy.'

She takes my hand. 'He's travelling now,' she says.

28.

Going home

Maureen is on the sofa and Julie is kneeling at her feet, her head in Maureen's lap. Maureen strokes Julie's hair.

Maureen's eyes are closed. 'I want to go home, Julie,' she says.

'You are home,' Julie says. But we both know what Maureen means really.

These two go way back. Years. They bicker like an old married couple. Once, after a particularly volatile difference of opinion, Julie refused to go back to Maureen ever again. It was less than a fortnight before the tearful, pathetic reunion. Julie's always told me not to let Maureen give me the runaround. 'That bloody woman will keep you there for ever if you let her.' But I allowed Maureen to run me ragged because I don't have that kind of relationship with her. I couldn't answer back and get away with it even if Maureen deserved it. She'd never have had me back. Not like Julie.

Maureen's been sick before. Julie told the doctors it wasn't her time to go yet. The doctors didn't believe it, they insisted she'd not be here the other side of that weekend. 'She's a bloody ox,' Julie had said. 'I'll let you know when it's time, eh? You can give up then.' Julie and Maureen had laughed about it afterwards.

Today it's different. Maureen's been in hospital twice this month, weaker with each discharge, Julie spending ever more time in her flat between visits or late in the evening, anxious that she shouldn't be alone when Paddy is out. Sometimes I've accompanied her and thought of Beryl and Franklyn, two of my earliest customers who had died soon after I'd met them. I didn't really miss either Beryl or Franklyn because I didn't know them well and I was still fully occupied by just trying to do the job. And, of course, I'd told myself I didn't need to get attached to anyone in order to care for them. But now, like Julie, I have customers who I know inside out and they know me. I care deeply about them. It has been utterly impossible not to. I try to imagine how I'll feel if they die. Not if. When.

Maureen has family. As well as her brother Paddy, there's a daughter who lives far from London. They care about Maureen but it's Julie who Maureen asks for when she's scared, cross or wants to have a gossip or share a memory. Julie knows Maureen so well that she is relied upon to liaise with the doctor. Julie can understand more than anyone what Maureen feels is right or wrong, good or bad, tolerable or unbearable.

'I want to go home.'

'You are home.'

Maureen weighs so little now that Julie doesn't bother with a hoist. Against all the rules, she scoops Maureen up instead, like a lover with a sweetheart, out of the medical bed and into her arms and carries her. If it's warm they go into the garden but now that it's getting cold again they usually make it only as far as the sofa in the corner of Maureen's bedroom-cum-sitting room as they have today, Julie trying not to cry, and Maureen's voice getting smaller and smaller and smaller.

You were his favourite. You came only in the mornings at first. Sometimes he was loading the dishwasher. Very slowly. Later you came in the evenings too. He knows you well, through hours of chatting. Knows your family. That your daughter passed her driving test first time. That your husband keeps you awake with his snoring. You know where his children and grandchildren work. Cooed with him over the picture of his first great-grandchild. And the second, and the third, and the fourth.

Now you come at lunchtime and teatime too. He can no longer leave the bed. Stops eating. Drinks little. Becomes sleepy. Then agitated. Sleepy again. Doesn't want to be changed. Tells you you're fucking stupid. That you've always been fucking stupid and you're still stupid now. Afterwards, he apologizes. You tell him it doesn't matter. But later he starts the shouting. 'Fucking stop!' 'Get away from me, you bastard!' 'For God's sake hurry up, arsehole!' You shouldn't mind but you are hurt, not by his words, but by the hatred in his sunken eyes, and the spiteful mouth too soft and small, like a furious sock puppet without his false teeth inside it.

You ask that he not shout at you like that. 'I wasn't shouting at you,' he says. 'I'm sorry. I was shouting at that feeling that I'm going to be sick, and at the pain, and for my sleep to come. Proper sleep, I mean.'

Maureen's eyes are sunken deep, the upper sockets cavernous and full of shadow, her grey curls too big for her head.

'I want to go home.'

'You are home, Maureen.'

Julie doesn't take her red-rimmed eyes off Maureen. 'Remember when we first met and you told me to eff right off?'

'I want to go home.'

'And at the street party when Tina danced in front of you holding your hands and I was wheeling your chair and I fell and landed on my arse in front of everyone and you – you just bloody laughed.'

'I want to go home, Julie.'

I bend down. 'We know you do, Maureen,' I say.

'Kate, what'll I do?' Julie whispers.

Julie and I go into the kitchen and I put my arms around her and she sobs. Then we blow our noses and go back. Family arrive and Julie's in charge, allowing the littlest ones just a brief time before banning their noise to the other side of the door where their noses become bobbled against the textured brown glass. For a while I take Julie's place at Maureen's feet. I encircle her wrist with my thumb and forefinger, marvelling that this is possible. Think of the blood flowing beneath the thin, translucent skin, the heart pumping relentlessly, and wonder specifically how many beats are left. I stroke the soft patch between eyebrow and eyelash and feel the hardness of the socket, see the very skull. I tell Maureen I love her and that she's funny and I'm really proud that she was once a head cook and a wife and a mother.

'I want to go home.'

I smooth her forehead and think what it will be like to pass this house and never again go inside. The time when others will live here and how they will not know that Maureen once had us in hysterics when she farted really loudly and blamed it on the cat, and that time when I came in drenched and she told me off, and when she sang 'Unforgettable' and had the most beautiful voice and afterwards she said, 'That's for you, girls.'

I help Julie lift her back to bed. Take the too-big cardigan off. I wonder what Maureen really feels. How much she can hear. Whether time is slowing down, speeding up or replaying all of her days behind her closed eyes.

The day of the funeral, it's freezing. I sit shivering in the pew, willing Julie to make it through the reading. She just about manages to hold it together. Afterwards, when we go back for refreshments, Maureen's front room looks huge without the medical bed, wheelchair and hoist in it. There is a rectangle of slightly paler, fluffier carpet where the bed used to be, four circular indents at the corners where each of its legs were.

The table laden with sausage rolls and sandwiches nowhere near fills the gap.

When I arrive at the hospital the next afternoon, Greg has been moved to a quieter ward. They ask who I am. I tell them again I am his acting next of kin. As usual, I point out where they've written and underlined my name on his notes. They tell me he's had a sudden deterioration and is not expected to survive the night. My patience snaps. I scream, furious that had I not come in I would not have known. I am taken to him, but we have been denied the chance of saying goodbye. I ring a friend to ask that they come and sit with him before calling my husband and the office and going out to the two calls that cannot be cancelled.

On my return he lies, apparently asleep. I tell him I'm here. I know this has to happen. I know Greg cannot go on any longer. It has to end. I realize with a shock that I'll have to manage a funeral and I don't know anything about doing that except that it will be full of finality. I imagine Greg cold in the winter ground and the flat empty and inaccessible.

The door of the ward opens, I hear whispered voices and turn to look toward the dim light around the nurses' station where heads are bent together. My heart skips. I feel enormous relief. My husband walks toward me, pulls up another chair, sits down alongside me and takes my hand. 'I'm sorry, Kate,' he says. 'I'll help you. If you'll let me. You know, with everything that will need to be done. We can do it together.' I am flooded with gratitude.

Together we watch the chest rising and falling, nodding

to the nurses as they carry out their pointless observations and repositioning. I tell my husband how much I'd wanted to say a final goodbye. But Sheila's right. Greg's travelling now. Travelling the furthest any of us can ever travel. Further than the bed, further than the chair, further than the kitchen, further than the corner shop, further than the countryside.

Further even than a journey by aeroplane.

29.

Eighty quid

I didn't rest easily for some time after Greg had died. I was troubled by what had happened in his final days, the inability of ward staff to understand him that had made his hospital stay and passing traumatic, unbearable, lonely. I could see now why he had fought so long against being admitted and wished that he had died at home surrounded by music. Greg's wonderful GP appreciated this too. Dr Kott asked that I help write up a case study in an effort to improve the lot of those people who are disenfranchised from the system. To ask the system to see them as complex individuals with particular needs. As something other than nuisances.

I was also so used to going to bed late and surviving on so little rest that my brain could not slow down and switch off. I'd worked long and slept badly the day before I found Mr Rose searching for his favourite glass. 'I thought it was the little nieces. I seen them looking at it. They like its shining.'

Veronica Rose gets chilled easily, so Mr Rose keeps the house roasting. Coming in from the cold, it made my nose run. 'Maybe it was one of us. Someone broke it and put it in the rubbish because they were too scared to own up. Or they just forgot to.'

'No, I'm sure it was the kids.'

It was a wet and windy day. Margaret had been my first customer, and Veronica my second. By the time I got to

Stevie, the weather had worsened. To be honest, just this once, I was relying on Stevie's usual refusal to get up so that I could take things a bit easier. But, today of all days, Stevie was a changed man. He'd decided to take his medications *and* get out of bed *and* have a shower *and* put on a new outfit *and* eat. It was unprecedented.

'Jesus, that's everything we're actually supposed to do. What's got into you?'

'Carla's coming over. What you been up to?'

'Nothing.'

'Doesn't look like nothing to me. You been out all night? You look fucked.'

'Charming. What do you want for breakfast?'

'Eggs.'

'There's no eggs.'

'Ah, get me some eggs, Kate. Go on. And a bottle of brandy. You can have some. You look like you need it.'

'If there was ever a chance I was going to, it's gone now, mate.'

'Ah, away an' boil yer head.'

'You got Carla coming. Ask her. Anyway, I prefer gin.'

'Gin'll do,' he winked.

'Not a hope.'

'You're useless, you are.'

'You want your breakfast or not?'

'Eejit.'

'Muppet.' I went for the eggs.

The tasks, plus the eggs, plus the gentle bickering equalled an extra quarter of an hour on Stevie's call. I raced against the wind across the borough to get to Bridget by midday. She'd received a text message. 'Calm down,' I said, 'let me just put your lunch on first.' It would only have taken me about ten seconds to read the text out to Bridget, but I couldn't do that because Bridget was learning how to read text messages all by herself. She didn't get many, so we couldn't miss this opportunity to practise. She took up the phone, bent her grey head over it, dropped it, picked it up again.

'Press menu.'

'Where?'

'There. Now scroll down. It's boiling in here. Do you need the blower heaters on?'

She stabbed at the keypad, sharp and quick, as though it might electrocute her. 'This weather's going on for ever. Now where?'

'There.'

'I can't see what it says. Am I going blind?'

'Put your glasses on.'

'Do I look good in glasses?'

'You do. Scroll down.'

'Ah, OK. It says Phone Book.'

'Do you want that?'

'Do I?'

'No. You want Messages. Scroll down.'

'Call Log. Do I want that?'

'No. You want Messages. Scroll down.'

'Where?'

'There. What does it say?'

'It says Messages.'

'Well? Do you want that?'

'I don't know. Do I?'

Once we'd made the happy discovery that the phone company would carry Bridget's unused data over into the next month, I put an extra cardigan on her. Then I got frozen going back on my bike to Veronica's, thawed out in the oven of her house, and was drenched in a downpour during my return to Stevie. Stevie was cross. There was no sign of Carla.

'Brandy!'

'Coffee!'

'Useless, you are. Where you off to now?'

'Nightingale Road.'

'Eejit, why're you letting them make you go all that way? You take care of yourself out there in that.'

In Nightingale Road, I helped Lorna's dainty bare feet into shoes and, hoisting her into the wheelchair, we took the lift downstairs and set out for our regular afternoon constitutional around the ground floor of her building. I pushed her through the corridors and communal areas, occasionally stopping so we could chat to a neighbour or look out of the windows and marvel at the black trees, bent double in the storm against a pewter sky. When we got back to the flat again, I helped Lorna onto the sofa and tidied the living room. The rain on the windowpanes sounded like someone vacuuming up gravel. I pulled the blinds down over my drizzled reflection.

She asks if you can spare an extra couple of minutes. You can't really, but you say you can. She can manage the cards, but she needs a bit of help with the wrapping. Her hands can't do that. She plans it, bit by bit, through November, ordering online and asking the carers to help put everything together ready for her to give in December. 'For my little treasures,' she tells you. 'That's what all of you are.'

There's a big canvas shopper in the hall cupboard. It contains wrapping paper and those shiny stick-on bows and a variety of chocolates and lovely hand creams and a couple of bottles of scent. You bring the bag through to the living room and, instead of rushing on, spend a happy ten minutes wrapping one or two of them.

She writes the gift cards, and you stick them on and you giggle together about who will like what and at the end of the ten minutes she asks you what would be best for Jen and you consider this and suggest a rose-scented face cream. 'So give that to me,' she tells you, 'and I'll hide it here under my blanket because Jen's coming next.'

And you leave, wondering with some small excitement, what might have been hidden under that blanket while you were there.

I went on out into the rain again. On to Geoff. I hadn't been to Geoff before. He lived on the ground floor of a secure block of sheltered accommodation. I had to buzz the manager to let me in. There was a short, skinny, bearded man sitting naked on the bottom step of the stairs like a mischievous leprechaun. He said nothing, just grinned at me shedding my coat and gloves and stamping the feeling back into my feet.

Geoff's room was empty.

I sighed and went back to the stairs. 'Geoff,' I said, taking his hand, 'let's get you dressed, honey.'

After Geoff, I had a double-up with Julie. We estimated how much we'd get paid for the day while we changed Mrs Gibson.

'Eighty quid. Hold still, Mrs G.'

'Is it raining out?'

'It's pouring, Mrs G. It's got to be more than that.'

'Nope. Eighty quid. At the most.'

Mr Gibson came through from the kitchen. 'Want a cup of tea, girls?'

'No time for one today,' I told him. Feeling thirsty, I realized that, apart from my early-morning coffee, I hadn't had anything to eat or drink. That explained why I'd been able to avoid going to the toilet. I could have picked up some junk food from the corner shop where I bought a light bulb for Mr Radbert, but I no longer felt hungry and it's tricky to eat a meal whilst riding a bicycle, especially in the dark, so I didn't bother.

'Hey, you!' Mr Radbert yelled, when I opened his door.

'What?'

'Good news. Shelly's found my car.'

'Blimey,' I said, mopping my nose again, 'you mean, you really do have a car after all?'

'Of course. You all right? You look pale.'

'Just tired. And my throat's a bit sore.'

I changed Mr Radbert into pyjamas, got his meds, fitted his catheter bag and assisted him to bed, before finding a non-wobbly chair and pulling it under the kitchen lamp-shade. I spent the next ten minutes trying to fit the new bulb before I realized the old one had sheared off in the light fitting.

'I can't put the new bulb in. There's a piece of glass left in the socket.'

'That'll be Micky Donagh.'

'Micky Donagh's dead.'

'He is?'

'Yes. Car crash, remember? Dead as a doornail.'

'Oh yeah. Well, anyway, Shelly's found my driving licence.'

'You said she'd found your car.'

'Finding the licence is one stage closer to finding the car. And when we find that car, it's yours. Just so long as you drive me to St Lucia first. You won't be tired in St Lucia, Kate.'

'Good God, Mr Radbert,' I said. 'All my hopes are pinned on you, but it's always four steps forward and three steps back at your house, isn't it?'

Now here I am, back with Mr and Mrs Rose again.

'You know I said the missing glass was kids?' Mr Rose says, following me upstairs toward Veronica's room. 'Well, I was wrong. My friend stopped by this afternoon, and we went into the lounge. And there I found my glass. You know where he was? He was under the chair but pushed far back so he couldn't be seen. You know who found him? My foot.'

The wind screams around the top of the house like a phantom, rain crashing on the skylight above us. There is a vibration in my eyes, not a visual thing, but a texture like Velcro. 'I'm glad you found it,' I say. 'Everything'll be all right now.' I feel suddenly doomed.

'Yes. I use it for my concoction. Orange juice and cinnamon and a little rum. Good for my eyes and my sleeping.'

Looking down, I see the floor of the landing in great clarity. It is covered in fake vinyl pine, torn in patches by the wheels of the shower chair to reveal wooden boards underneath. Cracks run out from the torn patches like fissures in limestone. In the gaps between the floorboards, there is a little universe of fluff and scraps and human hairs. A kirby grip is wedged down there, alongside an obsolete halfpenny. There are no fake nails in the fake vinyl pine but there are real nails in the wooden boards. They have square heads. Hard heads, without thoughts, hit by hammers. Like mine. Pounded.

'Are you all right, Kate?'

I try to make myself be all right by squatting down on the oblong of yellow rug, a little woven raft in the fractured vinyl sea. I have one clear thought. The thought is that I am about to vomit. 'Give me a minute.' The rug is woollen threads worn flat. Close up, it's scattered with tiny polystyrene balls from a package opened downstairs and carried up here on slippers and shoe covers. Flakes of tissue are tangled in its trodden tufts. My brain distracts itself from wanting to lie down by trying to figure out where they came from. It takes a few minutes to remember that time an incontinence pad got in with the washing and shredded itself into all the clean clothes that came out of the machine.

'Kate?'

I want to be downstairs hiding in the ground-floor toilet until I don't have to breathe so heavily. The stairs are bare treads with white-painted edges and tacks down either side, some with small red threads still attached. Everything is burning except the back of my neck and my forehead. Rainwater coming in through the roof turns out to be sweat dripping from my eyebrows. The wooden floor is patched with dark spots. One drip falls precisely through the crack onto the halfpenny coin next to the hair grip. Get a grip, I think. But I cannot.

'Kate!' Mr Rose is more shocked than I.

I find myself lying near the bottom of the stairs and him scurrying to the kitchen and me sitting up and telling him not to call an ambulance. It wasn't my head that woke me. It was my arm. I caught the elbow on the banister as I went down and the pain was like a contraction during labour. Heavy agony compensated for by brevity. 'Would you rather have mild discomfort for ever or absolute torture for two minutes?' I ask him.

'Be quiet and drink,' he says. 'You're confused.'

My shrieking brain soaks up the sugar in the juice. I feel how white I am, and my lips blue. I taste oranges and cinnamon. Mr Rose helps me to sit. His gentle hands. The cut-glass beaker had been full. The decoration carved into its surface picks up light from the bare bulb overhead and throws its pattern over the blue walls. I hand it back, empty.

'Here,' I say, 'don't be losing your best glass twice in the one week now.'

30

No one thinks you feel things when you're old

Some people dislike birthdays. 'Another year older.' 'Don't want to be reminded.' Some take the day off. They're missing a trick, you think, when your birthday month rolls around. It's more special, a birthday, when you share it. This year, you carry cake to dole out as you go through your visits, happy with the anticipation of getting home to gifts and cards from your friends and family, and your favourite dinner. All day long you get hugs and kisses and greetings and give out cake in a warm, fuzzy haze of feeling special until you rock up at her door and say, as you've said the whole day, 'Guess what? It's my birthday.'

But she doesn't say 'Happy birthday,' she just smiles as you hoist her from chair to toilet. You go to the bedroom to remove the flowery cotton throw that turns the medical bed into a couch for visitors during daytime, replacing it with practical pillows and a square absorbent bed pad in case of accidents. You take empty plates and cutlery from the living room and wash them in the kitchen. You pull curtains closed and switch on cosy lamps and put water on the bedside table and help her brush her teeth before you hoist her into bed and find the right blanket and the right remote and the right bag full of all the right things for the night.

And you say, 'Socks on, yes? It's a bit chilly,' and she nods, still smiling, and with everything done just the way she likes it, you crouch down at her bedside ready to exchange a joke, an anecdote or a little moan about some annoyance that happened to one or other of you earlier in the day but instead she says, 'I have

something for you. It's in the drawer there.' And you say, 'Really?
Oh, you shouldn't have. I can't. It's against the rules.' And she just
says, 'Open the drawer,' so happily, almost smugly, wanting to see
your reaction. You pull out an envelope and a little box wrapped in
tissue paper. 'Open it,' she says again, and you can see now that
she has been thinking all day about you doing this.

The card is made of thick, heavy paper with a satisfying texture
to it. There is a charming verse inside and it is written to dearest
you from your good friend her but all the family have put their
names to it as well and you are trying not to cry while she is saying
'Open it,' again and again until you unwrap the pink tissue paper
and take the lid off the little box and inside there is a silver chain,
not a flimsy chain, but a more expensive, snakelike chain and on
the chain is a perfect, shining cross. 'To keep you safe,' she says,
'the way you keep me safe.' And you think this is the most memor-
able birthday you have had in such a long time, and you are utterly
happy at this moment, in this room, with this gentle, unassuming
woman and this friendship.

On the ground floor of William's block of sheltered housing,
there's an atrium with a residents' lounge and the manager's
office. The walls of the atrium are pale yellow, the walls of
the lounge are pale blue, the walls of the manager's office are
pale lilac and the carpets are pale green. All the doors are
glazed and there are large windows to the outside through
which you can see the external world going about its business in full Technicolor. But inside, colours are muted, sounds
are muffled, and fake greenery trails like pondweed from
pots on a bookshelf. It's like being in an aquarium.

There's a lift in the building, but I use the stairs. The stair
carpet is so pristine it looks brand new. Clearly, I'm the only
person who ever takes the stairs. On the fifth floor, in a flat
behind one of many identical blue doors, William's hallway

curves into an open-plan living room and kitchen with a bedroom and a bathroom leading off it. I first met William in March. He was, as he always is, silent and still in the far corner of the living room, an elderly man much smaller than his mustard-yellow armchair with his eyes closed and his chin on his chest. The television was, as it always is, I later realized, broadcasting football at full volume. A minuscule part of me wondered, as it always still does, if he had actually died.

'Hello,' I shouted, above the noise of cheering Millwall fans. William wore a formal shirt underneath a navy sweatshirt. His legs were bandaged beneath jogging bottoms, feet too puffy for slippers resting, bare, on a cushion on the floor. The carpet was covered in crumbs. A magnifying glass and an unopened tabloid newspaper lay among the remnants of tissues and pill packets on a table beside him. I turned down the telly and tapped him on the arm. He looked up slowly, through unblinking brown eyes enlarged by thick lenses. When his face met mine, he jumped almost out of the chair.

'Oops,' I said, 'sorry to startle you. I'm Kate.' He raised his eyebrows. 'Carer,' I shouted, shaping my mouth around the word so he could lip-read it. I soon found he could not see well enough to lip-read. Or to take his medications. I had to put them on a spoon and, as he tried to get them down, he dropped them in and out of his mouth like a fish nibbling gravel at the bottom of its tank. He refused the meal I offered.

'I'll just have tea and cake. I don't eat much apart from lunch.'

'You need to eat some protein to heal those legs.'

'What's protein?'

'It's in meat and beans. And eggs. Not much in tea and cake.'

'I don't suppose you'd fancy a cup, do you? Of tea, I mean.' His pessimistic frown had already decided that I wouldn't, but I didn't have another call for a whole hour and it was raining. I sat down in the crumbs on the floor in front of him and poured myself a mug. Now he looked bemused. 'The other carers are good,' he said, 'but they don't talk to me much.'

'Well, it must get very boring for them then,' I said, 'but I think they're just busy.'

William had difficulty finding the piece of cake I passed to him. As he ate it, more crumbs missed the plate and fell onto the floor. I was worried he would struggle to find the teacup too, but he picked that up just fine. It was a china cup on a proper saucer, and the teapot had a tea cosy over it. William was very particular about how I made the tea.

'What did you use to do?'

'Why?'

'I'm interested.'

'Blimey. I was in the forces. Then a bricklayer.'

I had difficulty following William's sentences. I could hear him, but his speech was as blurry to me as my face was to him. His mouth could not completely close for long enough to form all the words properly. When William brought his lips together, they immediately fell open again as though he was blowing bubbles. I kept asking him to repeat himself and we had a broken but complete conversation about work. After a while he said, 'How d'you manage to sit crouched down like that? Don't your knees hurt?'

'Nah,' I said, 'I can do the splits if you want. Look.'

William nearly coughed up his tea. 'Blimey.'

'I used to do gymnastics,' I said, 'a long time ago, of course.'

'Just because you did things a long time ago, doesn't mean

you don't want to do them any more,' William said. 'You're a strange woman, but I'm bloody pleased you came. It's made my day, talking to you.'

He was on my rota the following week too. And the one after that. He became my regular, seven o'clock, Monday evening call. Over the months, we learned about one another in thirty-minute instalments. My worst fear is fire and his is burglary. I like orange and he likes green. My family come from Norfolk and his from Scotland. William taught me how to replace hearing aid batteries, how to get the telly back onto the football channel and what kinds of cake the corner shop stocks. I taught him what each of his medications was for, that putting his feet up higher would stop them swelling and which of the other residents ever drifted down as far as the ground-floor lounge.

William was married for over sixty years. He was so long with his wife that his brain cannot help recreating her occasionally. 'She floats around the kitchen,' he said. 'I like it when she's here.' I decided not to teach him about bereavement hallucinations. 'She was very particular about making tea,' he added.

In July, William said, 'Never touching anyone makes you feel as though you don't exist,' and after that I always held his hand while we chatted. In August, I was drying dishes in the kitchen when I realized he'd crept up behind me. As I turned, he took my left hand in his right, hooked his other around my waist and we bobbed about in a wobbly waltz for a few seconds before I towed him slowly back to his chair.

In September, I got a shock. The flat was in darkness. William wasn't in the living room. Nor the bathroom. The outline in his bed was unmoving.

Tentatively, I nudged him. 'Hey, you OK?'

'Oh yeah,' he murmured dozily.

'God, you frightened the life out of me. Are you ill?'

'No, just tired. I'll get up, though.' He emerged groggily out of the blankets.

'Take your time,' I said, sitting down beside him.

Eventually, he shuffled through to the living room, one hand on my arm and the other on his walking stick. 'God,' he said, 'you don't know what that did to me. Sitting next to a woman on a bed. What I wouldn't give to lie down with a woman and have a cuddle.'

'I'm married,' I said. 'Watch out! Does that feeling never go away?'

'Never,' he was vehement. 'Can I tell you something? You won't be offended?'

'Go for it,' I said, taking a comb to the thin strands of white hair that rippled above the liver spots on his scalp.

'When I was young,' he began, 'I knew a woman who lived alone. Vera. She was in her seventies and she had the nurses come every day. She knew she was dying. I went to see her. I suppose I was about twenty-five. And, you know what? She asked me to make love to her.'

I stopped combing and held my breath.

'Of course, I was appalled,' said William. 'She seemed ancient. But, God, what did I bloody know at that age? She pleaded with me to do it. She wanted to feel close to some-one again before she died.' He stopped speaking and stared at his hands.

'And?' I said, angling for the end of the story. But William didn't hear me. Or maybe he just pretended not to.

I visited William every Monday. Never any other day. Eventually, December rolled around. My birthday came and went, me having doled out extra cake to William and Wil-liam protesting at my explanation that I wasn't allowed to accept a tenner as a gift, to get my hair done. 'Will you be here for Christmas?' I asked him a few weeks later.

'Where else would I be? You?'

'I'm working,' I said. 'But I'll go home between customers and open some presents and eat the dinner. The kids are going to cook it. It may not be edible.'

'Sounds perfect,' said William, and I was embarrassed that I'd complained about my home-cooked, roast dinner in front of this man, for whom Christmas Day would be just like all the other days. An old man, swimming in his gold-fish bowl.

The next afternoon, I got a surprise. The office called to say they'd had to make some changes to my rota. One of the other carers was ill. When the new schedule came through, I was delighted to see who had become my first customer on Christmas morning.

So, on Christmas Day, here I am, carrying a few chocolates, half a dozen eggs and some smoked salmon with me, and wearing a silly red-and-white Santa hat. It's early and dark when I leave everyone still sleeping at my house. Outside, the roads are empty all the way to William's block. I take the stairs to his flat and go to the bedroom. I watch him sleeping for a minute, savouring my anticipation of the pleasure he'll get when he sees me. Then I switch on the lamp and put my hand on his shoulder. 'Morning, William.'

He opens his eyes. 'Happy Christmas,' I say. But he doesn't smile. He's utterly terrified.

'Shit.' I take off the silly Santa hat. 'Sorry. It's me.'

'Blimey.' He rises slowly, then stops. 'Are you real?'

'Absolutely,' I say. 'I think I'm supposed to help you have a wash.'

We go arm in arm to the bathroom. I clear the pile of clothes from the perch stool and sit him down. Help him take off his clothes. Gently wash his back. Put cream on his poorly feet. Massage it into his hands and arms.

'What do you want to wear today?'

'Just put the old clothes back on.'

'Oh no. It's Christmas. Let me get fresh ones. What'll you have for breakfast?'

'I don't usually have much. A piece of toast.'

'How about poached eggs with it? For Christmas. For the legs.'

'I can't use a knife and fork.'

'Scrambled then,' and I cut up the smoked salmon to go with the eggs so he can eat it all with a spoon.

'William,' I say, 'I want to ask you something.'

'Oh yeah?'

'You won't be offended?'

'Spit it out.'

'I just have to know,' I say. 'That old woman. Vera.'

'What about her?'

'Well, did you?'

'Did I what?' He's teasing me.

'Go on, tell me. I'll give you a kiss.'

He takes the bait. 'Let's just say,' his slurred words are quiet, 'that those nurses who came every day said she suddenly looked very peaceful in the days before she passed away.'

'My God, William!' I squeak. 'You're extraordinary!' And I throw my arms around his shoulders and give him a big smacker on the cheek.

He grins his toothless grin. 'At the time,' he says, 'it was strange. Something to be ashamed of, even. But now I understand. Now I'm ninety-bloody-eight. No one thinks you feel things when you're old. But you do.'

31.

Toilet paper

I miss Greg. I miss the escape of going to his flat. I feel lost. And then something comes along to take my stupid mind off the whole lot of that.

We begin to seal people off long before everyone else does. The pub next door to Margaret's house is heaving as we shut them away like brittle creatures overwintering in twigs under protective mud while the rest of the city remains free. We tell the chemist not to deliver, that instead we will collect. We take on shopping for those for whom we don't already do it. We reassure families that it is the right decision not to visit. We avoid our friends. Still the restaurants are full to bursting. Wondering what's crept inside, it seems like a blessing that we can't afford to eat in them.

'Did you wash your hands?' It's a mark of Veronica's fear that she overcomes her embarrassment at feeling the need to check I'm doing my job properly.

'Of course,' I say, taking the blanket from her bed.

'Sorry to ask.'

'Don't be. It's really important.'

She's quiet as I hoist her into the shower. 'You OK?' I ask her. 'I'm scared.'

We've always laughed, but now we use laughter to take our minds off rumours of prevalence and predictions of death rates. 'At least you've got plenty of toilet paper,' I say, looking at the big multipack in the corner of the bathroom.

Veronica giggles. 'I heard people were buying it up by the carload.'

Across from Margaret's house, there's a new-build flat with a floor-to-ceiling glass window. Inside, packs of toilet paper line one wall like a layer of soundproofing. We were ridiculing them yesterday but today Margaret isn't laughing. She's heard the announcement that families may lose loved ones and is in tears. 'They meant me,' she says. 'I'm scared.'

'Cancel the hairdresser's visits,' I say, 'and tell your friend who comes to clean not to bother. Check we've washed our hands and if we aren't kitted up properly, throw us out. You ought to be the safest people in the country, if we behave well. By the time everyone else is told to isolate it might be too late, but you're already doing it.'

At Lorna's, I follow the instructions she pinned on the door a fortnight ago that tell callers to wash their hands immediately. In the bathroom, the anti-viral hand wash has been joined by a pile of new white towels. 'Use one,' Lorna calls, 'and put it in the washing basket as you leave.' She tells me she went to the doctor last week and, after taking her bloods, he told her to go straight home and not go out of her front door again for two months. At least. He forbade all visitors. Apart from carers. Who should keep two metres from her whenever possible. It sounds ridiculous. Like house arrest. 'This is really alarming,' I say.

'I'm scared,' says Lorna.

'Morning,' says Stevie, exhaling cigarette smoke as I come in the door. 'Washed your hands?'

'Bloody hell,' I say, 'I didn't expect you to be so hot on it. Well done. Yes, I did.'

He gestures at the telly. 'No fucking sport. None.'

'It's odd out there. Quietish. I went through town yesterday and it was like that week between Christmas and New Year.'

'Except for the supermarkets,' says Stevie. 'I heard there's no toilet paper left.'

'I'd choose something like baked beans over toilet paper. I bet I could manage without toilet paper.'

'Not if you go eating too many baked beans, eejit,' says Stevie.

'Oh, ha ha,' I say. 'How do you feel, anyway?'

'Fucking scared,' he says.

Julie encourages a family to admit their mother, with dementia, into a nursing home. Kathleen has become too much for them to manage, even with Julie's help. Julie is fond of Kathleen, and is almost a member of her family. She doesn't want to stop caring for Kathleen, but Kathleen's husband is exhausted. Sometimes Julie's the only one who can keep things manageable now. She tells the husband he should think of himself as well as the wife that he loves, and that Kathleen will be safe in the nursing home. It's a local one and he'll be able to visit whenever he wishes. I think, too, that this lady will be better off there now.

Instead of going to the pub this payday, we decide to go to Gina's house. Get a takeaway. Be out of the crowds.

One of your friends says, 'They're of no use. Old. Infirm. Perhaps their time has come.' You want her to understand the way you now understand. You explain that William once fought for us, Veronica cared for our babies, Mr and Mrs Seddon protected our communities, Patrick put himself on the line for others, Maureen cooked for our children, Margaret worked until the age of seventy-six. Even Mr Radbert and Stevie and Ina with their problems and misdemeanours have value and feelings and lively personalities. You explain that they aren't just statistics and nuisances. They're warm, funny, happy and sad and they are us and our friends and our families. It isn't for us to decide who is precious and who is not. It isn't humane.

Greg would have agreed with you. He'd always accepted anyone and everyone. 'Every kind of people,' he'd once told you, 'each one has their place in the world. I love them all. They're all interesting. Well, all except Marble, perhaps. Unfortunately, as you know, Marble has absolutely no point whatsoever. But still, he has a place.'

'Everyone has a place,' you say. 'Everyone is important.' Fiercely. Protectively.

As things heat up, we cancel the night at Gina's house, not knowing that we will never meet again as a group of colleagues.

At last, the announcement comes. The roads empty. I take to the car. Pin a note on the dashboard that says, *I'm a care worker looking after someone like your ma, please do not ticket me.* I tell the office that I think we should cut as many double-ups as possible to just single-carer calls and restrict the number of carers going to each customer to no more than two or three overall. The office agree but remind me I'll have to cover all visits if colleagues go off sick. I don't really think about what this means until I'm exhausted four weeks later.

Personal protective equipment becomes freely available from cardboard boxes in the office. Except for masks. We have to ask for those and they are given only to carers going to people deemed most vulnerable. This confuses me because I can't think which of our customers is not.

Kathleen dies alone having contracted the virus in the nursing home. Julie is distraught. I try to explain that some-times you just make the wrong call. That this happened to me in another life. I once agreed with guidelines and the opinion of a consultant not to interrupt the tube feed of a patient with suspected Norovirus who then aspirated on his own vomit overnight. I was told to respect another patient's wish not to be tube fed and had them perish of malnutrition. I accepted firm assurance that a woman could safely be handed over to an eating disorder clinic only to have her return and worsen on my watch. I never forget these people's names but seeing Julie makes me understand that I didn't ever choose the wrong option. That sometimes things end in disaster even though you've taken the most logical course of action. 'It's not your fault,' I tell Julie. And I try to convince myself that this is, and was, the truth.

I talk to my husband about being frightened of this thing. Of how much I would hate for any of my customers to catch it and to be identified as the person who carried it into their homes. One night we watch a documentary filmed in China and are horrified. When he goes on furlough, *he's* suddenly the one making days out of cleaning an already spotless house, doing the laundry, cooking up gastronomic delights night after night and putting the bins out on time. The only thing I must focus on is going out there and doing my job. One day, I arrive home to find a silver-grey line gaffer-taped across the hall floor, an empty plastic crate on my side of it.

'Wait there. Don't cross the line,' my husband says.

'Why? What is it?' I see that on his side of the line there's another box with my spare, clean uniform tunic in it. And clean black trousers, shirts and socks.

'Take your clothes off. Put them in the crate. Shower. I'll wash them all and put them back in here ready to wear when they're dry. That way everything stays uncontaminated.'

'That's a bit much, isn't it?' I giggle.

'You never know, Kate,' he says. 'We want you as safe as possible. And your customers too.'

Work becomes like walking through a blizzard, my feet trudging forward through deep snow one slow step at a time. When I look up, I see only whirling flakes. There is no horizon, just my feet going ever forward and never getting any nearer to an unknowable, invisible destination. I don't question anything, just keep doing as I'm told and seeing who needs to be seen. Our customers no longer match our rotas as we cover for colleagues about whom we worry when they temporarily disappear. Reasons for absence are confidential and it is a relief when these colleagues return again reporting how fed up they've been to be off work and earning nothing while they wait for their isolation to be over. Julie and I make a texted list of the carers we think will stay the course. Those who will never be too scared or too tired to be on duty. The Hardcore List.

Sometimes members of the public notice you in your uniform, people give you a thumbs-up. A neighbour leaves you flowers. You're grateful. It helps keep you going. It seems that carers are recognized after all. But at other times when people speak to you it is crushing.

'Are you a nurse?' A woman asks you one evening, several weeks into the pandemic.

'No,' you smile, 'I'm a care worker.'

'Oh.' Confused, she frowns and then says, but gently, apologetically, 'I won't clap you then.'

I'm approaching the door of Geoff's block of sheltered housing when I see her ahead of me. I scream. She looks back and shrieks. We run full pelt at one another, almost forgetting to stop two metres apart. So few of our calls are now deemed to require two carers, that I had forgotten this one was a double-up. It's a joy to see Chrissy. Beautiful, funny, happy Chrissy with her long eyelashes. The desire to hug one another is ridiculous.

Geoff's sheltered accommodation is a bit rough round

the edges. We are strict in people's homes, but we don't have control of this building. Staff come and go from room to room and Geoff roams the building so there is ample opportunity for a virus to spread here. Geoff has a wet cough. It isn't possible to stay out of range of it in his small self-contained room. Somehow, even he is not deemed vulnerable enough for us to wear masks. It's taken time for him, previously a rough sleeper, to trust us and come out of his shell. Chrissy is his main carer. We help Geoff take his medications, change his incontinence pad, make him a meal. I mop the bathroom and Chrissy remakes the bed. I chat, but she is quiet. 'What's the matter?'

'I don't know how much longer I can go on doing this.'

'Chrissy, you can't stop. People need you. Plus, you're on the Hardcore List.'

'I've got a heart condition,' she says. 'I feel scared and for-gotten.' Geoff looks up. 'Oh, I don't mean it, honey.'

'You need a rest,' I say, 'we're done. Ready to go?'

'I've got a bit of time to keep Geoff company,' says Chrissy. 'I think I should stay here a bit longer.'

Driving away, I calculate that it is almost six weeks since I've had a day without any calls in it. In a hurry to get to William, some miles away, I have to slow down to a crawl. A man and two children are cycling across the entire breadth of the road. I beep the horn. They stop. The man gets off his bicycle, stomps up to my car, motions for me to roll down the window.

'For goodness' sake,' he says. 'Do you bloody mind? My kids are trying to have a Sunday evening here.'

32.

Wait, meekly wait, and murmur not

I've never been good at waiting. Couldn't wait for summer holidays, couldn't wait for kittens and rabbits and hamsters, couldn't wait for new shoes, for snow, for Christmas. Couldn't wait until the next episode of *Doctor Who*. Couldn't wait for the weekend, to go to New York, for morning sickness to end. Couldn't wait for scan results that invalidated a cancer scare. And now this boring, scary sci-fi movie has turned into one long wait. My customers, used to waiting, are better at it than me, but their imagination runs away with them. It drives me nuts.

I like it when I have to wake up Margaret. It means I tucked her in really comfortably the night before. The first thing Margaret always says is, 'Hegyo, Gate,' as she's shoving her false teeth back into place with her tongue. Now, the second thing she always says is, 'It's going up again. There were hundreds more yesterday.'

'The people who died yesterday caught it well over a week ago,' I say. 'The infection rate's definitely going down.'

'It is?'

'Yes. It definitely is.'

'They say this thing's man-made,' says Stevie as I fix his breakfast.

'I don't think there's any proof of that.'

'You don't?'

'No. I think it came from an animal and we've been lucky it hasn't happened sooner.'

'I cannot bear this bloody waiting,' I say to Veronica. 'I want to go to the pub. See my friends. I mean, someone had bought me a theatre ticket.' Immediately, I feel guilty for saying this. It has been a long time since Veronica has been able to do any of those things.

She is far too gracious to make me feel ashamed of myself. 'I know a song about waiting,' she says gently. 'It is a song from my childhood. It's called "Wait, Meekly Wait, and Murmur Not".'

'Sing it for me,' I say. At first, she refuses but I press her. She is shy as she sings it, but her voice is as lovely as she is.

As usual, William's asleep when I arrive, chin on chest in his armchair. I shout, 'William, it's me,' into his hard-of-hearing ears, put my gloved hand on his shoulder, crouch down at his feet and squeeze his knee. Eventually, he raises his head. I smile. He doesn't. 'Are you ill?'

He looks confused. 'Linda hasn't been. She never comes any more.'

'She can't. They're not allowed to. Virus.'

'I'm sick of hearing about this ruddy virus.'

He's puzzled by the television. I try to explain why the football is odd. 'It's not live.'

'But it's on Sky.'

'Have the crime channel instead?'

'Kenny put that on the other night. Frightened the life out of me.'

'What about cookery?' I suggest. William snorts. 'News? Oh no, too much virus. Comedy channel?'

'When,' he says, 'will Linda come again?'

'Don't know. There's really only one thing we can do right now.'

He raises an eyebrow. Still unsmiling.

'Wait, meekly wait, and murmur not,' I say.

And so it goes on. And on and on, but we have not lost one single person and I just can't believe it. Then it happens.

'Kate, it's Sheila. I'm outside Geoff's and they've just brought his neighbour out on a stretcher. I'm scared. What shall I do?'

'Don't go in.'

I ring the office. My mouth is dry. 'We have to cut this visit.'

'We have to care,' Maggs says firmly.

I might once have found it difficult to argue, but doing this job all these months has turned me into someone different. I have no qualms about standing my ground. I'm anxious that I won't be able to make her listen, but I'm confident in questioning her. I don't mind looking difficult or even stupid. I'm surprised to find I am no longer scared at all about this.

'No,' I say, 'not until we've thought about it. Stop. Please. You must understand. I know you do, Maggs. This is the entry point, right here. You're looking at it. I don't go to Geoff now, but Sheila goes to Veronica. And to Bridget. We've done so well. Think about it. Don't let it happen.'

There is a long silence at the other end of the phone. 'Let me speak to people here,' she says. 'I'll call you back.'

I wait. Go to the shop. Buy cigarettes. Smoke one. Put the rest in the bin. Sheila rings again. 'Don't move,' I tell her.

The phone rings. 'We've split all his double-ups to a single call,' says Maggs. 'Done by just two carers who go nowhere else. And I'm sending masks and arranging visits so there's time for those carers to go home, shower and change their clothing afterwards.'

I sit down on the pavement, so grateful for the good sense and support of our office colleagues. 'My God, thanks.'

'No,' she says. 'Thank you. You're right. And the only way we'll get through this is by being a team. We're here whenever you need us, Kate.'

My next call is with Mr Radbert. I don't notice at first. I just go in with my cheery hello and give him a bit of joshing about not being able to get into any trouble while he's stuck inside. After fifteen minutes I notice his eyes are all red. He's barely speaking. Even then I don't ask about it. It isn't until I've hoisted him onto the toilet that he tells me.

He starts to cry. I've never even imagined Mr Radbert crying. I want to put my arms around him, but I can't. 'I lost my friend,' he sobs, 'the one who comes to take me to church on Sundays. I been weeping like a baby all day. I'll never go to church again. Even if there's someone else who can take me, this virus is in the air out there.'

'It's not. It's in people and if we don't mix with one another, it'll stop.'

'It will?'

'It will, yes.'

We are ever more bored, ever more sick of being the only face people see and on to which they can unload their fears. We hear the same stories over and over. We take on extra tasks that customers need doing. Wheel people out into their gardens on sunny days and weed under a watchful eye. Fetch newspapers and birthday cards for them to send. Mow lawns. Dye hair. Give manicures. Go in for unscheduled cups of tea. Buy cakes. Sub them money for shopping in exchange for cheques we lose money on because we cannot bank them when there is too little time to queue at banks with newly limited opening hours.

On the day my bike gets a flat Phil calls. 'Cancel Stevie. You have to go to Terry.' I've never been to Terry before. He lives several miles away. It takes two buses to get there and then I have to figure out how to get a well-to-do chap with alcohol dependence washed and fed and medicated. Terry turns out to have vascular dementia that I don't detect until I'm halfway through the visit because his intelligence and comfortable surroundings don't immediately make it obvious. He talks to me about biochemistry. A subject I don't often get to discuss. I'd really enjoy it if I had the time but I'm too busy trying to work out how mobile he is and find incontinence pads, blister packs and fresh clothing in this unfamiliar house.

It takes an hour and two more buses to do the half-hour call and get back on to my normal patch. I've spent six quid on bus fares and only earned a fiver so I've actually paid to do the job. I try to work out who I've paid. Terry? My company? I conclude it must somehow be the council, or the government, and this makes me furious but at least Terry understood, even through his dementia, that we are battling a virus and not the 5G network.

Toward the end of the day, Mr Rose is sitting in his chair with a mug of tea looking out the window, his expression serious.

'Did you go into the garden today?' I ask him. 'I know it's cold, but the sun was lovely.'

'I couldn't go out there, not with that.'

'What?'

'That sickness falling from space.'

'It isn't falling from space.'

'Come here,' he says. 'Look out of the window. See it? Hanging in the air. Making the clouds look strange. Brownish stuff.'

'Mr Rose,' I say, 'I might just have a spare hour next Thursday. Why don't we clean those windows?'

33.

Heavy bread

Personal protective equipment is moved outside the office into the corridor. Except for masks. Masks remain special. In short supply. You still need to ask for those. And they are still not given freely so my friend buys Nigerian fabrics the colour of sunshine from the market and makes some for me. I love them. I ask for more for my colleagues. My husband washes them between visits.

It all becomes normal. Where my customers and I once swapped moans about aches and pains and families, now we just talk about coronavirus. They tell me what they've seen on the news when they can't sleep at night and I tell them how little traffic there is and which of the shops are shut. All of us are operating like little spaceships in a void manned by just one astronaut, in a plastic spacesuit, whizzing about from one customer-planet to another. It's become normal not to see any other healthcare practitioners either, and challenging to get medical attention for customers. Not impossible, but time-consuming. I'm worried about Mr Radbert.

'You asked to see him for a review four months ago. We sent the form back but haven't heard anything.'

'We don't do in-person consultations at the moment. He has to go online.'

'He doesn't have a computer.'

'Over the phone then.'

'He's not good on the phone.'

'But you're on the phone.'

'Yes. I'm his carer. I have a phone. Do you want me to help him to speak to you on mine?'

'That would be fine.'

'Hold on then.'

'Oh, not now. We need to book an appointment for the call.'

'Right. Today?'

She is beginning to sound cross. 'No, of course not today. We're very busy.'

'Tuesday?'

'I'll see.'

'What time?'

'Oh, I can't give a time. It'll be between eight and twelve in the morning.'

'But I'm only here for an hour.'

'We are very busy. I will book you in for Friday at nine but I cannot guarantee the doctor calling at that time.'

'But I don't see Mr Radbert on Fridays.'

Ina takes so long to answer the door I think she might be in hospital. Eventually, she opens up, pushing a metal walker and carrying a bag that trails liquid. 'Whoa there, you've got a catheter?' I close the plastic tap on the bag, clip it back onto the walker and shove the dirty clothes into the washing basket. Ina follows me about, loosening the catheter bag again. I have no idea where it's come from, there being no note or warning from hospital or doctor. I make Ina comfortable on the sofa, get her meds and breakfast. I put snacks within reach so she doesn't have to get up until the lunchtime visit and knock the catheter around again. I wouldn't usually leave without making enquiries about it, but I'm now running late and my rota is overflowing.

Everything that goes smoothly takes more time. Everything that doesn't takes for ever. More time washing hands between tasks, between rooms, between houses. More time changing gloves, aprons, shoe covers and those annoying plastic sleeves. More time queuing for medications and food. More time reassuring anxious people and chatting to lonely ones. A few days later, I'm already running late again by the time I reach Ina, and later still when she's finally answered the door.

'Oh,' I say, 'what's happened to the catheter?' The flat smells of urine and as Ina walks, the bag dangles, empty again, from her walking frame.

'No good, missus. Not a hope of keeping it straight. I've been changing my clothes all bloody night. Family all well? I keep hearing about this virus.'

'They're fine,' I say. 'Ina, do you really not have a discharge summary for that?'

We search fruitlessly for clues about who should be checking the catheter. I pick up sodden linen with one hand and call the GP with the other. No answer. I try the office.

'Ring the nurses,' they say, 'we're a bit frantic.'

'Number?'

'Check the discharge summary.' They put the phone down.

'You all right there, missus? You look a bit pasty.'

I finally get an answerphone on the surgery number and leave a message. We rummage among Ina's dwindling wardrobe for a fresh outfit. 'You're next for washing, Ina,' I say and, when the GP calls back, we are mid-shower. It takes ages to talk through a referral to the district nurses with one hand on the phone and the other on Ina's flannel. On the plus side, all this has given the first clothes wash time to finish. I put on a second and pile up a third when I realize the time.

'Crikey, Ina, it's eleven o'clock. You need some breakfast.'

'No cereal, I'm afraid. Just do hot chocolate.'

'I'll go to the shop,' I say, fixing a plastic apron over the sofa and sitting her down in front of the telly.

'Get flour. We'll make bread. I'd like some toast. And eggs.'

'Ina,' I say, 'do you really think we need to add baking to the day? It's already quite complicated and I've just cleaned the entire kitchen.'

'Flour,' she repeats firmly. 'White. Self-raising.'

I buy cornflakes and trek around enough chemists to find a solitary pack of bed protectors. There appears to be no bread at all and I curse having to add breadmaking to my rota before delighting in the discovery that there's no flour either. In the very last corner shop, I whoop. There's a single, small, dark rye loaf on an otherwise empty bakery shelf.

Back at Ina's, another wash has completed its cycle. I take out cushion covers and reload more clothing.

'Did you get flour?'

'No flour.'

'You're joking, missus.'

'I'm not. I got this, though,' I hold up my precious prize of dark rye bread with a good degree of triumph.

Ina stares at it for a few minutes, sighs and shakes her head. 'Ah no, missus,' she says morosely, 'that's heavy bread, you know.'

'Right,' I sigh. 'Well, it's lunchtime now, anyway. Stay on this bed pad and I'll do a ready meal. But I'm leaving the bread in case you get desperate later. It's probably good for you.'

I go on to Stevie and William, go home to eat and out again, and finish the evening calls just before ten. My phone rings as I'm heading for home and thinking of precious sleep.

'Kate. You still out?'

'Yes,' I say cautiously.

'It's Ina. She's pressed her emergency button . . .'

'Oh God.'

'Please . . .'

'I'm on my way.'

At Ina's, I'm ecstatic to find that during the day the nurses have called. They've done a great job. The catheter is securely attached to its bag, now strapped neatly to her leg, and it functions perfectly. Ina has simply got into a muddle again over how to empty it and has panicked. Panic sets in easily now. Especially for customers who live alone. I empty the bag and we have a cup of tea to calm ourselves down.

'I'll be off then.'

'Wait, missus,' says Ina, 'let me give you something for all your trouble.'

You're so tired her generosity makes you feel weepy. The kindness of this woman with whom you have a bond that comes from having fought battles that have welded you together in this ridiculous version of normality. Adventures you didn't ask for that have tested you both. The people up there with all the money who pay so little do not know of these challenges. They must surely know nothing of them because, if they did, they would change things. Make lives easier. Your difficulties do not touch them in their privilege. If they require a carer, they pay a private carer a decent wage. A carer dedicated only to them.

They do not see you, here, on the ground, in this fragmented version of care. On paper maybe. Not in your sweating, exhausted,

*frustrated actuality. But they are not as fortunate as they think
they are. You are consoled in some small way by believing that they
know nothing of the richness of this humanity, those people who
pay so little. They know nothing of the depth of feeling down here
where it is often the poor who care for the poor. They know nothing
of this curious but solid love and respect between unrelated people
who have to fight to keep going. Those privileged people do not
have to cry as you do when things go wrong. But they surely do not
feel the triumph you do when things go right. They surely don't
laugh like you do when the laughter comes. You choose to believe
they never will. It makes you feel a tiny bit less angry with them.*

'You don't have to give me anything.'

'I must, missus.'

'Really, it's quite all right. You've already given me a cup
of tea.'

'Hang on,' says Ina.

I stand just outside her door taking off my gloves, apron,
shoe covers and those annoying plastic sleeves. Ina returns
from the kitchen. 'Here,' she says beaming, 'you can have
this.' She hands over a carrier bag that contains something
small but weighty.

'I think it's probably good for you, missus,' she says.

*You cycle home along empty streets and, though it is dark, there is
no breeze so you are not cold, and everything is still except for you,
and everything silent except for your breathing and the sound of
your wheels treading tarmac. You take great delight in going
through all the red lights because there is no point to red lights any
more and you swerve into the very centre of the road, careful to
stay exactly in the middle of it, looking mostly down at the broken
white lines disappearing under your tyres, when you realize you
are not alone.*

You look to your right. Beside you a group of city foxes, four of them, are keeping pace with your bike. Running smooth and slick and fast. City foxes used to be skinny, threadbare, mangy things, battered by traffic. You once found one with its jaw missing, crawling in agony in the park. They used to keep their distance, pick the bins before dawn and be off with the light but foxes are no longer like that. Foxes, having been given the run of the emptied city for weeks, have become fat and sleek and unafraid.

You look at the foxes and the foxes glance up at you as they run. Every now and again they peel off to yelp and roll with one another before coming back to escort you home, you, part of the pack, and it feels wild and you think that no one, absolutely no one else is out here tonight racing with foxes except for me.

34.
Plastic robots

Masks finally make it out into the corridor with all the other personal protective equipment. No one has to ask for them any more and absolutely every customer is deemed to need one.

Putting on plastic is tiresome. The mask goes on before I enter the house. Then I don blue shoe covers, a white apron, green sleeves elasticated at either end that run from above my elbows to my wrists, and navy gloves. Eight pieces in a specific order, punctuated by the washing of hands.

I walk through to Margaret like a plastic robot. My voice sounds normal to me, but I know it's muffled because she's puzzled by my familiar questions. It's like when you're in a cheese shop in a foreign country and you say, 'I'd like to buy cheese, please,' and, because your Spanish is so terrible, the shopkeeper looks confused even though what else would you be doing in a cheese shop except buying cheese?

'Hegyo, Gate.'

'Pop your teeth in. Shall I put the light on?'

'What?'

'May I put the light on?'

'Huh?'

'Light? Put the light on?'

'Oh. Yes, of course.'

We go through to the bathroom, Margaret in her nightie and me behind, rustling like a crisp packet. It's seven thirty on Saturday. Margaret's slow speed gives me time to check my phone when the text comes through.

Morning. Phil here. Need help. Can you cover Radbert at three and seven, plus all Stevie's calls? I know you'll get no break but I'm stuck. The next text comes in before I've finished considering how to object to the first: I'll buy you a bottle of wine. Please.

I help Margaret wash, dress and make breakfast before doing the same for Veronica and Stevie.

You feel suddenly dizzy, waiting at the lights, and pull to a stop at the edge of the road beyond them. Put down your bike and sit on the pavement, head between your knees.

'Are you all right, miss?'

You look up into the concerned face of an elderly man. You tell him you're not ill, that you're a care worker who just needs a bit of a rest, and slump back onto the recycling bin as though you're relaxing on a sofa and not sitting on a paving slab among the fag butts. He tells you he cares for his wife, that she also has a care worker and that he understands your exhaustion. You swap experiences about the pleasure of the job but the challenges of doing it.

'It's criminal,' he says, 'what you earn. They shouldn't tax you so much. They need to raise the tax band.'

You gently explain that you earn so little that it won't do you much good, raising the tax band. He shakes his head, holds out a hand. You take it, draw a breath and stand.

The sky darkens as I go across the borough to fix Bridget's lunch, and it's drizzling as I return to give Stevie his midday medications. The rain is heavier on my way back to Veronica and by the time I get to Mr Radbert I'm soaked.

'Who's there?'

'It's me –' I push the door – 'just washing my hands.'

'God help me. Who are you?'

'Kate,' I say. Mr Radbert looks as though he's aged a decade since my last visit.

'Oh Lord, Lord,' he cries. 'I'm in pain. Kate. Help.'

I don the sleeves, wash my hands again and put on gloves. Gloves are always difficult to get on because there's no time for my hands to get absolutely dry after washing them. They rip as they stick to my fingers and I have to start again. 'Hold on, Mr Radbert. I'm here.'

'Lord, please.' He starts to pray out loud. Not just made-up praying but the Lord's Prayer. It frightens me. I talk reassuring words, find out where the pain is coming from, take a urine sample from his catheter bag and call the doctor. Mr Radbert becomes quiet. After a while he says, 'I love you, Kate.'

'I love you too.'

'I love Sheila and I love Itzie and I love you.'

'We love you too, Mr Radbert.'

'Kate, I want you to go to St Lucia.'

I wonder if he is perhaps, outside his dementia, a little delirious. 'I'd like that,' I say. 'When shall we go?'

'No, Kate,' he says, 'I want you to go to St Lucia and ask for me. You'll see that everyone in St Lucia knows me. Go to St Lucia and ask for me. Promise me you'll do that.'

I suddenly feel tearful and afraid and honoured all at the same time, even though I'm not sure what my friend means. It sounds like a declaration of pride or a placement of trust, but it also feels like a farewell. 'I'd be glad to do that, Mr Radbert,' I say, squeezing his hand through my glove.

Unnerved, I head back to Stevie's teatime call.

'Is it raining?'

'What do you think?'

273

'I think you're all wet but it's hard to tell with all that shite you're wearing.'

It's bucketing on the way to Lorna. I arrive drowned. Put on the mask. Go inside. 'Just washing my hands.' Gown up. Go through to her room. 'Oh,' I say. 'Whatever's wrong?'

'I'm dizzy. I feel sick. It's horrible.'

This is the moment my rota, stretched to breaking point, has snapped. It's all over. I want to hug Lorna, but I'm not allowed close enough to do that. We talk through a reassessment of her condition, concluding that an ambulance is not necessary, but the doctor is.

'Lorna?' She's pale and weepy. 'I've got to go.' She's pale and weepy. 'It's going to be all right.' She's pale and weepy.

'Listen,' I say, 'no matter what happens I'll whizz back up when I'm done tonight and check you're OK.' She gives me a sad smile with her mouth and I give her a happy smile with my eyes.

Tattered schedule well and truly shot, I've only been gone two minutes when the phone rings again.

'I need you to go to Mrs Lyle. We're short of carers again.'

'But I'm on my way back to Radbert.'

'Do Lyle on the way.'

'Phil,' I say, 'I haven't been to Lyle before. What do I do with Lyle?'

'Meds and bedtime snack. Dementia. It's straightforward. I'll text you the address but it's near Friary Road.' I hover around the estate swearing for ten minutes, like an aeroplane waiting for a runway, until I get the address. Inside, an elderly woman sits, grinning, on a wooden chair. Mrs Lyle and I happily make our way through her medications. As I'm serving tea and cake the phone rings. My ears are sore at the back where the masks rub, and around my lips is all chapped and itchy. I move the elastic bands of the mask to a less irritated part of my ears, but they just slip back onto the same, painful place.

'Are you still with Lorna?'

'No, Phil, I'm with Mrs Lyle, remember? And then I'm going back to Radbert.'

'Sorry, but can you go to Alice? It's a double-up. The other carer was waiting for Sheila, but Sheila's become unwell.'

At Alice's, the door is answered by a plastic robot with frightened eyes. 'I've got her changed,' the robot whispers, 'but I don't know what to do about the meds. I've been here since six thirty.'

Six thirty was an hour ago. The robot looks young. Unlike most of my fellow carers, she doesn't curse the unpaid time this call is costing her. 'You've not been doing this long, have you?' I say.

'It's my first week.'

A yell shoots down the stairs into the hall where we are standing: 'This is bloody ridiculous! You need to get this sorted out. This bleeding minute.'

I put a gloved hand on the young robot's aproned shoulder. 'You've done brilliantly,' I say. 'It's been a terrible day but we'll sort this bit out together. Let's go.'

The stairs are narrow and carpeted in a floral pattern that is dark instead of pretty. A stairlift is parked at the top. I squash around it, tear my plastic apron on its metal arms, return to the hall, find another apron and, squeezing around the stairlift again, reach for the banister to steady myself. The banister comes away in my hand and I nearly tumble down the stairs again before pushing it back into place where it is merely wedged. Inside a bedroom, a woman in late middle age is sitting alongside Alice's bed.

'I'm terribly sorry,' I say, 'it's been a difficult day. We've had people become sick and when that happens they have to go off duty and it takes time to get cover.'

'My mother is in pain.'

'I'm terribly sorry.'

'She's just left here? While you take too much bloody time.'

I want to tell the woman that I haven't had anything to eat since yesterday, but I know she will neither believe me nor care. 'May I ask your name?' She looks blank. 'Your name? What's your name?'

'Lilian.'

'Hello, Lilian.' I smile with my eyes. 'I'm Kate, what's happened?'

What has happened is that Alice has returned from hospital with a fractured hip, a lot of pain, a fresh blister pack of medications, eye drops, painkillers and new laxatives that nobody thought to mention. Lilian isn't interested in the new blister pack that has no evening medications in it. She wants her mother to have the evening medications she's always had that are in the old blister pack.

I call the office. 'Phil?'

'Kate.'

I smile with my eyes at Lilian. 'Alice's daughter wishes her mother to be given her previous evening medications. She usually has lansoprazole and a statin. Those aren't critical, are they? And they're still in date. Can I give them, document it and you speak to the hospital tomorrow?'

'She really wants Alice to have them?'

'Oh yes,' I say. 'She really does.'

'Just ask her,' says Phil, 'so I can hear, and I'll try to ring the hospital and check. Otherwise, we can't give them no matter how much she wants us to.'

I hold the phone in the air and take a deep breath. 'Do

you really wish us to give the two evening medications even though they are not in the current blister pack, Lilian?'

'Of course I fucking do!' screams Lilian. 'I've been saying that for the last fucking hour.'

'That OK for you, Phil?'

I turn to my young robot companion. 'Nip to the kitchen and get a spoon and a glass of water.'

'I don't want that new one,' screams Alice. 'I'm taking that other one.'

'What does she mean?' I ask Lilian.

'She doesn't want the new laxative. She wants one of her old ones. They're in the kitchen cabinet.'

Both of us robots go downstairs, rummage in the kitchen cabinets and find an ancient pack of sachets of powder. 'They don't look good,' whispers the younger robot. I agree. We look seriously into one another's eyes and then burst into hysterical laughter. Tension floods out in something that's a mix of hilarity, exhaustion and desperation. We go back up with two glasses of water and a teaspoon stained brown. We pour a new sachet into the glass of water under the watchful glare of Lilian but out of sight of Alice.

Alice has a long face. It looks as though it's made of melted wax. I remember it being rounder when I last saw her almost a year ago. She was soft and friendly then. Her eyes are brown marbles on a creamy bed in a puddle of red, the tear ducts big enough to slot matchsticks in. Her hair is white, and her nightdress pink cotton, with sleeves that come down to just past her elbows so that her long brown arms stick out. It's not overly warm in the room, but inside my plastic sleeves, sweat has pooled around my wrists into bags of water that feel deep enough to float goldfish in.

'I remember you,' I shout at Alice. She shrugs. 'You told me about your cat. What was he called again?'

'She's stone deaf,' yells Lilian. 'She's asking about the cat, Ma.'

'I bleeding know that,' yells Alice. And to me, 'Barneeeeeee.'

'That's right. Barney. Alice, I need to put your eye drops in.' Even with her head only slightly tilted back, it's easy to put a drop into each of the gloopy red sockets. Afterwards, it takes for ever adjusting the bed inch by inch up and down until Alice's hip is comfortable.

'Are we OK now?' I ask Lilian, having had to explain against her fury why we cannot give the medications she obstinately wants her mother to have.

'Why,' she asks, 'do they send her home like this?'

'They don't want to keep people in for longer than necessary with this virus about. It's not their fault. Is there somewhere we can wash our hands?'

'Next door.'

Off the landing is a little bathroom. There is a shelf below the window that contains a collection of medications including those for diabetes, high blood pressure and hypothyroidism. Alice's medications all come in blister packs so these must be for her daughter. At an age when, with her own chronic health conditions, she might welcome some care for herself, she is having to nurse her mother through a fractured femur.

When I go back to say goodbye, Lilian stands, racked with arthritis. She looks about the room for a way to keep us. 'Mum needs an enema,' she says optimistically.

'Call the doctor in the morning.'

We two robots creep downstairs. The tips of the fingers of my gloves are puffy with sweat. When I take them off, it drains onto the doormat and my fingers are as wrinkled as if they've been too long in the bath. Just as we are opening the door there is a yell from upstairs.

'Heyyyyyy! Mum says she's not comfortable. Get up here.'

'You go,' I say to my fellow robot. 'I'll see to it.'

After another ten minutes, I'm on my way back to Mr Radbert. Despite the doctor's visit, he has worsened. He's shivery. I cannot attach his convene catheter because of the pain. I do my best to keep my distance while trying to comfort him. I am afraid. Not of catching the virus, I'm confident it isn't that. I'm frightened that Mr Radbert may have to go into hospital. I call the doctor again, but cannot wait for him to arrive because I'm so terribly late. It's ten fifteen in the evening. I ring the office. 'Can you call Margaret and tell her I'm nearly there now?'

At eleven o'clock, my rota is complete, but I can't go home. I've seen everyone the office has told me to see, but there's still someone left. As I make my way to Lorna I can barely keep my eyes open.

No matter how well you know someone, how much you laugh and joke with them, an official visit still has formality. All your customers have become friends, but the professional relationship remains in place. Here and now, it's different.

The hoist is invisible in the cosy darkness of her room. It feels as though you have special permission to be here, like being in a school at the weekend when the caretaker is the only other person left in the building. You tell her that it's no bother to have come back. This isn't so. You're exhausted. But you'd have worried about her all night if you hadn't come.

Refilling the hot water bottle means extricating it from the bed, taking it into the kitchen, avoiding tripping over the laundry basket, skirting the hall table, boiling the kettle and pouring the water in over the sink so as not to spill any of it onto the tiled floor, but you do all of this and return without switching on any of the lights because you know her home so well. Because you are a part of it.

As I leave Lorna's house, I receive a message from the office. I fret about it as I take off the seventeenth apron and pair of shoe covers and plastic sleeves, and the twenty-fourth pair of gloves I've worn today. Mr Radbert is in hospital.

35.

Love, truth or caring?

When the general population comes out of hibernation, for us the situation doesn't change. It seems we will be encased in plastic for ever. We still don't meet, don't go inside the office unless it's absolutely necessary, and keep ourselves away from others. For most of our customers there is no going outside anyway – these are people in permanent lockdown, many of them in isolation except for carers' visits.

Just as you're beginning to expect him home again, the office call.

You remember all those months before when you'd thought you were taking on a dead-end job to punish yourself. Well, this is punishing. But not in that way. His death is not distant to you like those of customers you barely knew, or vague like those you visited less. Franklyn's was a sigh. Beryl's a nasty pinch. Eddie's a slap. Maureen's was more painful. But Mr Radbert's is a punch, a flying tackle. You're winded by it.

And yet his death is not full to you like Maureen's was. It is huge but also empty. No exchange of words, no holding of hands, no telling him how fine he is, how well he's done, what you liked about him so much, how grateful you were for his ridiculous good humour. He is gone in ten words but no goodbye. 'I'm sorry to tell you Mr Radbert has passed away.' It hurts.

You also get that sinking feeling that you made the wrong call. Perhaps, if you hadn't telephoned the doctor whose visit led to the ambulance and then the hospital, your friend would have remained uninfected. He would be alive at home. Then you remember Kathleen and you know, you truly know, that sometimes things go badly even though you did the only thing you could. And it's not because you weren't good enough at your job.

Question of the Day today is, 'What's most important – love, truth or caring?'

I know what Mr Radbert would have said. 'I need the truth, where's my bloody car?'

Stevie just says, 'Oh, fuck off, Kate, stop talking bollocks.'

Predictably, Margaret says love. She was married for sixty-eight years, after all. Veronica also says love and, since she is the wisest of all my customers, perhaps that's the correct answer if there really is one. The new co-worker I train at Veronica's also says love. For training her, I will be paid an extra pound. One single pound for teaching a keen new co-worker the fundamentals of keeping a vulnerable member of our society safe and comfortable in their own home.

I travel on. By this time people are up and about. People paid far more than the money we earn. Money that, when the costs of poorly subsidized travel are deducted, can be even lower than the minimum wage. Scant recompense for work that is also a vital contribution to the UK. Except obviously it's not. Yet we have done it for months on end, as much of the population has had its enforced downtime on their higher wages. And while we've been doing this job of so little monetary value, we've also been doing the jobs of others and, indeed, are still doing them. Cleaning, hairdressing, bandaging. Cutting toenails sounds simple but when your customer's nails are thick and brittle and they are taking warfarin it is difficult and risky, never mind against the rules. A chiropodist suggests we might cut out corns with the aid of a video downloaded from YouTube, add it to the task list and accept responsibility for no additional recompense and absolutely no insurance. It makes me furious. Then I think of William and pull myself together. William is due to be discharged from hospital this afternoon and I am keen as mustard to see him home.

'What's most important – love, truth or caring?' I ask Bridget.

She just starts to cry. 'I never had any love in my life. Just brutality and truth. No one ever understood.' She tuts into her palm three times. 'I wish I'd not had the brutality but, to be honest, I could've done with a bit less of the truth as well. Would you really say I'm pretty?'

'Of course you are,' I tell her. 'Hey! I know! Would you like to see?'

'See myself? But there's no mirror.'

'I can take a picture of you. On my phone.' I can't believe I've never thought of it before. We're not allowed to take photographs of people inside their homes, but I can delete it as soon as she's looked at it. 'Hold on.' I sit down next to her, snap a selfie of us both and hand her the phone. She pulls it close up to her face, looks puzzled.

'See?' I say.

'Where?' She squints. Picks up the magnifying lens from the bedside cabinet.

'There.'

'Who's that? I know that's you, but who's that?'

'That's you.'

'Me? *Me?* My goodness. I look so old. I look so, I look so . . .'

'Beautiful.' I snatch back the phone. 'You are beautiful. Very.'

Next, I ask Lorna. 'What's most important – love, truth or caring?' I say. 'Love, of course,' she says, 'and not just the sexy kind. Love as in kindness to all and the world will be a much better place.'

And all through the day I continue to ask everyone this same question, thinking all the time of William, until I rock up at his door in need of the loo. I'm the first carer to call on him following his latest hospital discharge. He is one of the oldest old. A delightful man, almost blind and very deaf but with a wicked sense of humour and plenty of stories. William whom I had wheeled to the park in spring because he can no longer go outdoors without help. William, whose children are also elderly and who do as much for him as they can but who cannot perform miracles. William, with whom I spent my first waking hour of Christmas morning while my family were still sleeping because care doesn't stop for Christmas. It doesn't stop for coronavirus. It doesn't stop for poor pay. It just doesn't stop.

William had been plonked in his armchair by the ambulance crew who'd left a short time ago. It's now just me, him and a bundle of new medications.

'Cup of tea?' I check that the falls alarm still works and try to puzzle out what to do first. William had had to leave in a hurry, so the kitchen needs tidying, and the washing has to be put on and, of course, he's hungry.

He looks dazed and not quite himself. 'Where am I?'

Having worked out which medications are now due, we handle those and then I spoon-feed him since he cannot feed himself at all in this exhausted state. It takes an age because his dentures have gone missing during his hospital stay and his hearing aid no longer works.

At the end of a long hour, I suggest he ought to go to bed. William doesn't like it. 'Let's make a deal,' I say. 'If you can walk to the kitchen then I'll leave you, but if you can't I'll help you get to bed.'

'Deal,' he says, pushing his hands down onto the armchair to lever himself up.

Nothing happens.

Again.

Nothing happens.

He's more shocked than me. I've seen it many times before, this bemusement at your legs not obeying your brain.

It takes skill to help a person stand and is more hazardous than it looks. Even people as thin and frail as William are heavy to hold upright. For twenty minutes I make sure William doesn't fall, while also making sure I don't break his shoulders and he doesn't break my back. Eventually he concedes he isn't going to be walking anywhere any time soon. I fetch the wheelchair, bring it alongside.

'What will I do?' William says. 'When you're gone.'

'Don't worry,' I say cheerfully, feeling terrified for him, 'you'll be in bed.'

'How?'

'We'll do it together,' I say, not knowing how. I manage to get him into the wheelchair. 'You need to pee,' I say. 'Did they give you a urine bottle?'

'No,' says William as I wheel him to his bedside.

I manage to get him to rise a couple of inches off the chair. Enough to pull his trousers down and hold out a plastic jug, fetched from the kitchen, for him to pee in. 'I'm sorry.' He's crying, this forgotten man who once, like the celebrated Captain Tom, also fought in a war for us.

'It doesn't matter,' I say. 'You're exhausted, just concentrate on getting into bed.'

'I love you,' he says.

'I love you too,' I say.

'I can't do it any more,' he says. He stares into the air with his near-blind eyes. 'I can see Florrie,' he says. 'I'm going to die,' he tells his wife. 'Kate's here, but I'm going to die.'

'William,' I say, 'relax. I'm going to move the bed and work some magic on the chair and we're going to get you tucked in and you're going to sleep and in the morning things will be different.'

'Thanks, Kate,' he says. 'I don't know what I'd do without you.'

'Nor I you,' I say, manhandling the heavy, non-medical, non-wheeled bed so that we can get the wheelchair round it with his better side close up. 'Did they give you a sliding board?' I ask hopefully.

'No.'

I spend ten minutes working the arms of the wheelchair off and wedge a pillow tight over the exposed metalwork so William won't hurt himself if he falls on it. On a count of three I get him to standing again and, taking much of his weight on my screaming arms, rotate him around to sit down on the bed. Then I have to position him correctly whilst avoiding damage to his ulcerated legs. I put on his pyjamas with him supine, going from one side of the bed to the other, rolling and turning him and pulling the bottoms up and the top down.

At last we're done. Two hours after I first walked in the door. Two hours for a call that was allotted thirty minutes to complete. I'm fragile now. It's been exhausting, stressful and emotionally charged. I want to go home and have a stiff drink. But I have several more customers to see, all of whom I'm now very late for.

'Kate, can you fetch my wallet?' William says.

I assume he wants to be reassured it is safe. 'Here.'

He scrabbles inside. Brings out the twenty-pound note. 'Get yourself something, love. Have your hair done.'

'Oh, William, I can't take that. I'm not allowed.'

'No one will know.'

'I'll know,' I say.

'That's bloody daft,' he says, offended at not being permitted to use this gift both in order to thank me and to recover some of his dignity.

'You being asleep is all I need,' I say. Mercifully he is. About five seconds later. It's too late to ask him my Question of the Day, but I know what he would say. I wait another few minutes to make sure William is sound before I leave and then I cycle on to Mr and Mrs Gibson's tower block.

I take the slow lift to the top. From here at night, the city looks magical with its skyscrapers and giant Ferris wheel and stadiums. I briefly stop and gaze and think of the people in all the flats and streets and houses and parks and offices beneath me. Most going about their business independently, but many reliant on others. Pedestrians cross the road below, tiny from this height but every one of them an individual life with hopes and dreams, worries and fears. Each of them significant, adding one tiny part to an enormous whole. The lights over the city are yellow at the bottom, white in the middle and red at the top where they pepper the towers and dangle like baubles from cranes. A silver scratch left by a plane crosses a sky that fades from black to blue to grey, the sun already having fallen beyond it all. As ever, the view takes my breath away.

With Mrs Gibson safely changed, Mr Gibson is in the kitchen. We've called to their home three times a day for years now. But Mr Gibson was here from the start. He saw the first signs. The change in gait. That weird fall when she broke her ankle during the simple step down from pavement to road. He watched her become too tired to cook, in too much pain to clean. Shared the load. Observed the legs swell and the fingers fumble. Took over the running of the home. And then the running of the wife. He felt the wetness in the bed and changed the sheets around her body. Called the ambulance when she had the stroke that finally felled her. Then we came with our routines. He had to get used to us invading his privacy. Making him ashamed when his temper was short. Us, with our ability to walk away. We make things easier in the day but in the night, in the dark, his sleep is often broken, his dreams of a shared, active retirement long destroyed.

'What's most important – love, truth or caring?' I say when I take the empty mug through to the kitchen.

'Love?' says Mr Gibson. 'What is love? What an unimportant word. I love you, I love that coat, those shoes, that silly toy. I love him, I love her. And now I don't. Look at me now, this tired old body, going up and down this ruddy building. I can barely see when I trek out to the shops. The endless work. The fetching and carrying. I once knew love and what good was it? But caring. It takes but gives more back. Caring is solid, it does not end. Truth is important and the truth is that love is easy to say. Insubstantial. Dissolves like smoke. But caring . . .'

He slumps heavily into the kitchen chair.

You stand alongside him and think of a slim woman, a pretty woman who was bringing up children and took a job a bit like this during term times to make ends meet. A woman who used to tell you about the people in her day and went to work in flats and was always doing things that weren't on the task list. A woman doing a job that you are embarrassed to admit, even to yourself, you were possibly a little ashamed of. A woman who, along with your father, seems to have embedded in you the need to see that no one goes cold or hungry or lonely. Who taught you the value of compassion and companionship, the importance of making people feel needed and dignified and included. Who illustrated the significance of not only telling people you care but of doing the difficult things that show it. And the pleasure and satisfaction to be found in doing them.

Mr Gibson sighs. 'Caring,' he says, 'is the most important thing. Because caring is real. Caring matters.'

I remember all those months ago when Maggs had asked me why I wanted to be a carer and I hadn't been able to answer her question. I'd barely bothered to respond. Now I cannot imagine doing anything else. I'd thought caring would be monotonous. Grey. But it has turned out to be rich and vibrant. Multicoloured. I feel love as a delight and I know that one should always try to tell the truth. But, now, these seem only part of caring. Caring feels weightier than both.

I put a hand on Mr Gibson's shoulder. 'My God, you're right. It's the caring that matters. The answer is caring. Of course it is.'

Mr Gibson smiles, but he looks exhausted.

'How about I make you a cup of tea?' I say.

Author's note

Care occurs in different settings. This is my experience of working in domiciliary care, visiting people in their own homes. Most of the initial writing was done at the time when these events were happening, with the customers and Greg aware that I was writing about them, indeed urging me to write about them, as part of my own story. Sadly, many of these people have now passed away. Their names and many personal details have been changed to protect their identities but, since there are over ten thousand home-care agencies in England employing around half a million care workers supporting many thousands of vulnerable people, it is likely that the challenges faced by those in this book are replicated throughout the country on a daily basis.

Throughout this journey I have wondered why so little value is placed on caring. Taking into account largely unpaid travel time, my domiciliary care work was one of the worst paid jobs in the country. Shortly after I became a home carer, my daughter got a job looking after pets when their owners were away. After one bank holiday, we compared our earnings. I had been on the go for fourteen hours and was pleased to have earned one hundred and twenty-three pounds at the higher-than-normal bank holiday rate. But my daughter had worked only eight hours and had earned one hundred and fifty-three pounds. Arguably, therefore, the value of keeping fourteen people safe and comfortable in their own homes on Christmas Day was deemed less than that given to feeding nine cats.

It is clear we are aware that care work is undervalued. Plenty of stories about social care appear in the media that highlight the failure of wages against rising inflation, the failure of staffing levels against rising demand and the failure of morale against retention rates that see so many skilled workers leaving a job they love in droves. Yet little changes for those on the front line of social care. Care workers are largely, in the long term, ignored. Why is this so? Maybe it's because they work with real bodies, old bodies, disabled bodies, sick bodies, bodies that excrete and squirm and flop and ooze. Maybe it's because we feel shame at allowing someone else to care for relatives who can no longer care for themselves. Maybe it's because we don't want to think about the day we too might need care. Or maybe it's because, unlike nurses and doctors, carers are not in the fixing business. They don't mend bones and bodies. They don't, generally, bring people back to life.

But perhaps it's just that carers are so easy to ignore. In time I would understand that my colleagues could not shout out at the injustice of the low pay and poor conditions meted out to them. They were too busy struggling to help support their own families within the constraints of a low wage. One lived on a friend's sofa, unable to afford to rent even a room of her own. Several were bringing up children alone. Others were unfamiliar with technology and did not own computers. Often English was not their first language. They, disparately going about their job in the community, could not come together to organize themselves into a fighting force. Few of them were members of a union and anyway many were working at times when union meetings and discussions were held. They could not begin to lobby for change. And neither could I, once I was in the thick of it. It was just too difficult. I also want to add that although we understand the reasons that others may go on strike it is apparent that my colleagues, like myself, cannot consider it. Even if we could afford to strike, we are the safety net for people to whom we become deeply connected. If we joined those striking workers, many of our customers would have no one left. It would be as though we had deserted our own families.

I feel it is important to state here that the low wage paid to domiciliary care workers is unlikely to be due to the care agencies paying it. My agency was always supportive of me, particularly during the challenges of the pandemic. I believe that they were only doing their best with what they had to offer, and that their job of scheduling carers, within the difficulties of maintaining enough staff who sometimes had to cancel work at a moment's notice, was really challenging. I have heard that the tenders put out for care work contracts are often so low it is almost impossible to meet them and, of course, these low tenders are themselves due to low levels of funding allocated to social care as a whole. I know that some domiciliary carers are at last being paid for travel time and that rates of pay have risen since this book was written but, nevertheless, there is a long way to go to ensure that people can easily earn a living from home care work. I am a care worker and not an economist. This is a memoir and not a polemic. I do not know what the solution to poor funding is. I only know that it must be found.

By the end of that first year of the pandemic, we had achieved the unimaginable. Not a single one of our company's customers contracted Covid in their own homes in the community on our watch. Not one. Secretly, I was waiting for a thank you from our company for the work we had done. Not from the admin staff but from the management. I'd wondered if it would come in the form of a Christmas card. Granted, so many cards would have taken a bit of time to write, but it would have meant a lot to have received one. Instead, we were all sent a brief text message saying we could come and collect a gift from a box left in the office. The box was half full of unwrapped tins of lip balm and little tubes of hand cream. We should not, we were told, take more than one.

I chose a lip balm. I keep it, unopened, as a reminder of the worth that was placed on me during the time my colleagues and I gave everything we had to keep people safe.

It likely cost less than a pound.

Acknowledgements

This book was written by me but, of course, made possible by every kind of people.

I must firstly thank those who were there at the very beginning – the hard-working staff of home-care agencies, my colleagues, my customers and their families. I owe a huge debt of gratitude to Lana Citron at Morley College for her inestimable writing tuition, advice and honest feedback, and to my friend and fellow writer Felicity for her listening ear, critiquing and steadfast encouragement.

The manuscript was championed in its early stages by being elected winner of the Mslexia Memoir Prize and I am grateful to the judges and to Debbie Taylor and the team at Mslexia, without whom I would have struggled to find the courage or the resources to take it further. Along the way, my children – Edie, Dottie and Joe – and my niece Fiona have been patient in listening to chunks of the evolving manuscript being dictated to them for their opinions.

Thank you also to my husband, Adam, to Haidee, Mic and Salvatore, to my dear friend and poet Nicola Hilliard and to my three wonderful Sarahs for all their support, and to Yael for her kind and diligent proofreading.

Most importantly, I thank my brilliant agent Isobel Dixon of the Blake Friedmann Literary Agency for her expert knowledge, guidance, advocacy and endless, reassuring patience; Helen Garnons-Williams and everyone at Fig Tree for their belief, support, dedication and warm welcome;

and Mary Chamberlain for her especially insightful editing skills.

Lastly, I thank my mother and my father, Christine and David, still looking after people, plants, vegetable plots, baby birds, me, my sister and countless hedgehogs all these years later.